Snow, Flood and Tempest

A MIDLAND TRAIN SNOWED UP NEAR DENT (1881)

Snow, Flood and Tempest

Railways and Natural Disasters

P. J. G. Ransom

Ian Allan PUBLISHING

First published 2001

ISBN 0 7110 2833 8

© P. J. G. Ransom 2001

Published by Ian Allan Publishing

an imprint of Ian Allan Publishing Ltd, Hersham, Surrey KT12 4RG.

Printed by Ian Allan Printing Ltd, Hersham, Surrey KT12 4RG.

Code: 0111/B2

Acknowledgements

No book such as this can be written without the help of a great many people. I acknowledge with gratitude the assistance of:

Philip Atkins (NRM), John Barnes (Glenfinnan), Ed Bartholomew (NRM), Hugh and Biz Buxton, Laura Conrad (Railtrack), Jackie and Michael Cope (HRA), Paul Fathers (SVR), Keith Fenwick (HR Society), Robert Forsythe, Howard Geddes (HR Society), Andy Guy (Beamish), Peter Hall, Michael Harris, Martin Harrison-Putnam (LT Museum), Edna Haydock, A. P. Hopkins, David Idle (NYMR), Dick Jackson (GNSR Association), Mark Kennedy (Ulster Folk & Transport Museum), Cyril A. Leathers (Downpatrick RS), Don Martin (William Patrick Library, Kirkintilloch), Steve Martin (WSR), Nigel Massey (Snowdon MR), Dr W. R. Mitchell, Sarah Norville (NRM), Graham Oliver (GCR), Nelson Poots (RPSI), John Potter (Bluebell Railway), Bill Roberton, John Rowley, Stuart Sellar, Sandy Simpson, Brian Stephenson, David Stirling (SRPS), Brian Sutcliffe (Friends of the S&C Line), Dennis H. Taylor (WSR), Keith Verden-Anderson, Ron White (Colour-Rail), David Williams (SVR), Terry Worrall, Michael Wrottesley, John Yellowlees (ScotRail).

My wife Elisabeth and my agent Duncan McAra have once more given me every support. Every effort has been made to trace the holders of copyright in the illustrations, but if anyone considers they have been overlooked the author apologises and will be pleased to hear from them.

Other books about railways by P. J. G. Ransom

Railways Revived
The Archæology of Railways
Your Book of Steam Railway Preservation
The Archæology of the Transport Revolution 1750-1850
Transport in Scotland through the Ages
The Victorian Railway and How It Evolved
Scottish Steam Today
Narrow Gauge Steam: Its origins and world-wide development
The Mont Cenis Fell Railway
Locomotion: Two Centuries of Train Travel (Anthology)

Contents

Introduction:

Natural Disasters

It is unusual for a train in Britain to encounter a tidal wave. It is still less usual for there to come riding, on the crest of the wave, a bungalow — and for the bungalow to crash into the locomotive.

Yet that was what happened to the 7.27pm train from Hunstanton to King's Lynn on 31 January 1953, three-quarters of a mile into its journey on a stormy night. The bungalow was, presumably, one of the wooden sort that people put up at the seaside. When it collided with the engine, it damaged the vacuum brake hose. That put the brakes on and brought the train to a stand. The water was rising rapidly, and extinguished the fire in the locomotive. The lights went out in the carriages. The water rose quickly to the level of the seats. From time to time flotsam crashed against the train.

It was, apparently, a moonlit night, and for the next six hours the guard and the enginemen endeavoured to keep up the morale of the marooned passengers, of whom there were six including two very young children. It cannot have been easy.

At last the water started to recede. The enginemen managed to get to the front of the locomotive, and patched up the brakes. They broke up some of the wooden floorboards of the tender and, using them for kindling, relit the fire. They raised steam and started to propel the train back the way it had come. The guard got out from time to time to push out of the way debris such as floating huts. At 2.50am, after this horrifying experience, passengers and train crew were back where they had started.

This was one of the earliest and most dramatic events in the worst disaster, from a single natural cause, ever to have overtaken railways in Britain: the East Coast Floods of 1953. There is more about them in Chapter 9. Yet floods caused by wind and tide, as these were, are but one of several types of disaster brought about by natural hazards or 'Acts of God'. Wind and tide may equally cause massive damage to sea walls, and to the railways that in places run along them. Inland, running water in the form of flash floods can wash out bridges and culverts, erode away ballast and embankments and cause accidents. Lower down their courses, swollen rivers may inundate large tracts of ground, railways and all, placing them under water that is sometimes several feet deep. Trains become stranded, or have to traverse floods with extreme caution.

Heavy snowfall and hard frosts are an even worse hazard. Visibility is reduced, conductor rails become iced up, electric traction motors are harmed. Signals and telegraphs are damaged and accidents occur. Lines are blocked by snowdrifts, in which trains become snowed up and passengers are isolated. Such happenings are recurrent on lines such as the Highland, West Highland and Settle & Carlisle, but they may occur in any part of Britain during severe winters, such as those of 1894/5, 1946/7 and 1962/3.

Other natural hazards have also brought disaster. Strong gales have done severe damage to both structures and trains. Exceptional heat buckles track and causes accidents. Avalanches (occasionally) and landslips (more often) descend on railway lines. Autumn leaves falling on to rails

Left:
What the floods of August 1948 did to the East Coast main line at Grantshouse. National Railway Museum

Left:
Up to a point, snow is fun. Station staff at Leytonstone, on London Transport's Central Line, set about clearing the platform during the hard weather at the end of December 1962. *London Transport Museum*

Below left:
Accumulated snow causes cancellations. This is Miller's Dale in February 1940. *National Railway Museum*

Below:
Too much snow becomes impassable: a failed snowploughing expedition on the Far North line, probably near Altnabreac, in the 1890s. *The Wick Society*

degenerate under the weight of passing trains to form a non-stick coating, with disastrous effects on train adhesion. The timbers of Barmouth Bridge were uniquely (so far as I am aware) attacked by marine boring molluscs.

Many of these hazards are related to one another. Snowdrifts block cuttings when heavy snowfall is accompanied by gales. Deep snow followed by a quick thaw gives rise to extensive flooding. Heavy rain produces not only flooding but also avalanches and landslips.

Many natural disasters (but not all) are consequences of extremes of weather. At what precise point, one may ponder, does mere bad weather deteriorate into a natural disaster? But this is not a book of meteorology. The familiarity and apparent simplicity of the natural phenomena — sunshine, showers, wind, snow — that make up our weather are deceptive. Their causes are immensely complex. They include continuous and interrelated global changes in air pressure, air temperature, humidity, wind speed, wind direction, sea temperature, night/day and season. I shall leave to meteorologists the detailed consideration of the causes of the hazards and disasters I describe, and climatic change I shall leave to the experts. I make no predictions as to global warming, nor for that matter to the return of the Ice Age.

So this is a book not of causes, but of effects. The immediate effects of natural disasters upon railways are often dramatic, but true drama appears in the hard and sometimes

RAILWAY GOODS AND ... WAREHOUSE

heroic tasks of putting things right. Precautions against recurrence are laborious, expensive and impressive. Yet despite disasters, it is also a success story. Railways traditionally have kept going in conditions that have brought other means of transport to a standstill. Occasionally the conditions even bring benefit to railways. In January 1963

Above:
Low-lying districts close to big rivers are liable to flooding. This is the approach to Nottingham Midland in 1932. *Rail Archive Stephenson, T. G. Hepburn*

British Railways Western Region was reported to be doing a roaring trade in carrying back to London motor cars that had been abandoned by their drivers in the snowbound West Country!

It is noteworthy how problems tend to recur at the same locations. Clearly certain exposed locations are liable to be blocked regularly by snow, or certain low-lying ones to flood, and precautions are taken. But in other locations problems have recurred only at long and irregular intervals, to be forgotten in the meantime. When torrential rain flooded the East Coast main line at Grantshouse, between Berwick and Dunbar, on 28 August 2000 and trapped a Newcastle-Glasgow express, a spokesman for Great North Eastern Railway was quoted as referring to 'a freak weather storm'. Yet the location had been badly affected by floods before, in 1956, and on the very same day, 28 August. Eight years before that, on 12/13 August 1948, it was the principal scene for the worst series of washouts and storm damage, within a limited area, ever experienced on the railways of Britain. And many, many years before that, as early as 1846, a mere three months after the line was opened, a severe storm washed out many of the bridges on the same length.

Another example: in October 2000 newspaper pictures showed the tracks at Lewes station inundated almost to the level of the platforms. On the day that they appeared I was, in the course of researching this book, reading of just such a happening in November 1960.

With snow, although locations liable to problems may be predictable, the actual arrival of heavy snow occurs only at irregular intervals, and the locations in which it actually falls are varied again. I shall be enlarging on this theme in the next few chapters, but I do have a notion that in snow clearance there may be a classic instance of the applicability of the old saying — that things go wrong when the people who remember what went wrong last time have all retired. This evidently applies to natural disasters of other types too. So although this is no technical manual, as an account of how the problems have been tackled in the past, it may be of some value to those who have to tackle them in the future. For the rest of us, we can only marvel at how effectively railways and railwaymen have coped with past disasters, note how little validity there has often been in public criticism of them at such times, and wish them well for the future.

Chapter I

Snow: Railways' Greatest Hazard

Despite the extensive flooding of recent years, the greatest natural hazards with which railways and railwaymen have to contend remain snow, ice and extreme cold; snow particularly, for one of its main problems is that snowfall year on year in the British Isles varies markedly in quantity, quality, location and frequency.

Of its capricious arrival I had a good example while preparing this book. I chose to travel over the highest and most exposed section of the West Highland line, from Crianlarich over Rannoch Moor to Tulloch, two days after a severe blizzard had brought most of Scotland to a halt. Or so the papers said. I confidently expected to see deep drifts that had. been sliced through by snowploughs, and the snow shed at Cruach (unique in Britain) doing its stuff by preventing snow from accumulating in the cutting beneath. But of this sort of thing, on the heights of Rannoch Moor, there was no sign: patches of snow beside the line, but little more. Meanwhile, back at home at lower level, neighbours were snowbound in their home because of drifts that had blocked their driveway.

Many winters see little or no snow over much of Britain — then, just when everyone has been lulled into a false sense of security, there arrives a winter that brings forth headlines about Arctic Conditions or The Return to the Ice Age. Railways in the northern parts of Britain, and at high altitudes, are the most likely to be affected, yet railways as far south as Cornwall and the Isle of Wight have been blocked by snow, as have those close to sea level further north.

Snow also varies immensely in its physical properties. In *Railway Snowfighting Equipment and Methods* — one of surprisingly few books on the subject — G. R. Parkes points out that one cubic foot of snow may weigh between 7lb and 60lb. The specific gravity of snow, he says, varies between extremes of 0.05 and 0.85, and normally lies between 0.1 and 0.6, a ratio of 1:6. For sand, coke and similar movable materials, a ratio of 1:2 would be extreme. The cohesion of snow is at a minimum immediately it has fallen, and that is the time when it is easiest to clear. Snow is easily compressed at high temperatures, but compressible only with great force at low temperatures; once compressed, it does not recover.

Clearly it is most awkward stuff. Nevertheless, M. Harbottle, District Engineer at Inverness, writing in *The Railway Magazine* for January 1960, considered that snow could be classified into two main types, at least in his district: first, the light powdery type that, when accompanied by high winds, produces blizzards and, in consequence, extensive drifting; and second, 'wet' snow in large flakes that does not drift much but causes difficulties with point operation, semaphore signalling and snowploughing.

Even a light snowfall causes problems, particularly when accompanied by frost. It makes it difficult for railwaymen to get to work, and hampers moving around on foot once they have arrived. Couplings freeze up, and so did steam-heating equipment, with consequent delays in thawing them out. Bad weather inevitably brings a higher sickness rate. Problems accumulate: men and women have to stay on duty for longer hours than usual.

Snow and ice cause points to freeze up, resulting in delays and, in extreme circumstances, derailments. Compressed snow and ice in flangeways equally derail locomotives and rolling stock — often in locations where it is difficult to re-rail them. Wet and heavy snow clings to

Snow is ever capricious in the manner of its arrival — as is well shown by the shapes and locations of these drifts that accumulated on the Isle of Man Railway *(Left)* in 1939/40 and on the Festiniog Railway *(Below left)* in 1981/2. *Manx National Heritage/ N. F. Gurley*

Above right:
Even light snow causes problems. Despite this relaxed scene at Yeovil Town on 28 December 1964, staff will be finding it difficult to get in to work, the ground is slippery, and the water cranes risk freezing up. No 80035 is on the left, and 75001 on the right. *Rail Archive Stephenson, M. J. Fox*

Right:
Heavy snow brings down trees and telegraph wires. This is the Southern Railway at Haslemere in January 1940. *National Railway Museum*

telegraph and telephone wires, and rain freezes to them, encasing them in ice and bringing them down, causing failure of block telegraphs; poles fall as well, obstructing the track.

Exceptionally powdery snow enters the traction motors of electric multiple-unit trains with the cooling air, then thaws and short-circuits them. Early in February 1991 some 35% of Network SouthEast's units were disabled, mostly from this cause, with widespread disruption to train services as a result. This was, infamously, 'the wrong kind of snow' — yet the origin of this description is less straightforward than might be supposed, and I return to it in Chapter 2.

Snow, particularly the loss of visibility in blizzards, has been the cause of derailments, collisions, and accidents from signalling faults. Drifting snow blocks cuttings, closes lines and traps trains, leading to dramatic attempts at clearance and rescue. Where main lines were blocked and passenger trains trapped, the drama was self-evident, but even on a little-known freight-only branch the consequences of snow blockage could be serious when, for instance, supply of coal from an important colliery was interrupted just when it was most needed. A severe winter brings such problems on a colossal scale: in January 1940 the London Midland

& Scottish Railway (LMS) suffered snow blocks in no fewer than 313 places.

Blizzards form ice on conductor rails. Intense frost has been known to cause roadbeds to swell or heave, and rails to break. It causes water columns to freeze and, when there were water troughs, caused them to freeze up. Coal frozen into wagons had to be hacked out with picks instead of tipped. In severe frosts iced-up tunnels become a serious problem: drainage water in ventilating shafts freezes to form great icicles, dangerously within the loading gauge. They then, when there is a slight thaw, collapse on to the track and obstruct it.

Widespread snow changes travelling patterns: some passengers stay at home, but others are diverted from road and air. Since rail is generally more reliable than road and air in these circumstances, there is some small benefit to be had from snow.

Above:
Winter in the Highlands: just when and where is uncertain, but four or perhaps five locomotives are involved. *Highland Railway Society*

Below:
The snowplough has come to grief near Crowden on the Woodhead route in 1940, and troops are helping to clear the line. Gantries are already in position for overhead electrification, which would not be completed until after the war. *National Railway Museum*

Chapter 2

Snowfall: When, Where, and the Consequences

Let us now consider chronologically the occurrence of snow and ice problems throughout the British Isles. From this chapter, however, the Highlands of Scotland will be excluded, for problems there are both more severe and more frequent than elsewhere, and will get the following chapter to themselves. Subsequent chapters will describe how the problems were and are alleviated.

Snow was causing problems on tramroads even before there were steam railways. One of the objectors to the Liverpool & Manchester Railway's bill of 1826, a coal-owner who found water transport satisfactory, noted the problems on the tramroads connecting collieries to the Sankey Brook Navigation. They were severe enough for him to claim that 2 hours of snow would stop the proposed railway for a month.

The Cromford & High Peak Railway was built at the same period as the L&M, but laid out for operation by horses on the more-or-less level sections between its cable-worked inclined planes. By the 1820s tramroad builders had become adventurous, and during its crossing of the Peak District the C&HPR achieved an altitude of 1,266ft above sea level throughout its level 9-mile-long summit section. Other sections were almost as high, and these evidently soon gave trouble, for as early as 1832 the railway company was considering construction of a machine to clear snow.

Other tramroads habitually used gravity to power trains, and the Festiniog Railway retained this practice for down slate trains long after introduction of locomotives for other trains. December 1899 was so cold, however, that gravity trains were brought to a stand by ice on the rails, presumably snow frozen in lumps. A locomotive had to be brought down to propel the train into motion again, a task rendered the more difficult when wagon wheels were found to have frozen to the rails before it arrived.

Back on the Liverpool & Manchester Railway, snow and ice did indeed cause problems as early as the winter of 1830/1, the first winter of operation. Locomotives found it difficult to make progress through snow, and it had to be cleared off the track. When a storm coated the rails with ice on 31 December, locomotive wheels slipped so much, particularly on the railway's two steep inclines, that the usual journey time of 2 hours was doubled.

In January 1842 on the Cromford & High Peak — by then locomotive-operated, at least in part — repeated heavy falls of snow closed the summit section for almost a week. The following January saw further very heavy snowfall there. It was in January 1854, however, after the rapid expansion of the railway system in the 1840s, that snow first caused widespread disruption. According to the *Illustrated London News* (24 March 1866) the London & North Western Railway (LNWR) line to Manchester was impassable beyond Crewe, interrupting postal services between Manchester and London for two or three days, and the lines over the Pennines were blocked too. On the Great Northern Railway (GNR) the main line was blocked by snowdrifts from Peterborough to Newark, deepest in the cuttings south of Stoke Tunnel, and the loop line via Boston and Lincoln was also blocked. No trains from York reached London for two days.

These difficulties were small compared with the disaster that overtook the Great Northern 22 years later. In the early evening of 21 January 1876 a severe snowstorm accompanied by a northeasterly gale and extreme cold swept over the Fens and across the main line south of Peterborough. At Peterborough itself, where the snow began at about 4pm, the snowflakes were described as being as big as 2-shilling pieces, and sticky, seeming to adhere to everything they touched.

But the root cause of the trouble ahead lay in the signalling equipment. Semaphore signals had been, when first introduced 35 years before, of the slotted-post type: the normal position of the arm, when no danger was known to be present, was hanging vertical, hidden within the slot in the post. Only when danger was known to be present was it raised to horizontal, the 'danger' position. At night, lamps linked to the arm showed lights coloured respectively white and red.

By 1876 signalling on the GNR had developed a little. The earlier time-interval system had been replaced by block working, but the normal position for signals was still 'clear', the arms within their slots and lights showing white. The signals were worked from levers in the signalbox, which were linked by wires to balance-weights at the foot of the signal posts, which were linked in turn by rods to the signal arms above. Normally the wires held the signal arms in the 'clear' position: when a lever was reversed, tension in its wire was relaxed and the balance-weight caused the signal arm to rise to the 'danger' position. So far, so good: in normal circumstances, in the event of a fault, such as a broken wire, the signal would go to 'danger'.

Conditions on this particular night were very far from normal. At successive signalboxes on the main line south of Peterborough — Holme, Connington, Wood Walton and Abbots Ripton — snow accumulated on the wires to a thickness of 2in and its weight alone was enough to hold signal arms at clear. Worse still, snow and ice had so clogged the slots of the signal posts that the arms were in any case stuck within them, immobilised or at least prevented by the weight of snow clinging to them from rising fully to the horizontal. Even when a signalman moved a lever in his box to the danger position, the balance-weight was unable to raise the signal arm and the signal still showed clear, with a white light. (Some conflicting evidence emerged at the eventual court of inquiry, but this seems to have been the correct story.)

Of these appalling circumstances the driver and fireman of a heavy coal train, rumbling southwards from Peterborough, were sadly unaware. What they were aware of was that they had headed out into the storm 18 minutes late, at 5.53pm, and that the up Scotch express, due away from Peterborough at 6.18, was behind them and catching up. They expected to be shunted, setting back into a siding to allow the express to overtake, but no red danger signal was showing at Holme, and they carried on. Only at Abbots Ripton were they eventually stopped; the signalman waved a red light from the box, and indicated that they were to shunt. As the locomotive passed the box, setting back its long train into the siding, the signalman called out urgently, 'Shove them back — the "Scotsman's" standing at Wood Walton!'

But the 'Scotsman' was not standing anywhere. Its driver was lured on by white light after white light and the train was closing on Abbots Ripton at full speed. The signalman had scarcely finished shouting when the express burst out of the blizzard. The coal train was still shunting with six wagons on the main line. The express collided with these — its locomotive was thrown on its side, its tender across the down line and coaches piled against it.

On the down line, the 5.30pm King's Cross to Leeds express was now approaching, its driver running hard to try and keep time through the storm despite what he later said were the worst conditions he had ever encountered on the footplate. Despite every effort to warn him, it was only at the last minute that this was achieved. Too late for him to pull up completely, the locomotive of the down train struck the tender of the up express at about 20mph, and was thrown on to its side with its train piling up behind it. In this double collision, 14 lives were lost.

There were two important consequences that resulted from lessons learned from this accident. The GNR ceased to use slotted-post signals, and adopted instead the distinctive 'somersault' signal with centrally-pivoted arm. Slotted-post signals went out of use more gradually elsewhere and remained in use on some railways until recently — notably, and perhaps surprisingly, on the adjoining North Eastern Railway (NER), which was even more prone to snow problems than the Great Northern. Nor was Abbots Ripton the last occasion on

which hard frost would cause trouble with signals. As recently as March 1958 at Chinley, on the former Midland line from Derby to Manchester, a signal arm frozen into the clear position allowed one train to run into the back of another. Fortunately, injuries to passengers were few and light.

The other consequence of the Abbots Ripton accident was that Captain H. W. Tyler, the Inspecting Officer who inquired into the causes of the accident, recommended that signal arms should indicate 'danger' rather than 'clear' as their normal position. This recommendation was adopted, and remains the practice throughout the British Isles to this day.

Although this is not primarily a book about accident prevention, there is in the reaction to this accident a noteworthy example of how we have forgotten things the Victorians understood well. They investigated railway accidents to establish the cause and prevent, if possible, a recurrence. Today, more and more it seems, accidents are investigated with a view to apportioning blame. The more likely those involved in accidents are to be blamed, the less likely they are to speak frankly, and the more difficult it becomes to establish the causes.

* * *

When the Imperial Russian Commission came to inspect the Festiniog Railway in February 1870 the weather was intensely cold, the country snowbound, the sea in places frozen. This does not, however, seem to have hampered their approach, over the three-year-old Cambrian Railways Coast line, nor the trials and demonstrations of various types of train laid on for them on the FR itself — with one exception, that when some members of the Russian party felt that a further trial was needed before their departure, and attempted it at 4am, they were prevented by frozen pipework on double-Fairlie *Little Wonder*. But in general the performance of the FR on its narrow gauge in conditions that were (as *The Engineer*'s special correspondent famously reported) *plus Russe que dans la Russie méme* was evidently good enough to result in construction of a vast mileage of narrow-gauge railways in Russia.

Snow was more of a problem when W. H. Bishop, correspondent of the American *Scribner's Monthly*, visited the FR just before Christmas 1878. By that date in the USA, as in Russia, many thousands of miles of narrow-gauge railway had been built following the Festiniog example. Bishop attempted to travel on the Monday 6am up quarrymen's train from

Portmadoc in a heavy pre-dawn snowstorm, but first the locomotive slipped violently and found it impossible to get its long train under way, then the train was cancelled because the line higher up was blocked. Bishop accompanied the party going to the rescue on the footplate of *Little Wonder*, and describes the railway as 'two dark lines … drawn on the snow between low walls, like the trace of a single sled down a country lane'; a dismal crackling sound, as they traversed the long tunnel, proved to be that of icicles snapped off and falling on to the locomotive. At Tanygrisiau they found the 0-4-0 tank locomotive *Princess* derailed — he does not state the cause — and she was jacked up and pushed back over the track by muscle-power. The snow was no more than 2 or 3in deep, but wet enough and clinging enough to cause the problems.

* * *

Left:
The great snowstorm of January 1881 extended as far south as Ventnor station on the Isle of Wight.
National Railway Museum

In mid-January 1881 a great snowstorm swept across the South and West of England, affecting particularly the counties of Oxfordshire, Berkshire, Wiltshire, Dorset and Hampshire, and reaching as far south as the Isle of Wight. On that island snow fell for three days and nights and froze so hard that people could walk about on top of hedges and children were unable to reach school until Easter. A remarkable photograph shows Ventnor station largely submerged in snowdrifts.

In *Our Iron Roads* F. S. Williams quotes the experiences of a London & South Western Railway (LSWR) guard at this time:

'I went down from Waterloo in the morning to bring up a train coming from Exeter on from Salisbury to London. It was blowing wild enough when we started, and the snow whirling round and round us — not in big flakes, like you see it fall when in still weather, but in a sharp fine dust, just like glass ground down into powder. Long before we got to our down journey's end the snow had begun to gather deep in the cuttings, laying it in a sloping bank, running down far across the rails. It is an odd sensation when you are cutting through snow that is not quite enough to stop you, but very near. It is as if you were off the rails, going over stony ground, and something all the time trying hard to shove you back, and then letting you go clean ahead for a minute or two.

'But the worst of it hadn't come yet. Our engine made her way through it very fair, and we were not much above half an hour behind when we went into Salisbury station. There we

18

waited for the Exeter train, telegraphed from Gillingham only an hour late. When she came in I took her guard's place, and we started for Waterloo with nine or ten carriages, and a good many passengers, a little before five — just after dark, in fact. It had been snowing, snowing, snowing down there, as elsewhere, all day long; and as we went out of the lighted station right into the wild open country, I couldn't help thinking of what it would be like that night on the great chalk downs, or on the roads over Salisbury Plain, without a bit of shelter for miles and miles. Oh, how it did blow! and how the sharp snow-dust came sweeping down upon us as we went towards it in the teeth of the wind. We kept on at a good pace, at least on the embankments, where the line was swept by the gale as clean as twenty thousand brooms could have made it. On we went till we got into the cuttings the other side of Andover. There we were again rumbling as if over stones instead of iron rails, and being shoved back, and then again on with a start, and then rumbling and bumping, and then on again. I should think, with you, that the passengers found it unpleasant; but it was curious how quiet and contented they all seemed. Nobody cared apparently to peep out even for a moment. The ladies in the first-class carriages had got foot-warmers, and so had a good many people in the second and third class; but if they wanted anything more they didn't trouble themselves to make a sign, even when we stopped a moment at Andover...

'... I knew it would be worse when we got past Whitchurch, for the deep cuttings are about there; and so it was. Rumble, rumble we went again, and again something seemed shoving us back, and then on, and then back; and then we came to a dead stand in that comfortless hole, with the snow, that was continually sweeping down on us, now up above the foot-board and even against the lower part of the carriage doors. I got down with my lantern, and no sooner did I meet the cutting gale, than my beard and all the lower part of my face was covered over with a thick crust which you could neither rub nor pull off with the hand. The wind literally blew me backward, and forced me to keep my chin down on my chest and grope along holding by the carriage handles.

' "How are you getting on, Jack?" I asked my mate beside the engine as soon as I could get near enough to his ear to be heard.

' "Bad enough, Bill," he said."Turn your lantern down here, old man. It's the ash-pan all caked up with snow, and not a bit of draught can get into the fire."

'And so it was — hard as flint, too, in spite of the warmth. There was nothing to be done but to rake away with a long bent iron bar — all three of us, stoker included — till we had cleared a bit; and we began to make steam again.

' "Can you get on now, do you think?" I says.

' "Look at that snow in front of my engine," says he; "she'll never go through with the train behind her."

' "What'll you do, then?" I says.

' "You get into your van, Bill," says he, "and put the brake hard on while I unhook."

'So I did; and when Jack Randall had backed a trifle, or tried to do it, he unhooked, and leaving us behind in that dismal place, whistled and went bang at the snow, and right on, ploughing and cutting into it for three hundred yards or so. Then he backed again, and down we were once more, stoker and all, hooking on and peering with the lantern and clearing the ashpan. That is the way we got on; and patience it wanted too, with our numbed fingers and half-frozen faces.'

The troubles of the driver, wrote Williams, were greater even than those of the guard. The white ground reflected the light, it was difficult to see any signal when the air was full of snow driving straight against him, and he continually had to clear the snow off the two round glass spectacles in front of him. All down the line there were similar difficulties. Trains stuck fast in stations themselves from snow drifting up to the platforms.

On the Great Western Railway (GWR) the problems were as great, if not greater. Williams quoted the experience of a young lady *en route* from Oxford to London:

'...we came to a standstill, and on hearing voices upon the line, I opened the carriage window, and nervously inquired what was the matter, saying, "Snowed up, I suppose," and, receiving an answer in the affirmative, rejoined, in my simplicity, "That we should all turn out and help clear the snow away," to which a good-tempered man responded, "If they was all like you, miss, we should soon get it out." I closed the window, expecting every moment the train would proceed, and continued to amuse myself by reading; but hour after hour passed without the slightest indication of a movement, and I began to feel my lone and desolate position — cut off from all communication with my fellow-passengers, and with nothing visible on either side but snow, which insidiously crept in through the crevices of the windows and drifted to such an extent that I thought unless relief soon came I should become "snowed in".'

The light failed in the carriage, says Williams. Then:

'Cold, benumbed, and hungry, I lay myself prostrate on the seat, unconscious of what was going on around me, until I was aroused by a knock at the window, and on opening it a "Samaritan", in the form of a labouring man, asked me to take a little "whisky". At first I refused his proffered kindness, but on his assuring me it would do me good, and that some other ladies had drunk some, I, much against my will, yielded to his kind-hearted solicitations, and for the first time in my life swallowed what I have heard my gentlemen friends term a drop of the "crater". That it did me good I have no doubt … I offered a shilling to him, but, with a generosity I shall never forget, he declined to accept a farthing, and left me. On the departure of my well-intentioned benefactor, I took off my shoes and stockings and rubbed my feet, which were very benumbed, with all the energy I was possessed of. I made a pillow of some wraps strapped together, and tried to sleep; but in vain. Thoughts of home would come, and tears rolled down my cheeks, for up to this time I had not thoroughly realised my critical position. At 12.30 I heard someone talking to my next-door neighbours — some light-hearted youths going to Harrow — and asked where we were, for until then I had no idea, and was informed by the gentleman whose voice I had heard, that we were 200yd from Radley station. He inquired if I was alone, and on telling him of my position he asked if he could do anything for me, and suiting the action to the word climbed up to my window, literally covered with frozen snow, supplied me with some biscuits, and took my foot-warmer away and refilled it from the engine, a matter of considerable difficulty, as the snow had blocked up the train on either side, and was very deep… He advised me to try to sleep, and for half an hour I managed to do so, when he returned with some warm tea and bread and butter, saying that he believed the train was to be cleared, and passengers were to go either to Radley station or the inn. He remained with me for several hours, and, a way having been cut through the snow, we reached the inn…'

The travellers were subsequently evacuated still further, trudging 3 miles through the snow to the Crown & Thistle at Abingdon; there our heroine slept for 10 hours before being able to resume her journey, and eventually reached home in the small hours of the fourth day after she set out.

The extent of the snow blockages was so great that the mail trains for the West were held at Paddington for 24 hours until it had been reported that the line was clear enough for them to get through. The full significance of this is sadly lost on us today, when such a delay does not seem unlikely. But in the 1880s for a century the culture surrounding the carriage of mails, first by mail coaches on the roads and then by train, had been that, come what may, the mails must get through. Of all trains, the mail trains were the most important — such a delay was unprecedented.

As a consequence of this storm, the GWR suffered 51 passenger trains and 13 goods trains snowbound. Six of these were between Oxford and Reading. There were snow blocks at 141 places; the drifts covering the tracks ranged from 3ft to 10ft in depth, and their extent was 111 miles in total. The cost of clearing the snow, and all the associated expenses, was £56,000: the next dividend was half what it might otherwise have been.

* * *

The Settle & Carlisle line was opened to all traffic in 1876; it was the third main line from England to Scotland, the Midland Railway's rival to the East Coast and West Coast routes. Gradients and curves were made appropriately easy — or at least easier than they would have been for a purely local line. But the route of the S&C lies high among the Pennines — its summit is 1,151ft above sea level, and it was always going to be subject to the extremes of Pennine weather.

The engineer, Sharland by name, had a foretaste of this when still staking out the centre-line of the intended railway during the winter of 1869/70. While he was staying at an inn on Blea Moor, according to F. S. Williams in *The Midland Railway*, so much snow fell for so long that he became snowed up — all too literally, for the snow accumulated to a depth 18in higher than the lintel of the doorway. It was only by tunnelling through the snow that the engineer, his staff and the innkeeper and his family were able to obtain drinking water from a horse trough. They were cut off from the outside world; fortunately there was enough food in the house to last until conditions improved.

On 3 March 1881 — a few weeks after the great snowstorm in the South of England — heavy snow started to fall over the country traversed by the S&C, accompanied by a furious gale. This swept exposed hillsides clear, but snow accumulated in the cuttings. By 10pm the up line was blocked, and soon afterwards the down line became blocked too when a locomotive, which had been detached from its train to take a run at a drift, became embedded in the snow, immobilised. Over the next couple of days, despite every effort to clear the line, drifts increased, in places to a depth of 30ft. Then it alternately rained and froze, so that the surface of the snow would bear the weight of those walking upon it. All that could be seen of one train was the top of the engine chimney protruding from the snow. At least ten locomotives were stranded in the drifts.

* * *

Away to the east of the Settle & Carlisle lay the country served by the North Eastern Railway. Those of its branches that ascended into the hills were of course much troubled by snow, notably the line to Kirkby Stephen and beyond, which, at Stainmore summit, crossed the Pennines at 1,370ft; but even the East Coast main line, although at a relatively low altitude, has been far from immune.

On 5 March 1886 the main line was blocked by snow north of Newcastle. An up express was stuck in a snowdrift overnight at Forest Hall, eventually reaching Newcastle 12 hours late. But it fared better than a following one, which stuck in the snow at Acklington in the small hours of the following morning, and its passengers, who included those travelling in the Pullman sleeping car, were stranded aboard for 17 hours. Then they were taken to Acklington itself, but even there food was limited and it was two more days before they could continue to Newcastle. In the meantime first one and then another snowplough train sent to clear the line had themselves become stranded. It was

21

these events that led to the construction by the NER of large independent snowploughs, which will be described in Chapter 4.

They were in use two years later when a blizzard struck in March 1888. A down goods train became snowbound in a drift north of Longhirst, and the down 'Flying Scotsman' was held up behind it. The following express got as far as Morpeth, whence it was sent back to Newcastle, but had only got half way when it stuck in the snow at Annitsford near Killingworth. The attempt to rescue it resulted in a serious collision involving one of the large snowploughs; there is more about this in Chapter 4. The 'Flying Scotsman' was brought back as far as Morpeth, where most passengers spent the night on board. Meanwhile there had been problems with deep snow on the line near Consett, and five trains were snowed up between Tebay and Kirkby Stephen.

The Cromford & High Peak was getting its share of snow at this period, too. The line was blocked by snow in December 1882, and again in February 1888, when two trains were snowed up. The load of one of them included milk in churns, which provided vital nourishment for the train crew.

* * *

In 1891 it was the turn of the South of England again. On 9 March, after a spell of mild weather, a blizzard swept across the country from South Wales to Kent leaving snowdrifts and derailments in its wake, but worst affected was the West Country. The down broad-gauge 'Dutchman' express (in full 'Flying Dutchman', named after a Derby winner of long before) encountered the blizzard soon after Taunton, and by the time it reached Plymouth drifts were 5ft deep. It continued but, just short of Camborne station, all wheels of the locomotive (South Devon 4-4-0 saddle tank *Leopard*) left the track on a level crossing in deep snow and the train was stranded. An up train from Cornwall struggled as far as St Germans, but was there immobilised when the locomotive became entangled in telegraph wires from fallen poles. Numerous other trains were stranded on both the GWR and the LSWR, and it was 15 March before things were back to normal. The cost of this storm to the Great Western alone was calculated at some £3,500; this included additional wages and overtime, particularly for men clearing the line, refreshments both for them and for passengers, additional locomotive mileage, notably in piloting, and damaged telegraph equipment.

* * *

Less improbably, railways in southwest Scotland have had severe problems with snow from time to time. C. E. J. Fryer describes some of them in his two interesting books on the railways of the region, *The Portpatrick and Wigtownshire Railways* and *The Girvan & Portpatrick Junction Railway*.

On 6/7 February 1895 a snowstorm blocked many of the cuttings on the Portpatrick & Wigtownshire Joint Railway and passenger trains in both directions became snowbound. The 7.28pm from Dumfries on 6 February became marooned at Loch Skerrow for several days; its two (only) passengers and train crew were able to take refuge at nearby railwaymen's cottages, but when food ran short were obliged to make inroads into foodstuffs consigned in a van attached to the train.

In the up direction the 3.40pm from Stranraer had become stuck in the snow near Creetown. Conditions were so bad that some 24 hours elapsed before passengers could at last be evacuated from it and taken first to Creetown station, where there was warmth and hot food, then down to the village. It was three days before they could resume their journey. Fryer records that one passenger became so unnerved by the whole experience that he attempted to commit suicide by cutting his throat. Fortunately the razor was snatched from him in time, and he received medical attention.

While these trains were becoming snowbound on the Portpatrick & Wigtownshire, the 4.15pm from Stranraer to Glasgow was struggling northwards on the line to Girvan. It too eventually became stuck in the snow near the summit of the line between Glenwhilly and Barrhill. Passengers and train crew spent the night in the train; by daylight they were able with difficulty to cross snow-covered moorland to shelter in houses nearby. It was a week before the line could be reopened. At this time the Whithorn and Portpatrick branches also were blocked by snow for five and six days respectively.

The privations of those on the Stranraer-Glasgow train on 6 February 1895 were small compared to what was suffered a few years later by those on the 4.15pm Glasgow-Stranraer, on 28 December 1908. It was extremely cold and, by the time the train reached Barrhill, snowing hard. Snow lay thick on the ground and was drifting in the cuttings. But men were out trying to keep the line clear and the train set off. A mile south of Barrhill it became stuck in a drift, but by setting back then charging the drift it got through. Two miles south of Barrhill it stuck fast in a drift in a cutting and could not extricate itself. A light engine sent to the rescue from Barrhill got stuck in a drift itself. When a rescue party arrived on foot two hours after dawn the only way to get the food that they had brought to the passengers was by opening the lamp-holes in the carriage roofs; the space between the train and the sides of the cutting was now so full of snow that the carriage doors could not be opened. Valiant attempts were made to clear the line with a snowplough, but this itself became derailed a mile short of the stranded train, and the incarcerated passengers spent a second freezing night on board. The following day, after much effort, doors along one side of the train were dug clear of snow, the passengers extricated and escorted to a relief train that had approached as close as it could. Those who wished to continue their journey to Stranraer had to travel, eventually, by Kilmarnock and Dumfries. Sadly, one of these died the day after arrival, a consequence of her experiences.

Snow is rare in Ireland, but on the same day that these events overtook the Stranraer train, 28 December 1908, the Northern Counties Committee's Class J tank locomotive No 25 was caught in a snowdrift on the Ballyclare branch, so it appears that the same harsh weather was affecting Galloway and County Antrim.

* * *

Let us now take a brief excursion to the Snowdon Mountain Railway, the highest and most exposed of all railways in the British Isles (although the Cairngorm funicular will challenge this). The Snowdon railway uses the Abt rack system to reach an altitude of 3,493ft at Snowdon Summit. It was opened on Easter Monday, 6 April 1896 and, as is well known, was closed again almost immediately because of a serious accident. This accident was due, at least in part, to the severe climatic conditions at the top of the mountain. On Snowdon, above 2,000ft, temperatures are at or below freezing for much of the winter; snow freezes, and stays frozen. The railway follows the cold northwest slope of the mountain.

The locomotives were driven by their rack pinions; these were fitted with brakes that were applied automatically if the speed of descent became excessive. When the first descending passenger train was a little below the summit, the pinions of the locomotive rose relative to the rack, became disengaged from it, and the locomotive ran away. The automatic brakes came on and locked the pinions, but these skidded along the top of the rack, until the locomotive derailed and dived over a precipice. With the following train, the pinions became disengaged at the same place and the locomotive collided with the coaches from the first train. These, which had not been coupled to their locomotive, had been held by their brakes and the passengers had fortunately dismounted (although one, who had jumped from the coaches while still moving, was fatally injured). The shock of the collision re-engaged the pinions of the second locomotive, which was thus halted, but set the coaches off again to run away for some 800yd down the line.

The cause, or causes, of this accident have been the subject of much controversy. One contributory factor seems certain to have been construction of the line over ground that was frozen hard. Because construction had fallen behind schedule, the high-altitude part of the line was built during the winter, the track reaching the summit in January. While the ground beneath it gradually thawed with the onset of milder weather, heavy works trains were running. Eventually the track subsided and twisted sufficiently for the pinions to become disengaged. There were possibly other factors too.

The principal remedy adopted was to equip the line, before reopening, with safety girders alongside the rack. These are of inverted L-section, with safety grippers on the locomotives that pass beneath the horizontal part of the L. No other Abt rack railway is so equipped, and many operate, apparently safely, through deep snow. On Snowdon, when there is snow on the summit in early and late season, the Snowdon Railway prefers to terminate its trains below the snowline.

These two circumstances are not unconnected. The safety girders on either side of the rack form a convenient channel in which snow accumulates and ice forms, clogging the teeth. They also make it very difficult to clear the snow out again. High on Snowdon, heavy snowfall is often accompanied by high winds, and snow sufficient to start clogging the rack may accumulate in a few minutes. Even if there were equipment to clear the rack for a train to go up, the channel containing the rack would fill with snow again behind it. Where the line is located on a ledge cut into the mountainside, snow accumulates and often stays throughout the winter.

Winter maintenance of the railway during its closed season is also affected by conditions. It starts at high level and then, as weather conditions dictate, moves down to lower levels; in the spring, maintenance staff work their way back up the mountain as the weather improves. Snow above 2,000ft is not uncommon in April, and has been known in May and June, so it is usually late May before the upper section from Clogwyn to the Summit is reopened.

* * *

To return to the main story, at the end of December 1906 another widespread snowstorm affected much of the northern part of Scotland. As usual (and as will be seen in the next chapter) it brought problems to the Highland Railway. Less usually, it extended to the East Coast at Arbroath, where it brought chaos to the Dundee & Arbroath Joint line, owned jointly by the North British Railway and the Caledonian Railway. This chaos led, in turn, to one of the worst accidents, in terms of loss of life, to have arisen from such a cause.

The snow commenced on 26 December accompanied by a gale, and by nightfall on the following day there was 12 to 18in of snow lying on the level, with much drifting and a hard frost. Snow frozen on to telegraph wires brought them down, and many of the poles too. By the morning of 28 December, block working, telegraphs and telephones were all interrupted for several miles southwards from Arbroath, and trains were being operated by time interval. The snow continued intermittently, accompanied by violent squalls of wind, and rendered many points and signals inoperable. North of Arbroath the separate routes of the two railways were alike blocked by snowdrifts and by trains at a stand, unable to proceed.

The sequence of events that led to disaster commenced when an up goods train (which, in the prevailing conditions, had already taken almost 12 hours to travel from Aberdeen) ran into a snowdrift south of Elliot Junction, the next station south of Arbroath, about 7.30am. It broke into three parts. During attempts to reunite them, some of the wagons were propelled through the drifts and promptly became derailed. Then the locomotive tender also became derailed. This meant that single-line working, with a pilotman, had to be instituted over the section concerned. But there was a long delay in doing so, for attempts were first made to re-rail the derailed vehicles. Thus it was around 2pm before single-line working past the derailment was put into operation.

Meanwhile a down North British express from Edinburgh reached Arbroath at 10.41am, and there it was obliged to terminate. Also at Arbroath were an up local train waiting to leave for Dundee and, with the New Year holiday approaching, a great many delayed passengers. The staff at Arbroath, endeavouring to retrieve order from chaos, eventually dispatched the local train crowded with passengers at 3.13pm. Its driver later stated that the wind was blowing violently, with snow falling and drifting over the line. However, within a few minutes his train reached Elliot Junction. The home and distant signals were on, but an inspector on the footplate instructed the driver to pass the home signal and enter the station. And there the local train stood, awaiting the pilotman.

At Arbroath the stock from the down express was now prepared for its return south. The locomotive was obliged to run tender-first, for snow had rendered the turntable inaccessible and inoperable — or so it was considered. On the exposed footplate, the locomotive crew would face the freezing blizzard. They were warned that the time-interval system was in operation, to stop at every station and to keep a good lookout — no easy task, when to the blizzard was added the coal pile in the tender to obstruct the view. They were not warned of the possibility of additional delays at Elliot Junction from single-line working, because the signalman at Arbroath South was as yet unaware of this himself. But Driver Gourlay was an experienced man with 47 years' service; he had driven Royal Trains. During the long wait at Arbroath, however, he was rash enough to accept a dram or two — or possibly more — to keep out (one may assume) the cold. The express left 15 minutes after the local; visibility of signals and obstructions alike was appalling. The local was still standing at Elliot Junction when Gourlay's train passed the home signal at danger and emerged from the snowstorm at some 30mph to collide with it, destroying the three rear coaches. Twenty-two people were killed.

Gourlay himself was injured but survived. Released after half an hour spent trapped on the footplate and suffering from shock, he then had three-quarters of a glass of neat brandy poured into him by some well-meaning person. A quarter of an hour after that, he was examined by three doctors who not unnaturally concluded that he was under the influence of alcohol. Of his condition when he left Arbroath, however, there was much conflict of evidence. In his eventual inquiry report, Major Pringle, the Board of Trade's Inspecting Officer, wrote: 'I have therefore, most reluctantly, been forced … to give it as my opinion that the lack of intelligence, or of caution and alertness, displayed by driver Gourlay on this occasion were in part at all events induced by drink, the effects of which may possibly have been accentuated … by exposure to the weather.' Driver Gourlay, he wrote, was primarily responsible for the collision.

But Pringle was also bitterly critical of the administration of the joint line. For example, no extra men had been called out to help clear the snow. If the turntable at Arbroath had been cleared, not only could Gourlay's locomotive have been turned, but so could the snowploughs. These had been called out, but had ploughed fully only the down road from Dundee to Arbroath; they had returned to Dundee on the up road with the plough trailing. Had this road been properly ploughed, the freight train would probably not have come to grief in a drift and the whole sorry sequence of events would not have been initiated.

Nor had any hand-signalmen or fog-signalmen been called out. Had a detonator been placed at Elliot Junction up distant signal, its explosion would have alerted Gourlay to his position and in all probability prevented the accident. There was much more in the same vein. The root cause of it all appeared to be the divided responsibilities resulting from joint ownership, something that those responsible for today's far more fragmented railway system might well bear in mind.

Driver Gourlay was later arrested and charged with driving the train recklessly while intoxicated and against the warning of the Arbroath stationmaster, amounting to culpable homicide. (The case is described by Adrian Gray in his article 'Railway Accidents and the Courts', which appeared in the magazine *Back Track* in December 2000.)

Gourlay was convicted. His five-month sentence was, however, the shortest allowed, for there were many extenuating circumstances. But a petition in his favour attracted 70,000 signatures; Richard Bell MP, General Secretary of the Amalgamated Society of Railway Servants, went to see the Secretary of State for Scotland, and Gourlay's sentence was reduced from five months to three.

* * *

After 1908 the next three decades seem to have been relatively mild — relative, that is, not only to what had been before, but also to what would follow. But for the moment snow problems were few, and isolated. About the beginning of April 1916, for instance, the Midland main line was blocked by snow north of Kettering, and in February 1919 there was another outbreak of snow problems on the Cromford & High Peak, repeated a month later when the line was again blocked. Christmas 1927 brought a blizzard to the Home Counties, and the Southern Railway's suburban electric services were hard hit when snow became clogged between pick-up shoes and the third rail. In February 1929 a blizzard struck the Mull of Kintyre and brought the Campbeltown & Machrihanish Railway to a standstill for a week.

The Settle & Carlisle line, always at risk, was blocked by snowdrifts for a week in February 1931. The snowfall itself was not particularly heavy — it was the gale that accompanied it that brought the problems. Snowdrifts buried a locomotive, and Mallerstang signalbox too. On the Cambrian Coast line on 24 February 1933, a few days before the avalanche described in Chapter 10, a blizzard brought sufficient snow to require the attention of a snowplough. In December 1937, snow that blocked a facing points lock, reduced visibility and — perhaps — affected signals, was the root cause of the disastrous end-on collision at Castlecary on the Edinburgh & Glasgow line.

* * *

It was in the early 1940s, however, just when Britain had become engaged in a world war, that 'Arctic' winters returned with a vengeance. The first of these came in January 1940. There was intensely cold weather over most of Europe, but during the last week of that month in Britain exceptionally heavy snowfall was added. It put some 1,500 miles of railway out of action; snowdrifts up to 15ft deep were encountered, so *The Railway Magazine* for March 1940 reported, in places as far apart as Buntingford and Beattock, Fakenham and Garsdale, and scores of trains were snowed up.

The LMS was particularly hard hit. One up West Coast express that left Glasgow on a Saturday eventually reached Euston the following Tuesday. Even that was more fortunate than three following trains, which became snowed up near Beattock; passengers had to take shelter in nearby villages for five days. In total six passenger trains, two freight trains and a newspaper train were snowbound on that stretch of line. The Peak District was badly affected, particularly around Miller's Dale and Chapel-en-le-Frith, with 13 passenger and goods trains held up. On 28 January the 7.50am from Colne to Manchester became snowed up near Haslingden despite being double-headed, with 2-6-2T No 65 piloting 2-6-4T No 2431. It was eventually dug out four days later. There were blockages too on the Settle & Carlisle line. In all, there were 238 separate snow blockages on the LMS, affecting 1,056 route miles; 71 trains were snowbound.

On the London & North Eastern Railway (LNER) some 15 miles of the Manchester-Sheffield line were blocked by snow near Hadfield, and there were snow problems too on the Cheshire Lines. The Newcastle & Carlisle line and the Waverley Route were also blocked by

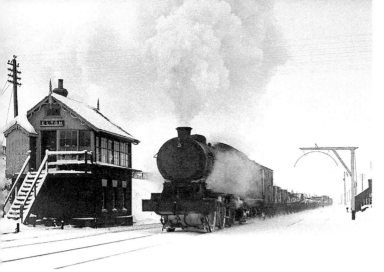

Left:
Despite widespread deep
snow, railways in many
parts of Britain kept going.
On 28 January 1940
'J39' class 0-6-0 No 2947
of the LNER heads a
goods train past Elton on
the Grantham-Nottingham
line. Snow is up to railhead
level, and almost
obliterates the siding
beneath the loading gauge.
*Rail Archive Stephenson,
T. G. Hepburn*

Left:
On the Isle of Man, the
former Manx Northern line
was hard hit by snow from
time to time where it
followed the West Coast.
Here a snow clearance
train headed by 0-6-0T
Caledonia stands at
(probably) Peel Road
during the winter of
1939/40.
Manx National Heritage

snow. The East Coast main line, however, was kept clear, and for some days provided the only
rail route between England and Scotland; a problem of a different sort arose when severe cold
caused sufficient ice to form beneath the water troughs at Wiske, near Northallerton, to force
them upwards off their mountings, which meant a 30mph speed restriction. The same cold
snap was causing havoc on the Southern Railway's electrified lines, and on the surface lines
of London Transport, with up to 2in of ice forming on conductor rails to interrupt power
supply. On 27 January the temperature at Cockfosters was as low as 7°F (-14°C). Even the Isle
of Man Railway was affected, with deep drifts blocking the St Johns-Ramsey line. The
conditions also brought damage to telegraph and telephone lines throughout much of Britain.
On the Somerset & Dorset Joint Railway alone, accumulation of snow and ice on the wires
brought down about 200 poles between Bath and Bournemouth.

* * *

January 1941 brought heavy snow to Lancashire and Yorkshire. Then in February it was the turn of the West Coast route to come to the rescue of the East Coast, for it remained open when a blizzard subjected northeast England to some of the worst conditions with which railwaymen have ever had to cope. G. R. Parkes, in *Railway Snowfighting Equipment and Methods*, quotes in full the report prepared shortly afterwards by Jenkin Jones, LNER Divisional General Manager, and the episode is also recorded in *The Railway Magazine* of April 1941.

The snow started to fall before dawn on Wednesday 19 February 1941, and continued without respite for 56 hours. When it eventually ceased falling around midday on Friday 21 February, it was lying to depths ranging from 1ft to 4ft, with drifting up to 14ft. During the storm, points rapidly became snowed up and shunting movements at Newcastle station took as long as one and a half hours, for the points over which a train had passed became snowed up again before the movement could be completed. The snow was wet and heavy, bringing down telegraph wires and breaking poles so that they fell, in many cases, across the track. By the morning of Thursday 20 February block telegraphs, telegraphs and telephones had failed throughout the area, extending to 600 route miles, and trains were being worked by time interval. Many became derailed and there were some collisions. But remarkably there were no serious accidents, and almost no injuries to passengers or railwaymen, the only exception being the very slight injuries sustained by half a dozen passengers in a collision.

At one stage on the Thursday afternoon the main line and all alternative routes between Darlington and Newcastle were blocked, and so were the lines into Newcastle from the west, north and east; at least 50 trains were stationary, waiting to move towards Newcastle. Trains from the south were then terminated at Darlington, and no further trains despatched from Scotland. Some sort of skeleton service was maintained on most branches, including steam trains over the electrified lines, but goods and mineral traffic was effectively at a standstill.

However, the permanent way staff were working doggedly to release trains blocked in snow; ten pairs of snowploughs were at work on 20 different routes, and tool vans were called out to deal with 25 derailments. The usually difficult conditions of wartime operation were for once turned to advantage: the railway's own staff was supplemented by no fewer than 1,000 soldiers. The only means of communication available were two Post Office trunk telephone lines, which linked divisional and district offices but not intermediate points; locations of trains could be little more than guessed at, by comparing those that had left, say, Darlington with those that had arrived at Durham, and similarly on other sections.

By these means passenger trains were gradually brought to stations where stranded passengers could alight. The down trains that suffered the worst delays were the 7.15pm, 8.20pm, 10.15pm and 11.30pm trains from King's Cross on the Wednesday; they eventually reached Newcastle on the Friday at 12.38am, 9.25am, 10.37am and 12.12pm respectively —

the 8.20 having spent 37hr 5min *en route*. In the up direction, the 10pm and 10.20pm trains from Edinburgh on Wednesday reached Newcastle on Thursday at 5.17pm and 7.26pm respectively. Some trains were evacuated and their passengers brought to Newcastle by bus. But even then the passengers could not immediately travel onward; the refreshment rooms at Newcastle were kept open night and day, and the LNER's hotel at Newcastle was packed with stranded travellers, with up to 120 people sleeping in the public rooms.

This succession of ever more staggering statistics is relieved, in Jenkin Jones's report, by his account of what befell one particular group of railwaymen — railwaymen, too, of a category seldom in the limelight. It had been realised on the Thursday morning, at the height of the storm, that three passenger trains were stranded near Durham, but a fleet of buses dispatched to rescue the passengers was defeated by snowbound roads and returned empty. Since it was thus impossible to bring the passengers to the food prepared for them at Newcastle, it was decided to send the food to the passengers. At 2.15pm a '4-ton motor' left Newcastle crewed by a cartage clerk in charge, with two motor drivers, four checkers and a loader; it was accompanied by a 2-ton motor with one motor driver for emergencies. The cargo of the 4-ton lorry comprised sandwiches, pork pies, biscuits, cakes, tea and milk for 600 passengers; the party was equipped with picks, shovels, chains and mats, and its instructions were to find the trains at all costs.

Four miles south of Newcastle the 4-ton lorry ran into a snowdrift, and the crew dug it out. It then encountered a tram, derailed and snowed up; the lorry's crew helped to get it back on the rails and (as Jones puts it) get it on its way — and out of theirs. They then found a bus stuck across the road, and dug that out too. They eventually reached Durham, a 14-mile journey, at 6.45pm, where they learned that the first of the trains was snowbound a mile to the south, and sent the 2-tonner back to Newcastle with the news. But the crew of the 4-tonner then discovered that the direct road to the train was blocked by three stranded buses and two Army lorries. However, they detoured, and managed to reach a farm half a mile from the train, which had left King's Cross at 10.25pm the previous night. This was the nearest point to the train that the lorry could reach. The party then waded waist-deep through the snow to carry hampers of food to the train. The tea, of course, was stone cold and the tea-urns too heavy to carry in this way, but nevertheless smaller containers were borrowed from the farm, and drink as well as food was delivered to the train. The lorry party subsequently located the second train, then the third, successfully delivering food and drink to them, in the latter case with the help of Durham station staff. They then set out to return to Newcastle, which they eventually reached soon after 2am, some 12 hours after they had left.

Jones wrote that the resource and determination of the men was beyond all praise — yet only typical of the spirit and devotion shown by all members of staff. What he does not add

— it would have been only too well known to his readers — was that all this was happening under wartime conditions of blackout, food rationing, fuel shortage and absence of many able-bodied young railwaymen in the armed forces.

Recovery was hindered by hard frost, which lasted until 26 February, then giving way to a sudden thaw resulting in floods. Priority was given to reinstating block telegraphs, and despite the difficulties the main line was working to 70% capacity by 25 February; block working had been restored over half the affected mileage by the 27th. This was aided by the loan of skilled staff, not only from the Southern and Scottish Areas of the LNER but also by the Royal Corps of Signals, while supplies of materials came from other areas of the LNER and also from the LMS. Nevertheless, it was expected that full repairs would take three months.

* * *

The year 1942 brought blizzards in February and March to Yorkshire and County Durham. Locomotives and a snowplough became snowbound near Barras on the Barnard Castle-Kirkby Stephen line, and less predictably a train was snowed up between Scarborough and Whitby, near Ravenscar. Snow brought transport in the Isle of Man to a stand early in the same year. Ian Macnab, in his history of the Isle of Man Railway, records that, furthermore, rough seas prevented the steamer from the mainland entering Douglas harbour, and it had instead to make for the more sheltered harbour at Peel. The passengers then had to be brought to Douglas. A special train was made up at Douglas comprising three coaches, double-headed by 2-4-0Ts Nos 13 and 11, and propelled additionally from the rear by two more locomotives, Nos 10 and 5. By charging the snowdrifts, this remarkable train successfully made its way to Peel, and carried the passengers to their destination.

Although conditions during the Newcastle blizzard of 1941 had been appalling, they were at least localised and of fairly short duration. By contrast, the exceptionally hard weather of early 1947 was not merely widespread but lasted for a long time. Looking back from the 1980s, Alex J. Robertson in *The Bleak Midwinter: 1947* suggests that it was a strong contender for the worst British winter on record.

The previous autumn had been dull, wet and muggy. By the end of the year an anticyclone from Russia was making conditions dry, bright and very cold; some snow fell on 5-7 January 1947, but mild weather reappeared. By mid-January it was cold again, and on the evening of Thursday 23 January, in southeast England, it began to snow. By morning, there was a covering of snow up to 6in deep; the snow continued, accompanied by frost and a bitter southeast wind, and on 26 January it spread northwards. By Monday 27 January there were snowdrifts up to 10ft deep in Kent. Surrey, Sussex and Essex were almost as bad, and further north most of England and Wales was covered in snow that ranged in depth from 1in to 4ft.

Things were to stay like that for the next seven weeks. Every day from 22 January until 17 March snow fell somewhere; snow cover as deep as 2ft became commonplace, and drifts 10ft deep became normal. Most of the snow came in a succession of snowstorms affecting different parts of the country. On 3/4 February a blizzard hit the North of England and the Midlands. On 8/9 February there was heavy snow in the Home Counties. On 20 February it was the turn of the West Country, and so on: on 26 February the North of England, and Scotland; on 4/5 March the South of England and the Midlands; on 12/13 March a final blizzard struck Northern Ireland, Southern Scotland and the North of England. As if that were not enough, the weather throughout February was extremely dull, with almost no sunshine, and cold with a raw penetrating wind from the east. Finally, relief came on 13 March, when a thaw started in the south and spread northwards.

The hard weather was not the only problem: the whole period was affected by a fuel crisis. In those days some 90% of the nation's domestic and industrial heating energy was derived from coal. For some years the mining industry had been having difficulty in meeting the demand for coal; the abortive campaign to convert substantial quantities of steam locomotives to burn oil (oil obtainable from within the Sterling Area) was one small facet of this, and it was abortive largely because the work of conversion was itself hampered by the coal shortage. Power cuts and temporary closures of factories were all too familiar. To the difficulties of the

Left:
On what looks like a typically gloomy, freezing day in February or early March 1947, LMS three-cylinder compound 4-4-0 No 1091 heads north on the Midland main line near Elstree. *Rail Archive Stephenson, C. R. L. Coles*

Left:
Despite deep snow and coal shortages, hard work by railwaymen kept some trains running in February 1947. LNER 'A2' class 4-6-2 No 511 *Airborne* approaches Bramhope Tunnel, between Harrogate and Leeds, with an up express. *Rail Archive Stephenson, M. N. Clay*

Left:
Railwaymen clear snow near Arten Gill, on the Settle & Carlisle line, in February 1947. *National Railway Museum*

mining industry were added the problems of distributing coal over a railway system that had yet to recover from wartime dilapidations of locomotives and rolling stock. On to these difficulties was further superimposed the dislocation caused by the snow. At the beginning of February not only was distribution of coal by rail brought almost to a halt, with around 20,000 loaded coal wagons stuck in colliery sidings, but also a large proportion of the East Coast collier fleet — the only substantial alternative means of transport — was stormbound in harbour. The railways themselves were not receiving the locomotive coal they needed, and later that month 15,000 tons of house coal in transit had to be commandeered for locomotive use.

Yet in 1947 railwaymen had had plenty of experience of clearing snow, and there was no shortage of snowploughs. The greater problem was the frequency of the task. Disruption was in many cases short-term — points frozen, electric circuits short-circuited by damp snow, long delays, cancellations. Passenger trains were cancelled so that priority might be given to coal. By 24 February, although the hard weather still had the country in its grip, bottlenecks on the railways had been cleared, and the number of loaded coal wagons in transit reverted to the usual for the time of year. The Government was quick to blame the weather for the fuel crisis, but it may be that in the weather it found to some extent a scapegoat for its own shortcomings.

Railways in the Peak District were among the first seriously affected by the snowfall, on 24 January. A St Pancras-Manchester express, hauled by a 'Jubilee' class locomotive, took 11hr 50min for its 189-mile journey. On, probably, the following day the Bristol-Manchester mail, which had left Derby at 9.15pm hauled by a 'Patriot', ran into a drift at Darley Dale; heroically, the fireman climbed down and with his shovel successfully cleared a way through the snow. It was to little avail, however; after struggling onward, the train eventually became snowbound near Chinley North Junction. The locomotive crew and some of the passengers managed to join the signalman in his box, equally snowbound, until troops arrived in the morning. The blizzard returned on 4 February and three trains became snowbound between Dove Holes and Buxton. Relief locomotives attempted to pull them clear, but the attempt had to be abandoned when the coaches of one of them became derailed. On the Cromford & High Peak, long sections of line were closed during February and March by deep snowdrifts. Dove Holes Tunnel, on the Derby-Manchester line, and nearby Cowburn Tunnel on the line from Sheffield, had to be closed because of long icicles hanging from the roof. There were similar problems elsewhere. The unfortunate fireman of the 6.23am from Huddersfield to Bradford on 29 January leaned out of his cab while the train was passing through a tunnel, or possibly beneath a bridge; his head was struck by a large icicle hanging from the arch and he was rendered unconscious.

The Settle & Carlisle line became blocked on 4 February and trains were diverted via Clapham, Low Gill and Shap while snowploughs strove to clear it. By 14 February the tracks were clear but lined on either side by high walls of snow. The late F. Slindon was personally involved as an inspector, and his reminiscences appeared in *Railway World* in February 1981. He considered that diversions should continue awhile, lest snow borne by gales blocked the lines again, but headquarters insisted that the trains must recommence. This perhaps reflected the urgent need to keep coal supplies moving. So trains did recommence, but the loads of freight trains were reduced by half, and they were preceded by snowploughs when necessary. The line did again become blocked, and in clearing it gangs of railwaymen were joined by soldiers and German and Italian prisoners of war, who had not yet returned home. When they eventually reached Dent, they found drifts so deep that the up home signal, on a 27ft post, had only about a yard standing clear of the snow. Aided by the eventual thaw, the line returned to normal about the end of March.

The LNER Barnard Castle-Kirkby Stephen and Scarborough-Whitby lines were blocked by snow for some weeks at this time. During February a snowplough propelled by a 'J12' 0-6-0 itself became snowbound at Barras on the Kirkby Stephen line. So severe were conditions that one locomotive, which became submerged in a drift near Stainmore, had to spend almost two months there before being extracted.

The blizzards of 5/6 March brought about 1ft of snow, with drifts up to 30ft. There were many delays and cancellations to suburban electric train services around London, but the effect on main-line trains through the Midlands was more marked. The 1.50pm from

Wolverhampton High Level on Wednesday 5 March finally reached Euston at 4.50pm on Thursday, the front footplate of the locomotive piled high with snow. The night train from Euston to Liverpool took more than 19 hours to reach its destination, and up trains were delayed up to 12 hours.

On the LNER, two passengers with a seven-month-old baby intending to join the 3.50pm from Manchester to Marylebone at Leicester had to wait 6 hours for it to arrive, which must have been well after midnight. But the worst was to come: the train encountered deep drifts near Aylesbury and by the time it reached London was 15 hours late. It seems they were lucky to get through at all, for 10 miles of line between Woodford and Quainton Road were then reported blocked by snow.

Serious snow problems were far more widespread than just the Midlands. In the East, the 8.50pm from Cromer to Norwich on 5 March ran into a snowdrift near Wroxham. Although railwaymen spent all night trying to clear the line, the passengers, who included the Bishop of Norwich, were obliged to stay on board until 8am the following morning. Then, according to *The Times* of 7 March, two locomotives were brought close enough to the stranded train for the bishop and the other passengers to travel the 3 miles to Wroxham on their footplates. One may express the hope, without belittling what must have been overall an unpleasant experience, that the bishop was sufficient of a railway enthusiast (as so many clergymen are) to appreciate the rarity of the event to the full. Probably light engines were brought close to the snowed-up train because of a reluctance to propel wagons or carriages through the snow, with the attendant risk of derailment.

To the West, lines of the Great Western in South Wales were suffering. Twenty-two men and women were marooned for 30 hours on a train on the Brecon & Merthyr line, until rescued by troops and railwaymen. There was deep snow on the Neath & Brecon, too, at Craig-y-nos, with at least two locomotives buried in it. Rail links to some 200 collieries were broken. Train services were interrupted in Devon and Cornwall as well.

By 7 March the Great Western had had 48 branch lines, in Wales and the West Midlands, blocked by snow. The LNER had had 34.

The final blizzard of 12/13 March brought problems to regions that had previously escaped the worst. It reached Galloway at dusk; the 5.10pm Glasgow-Stranraer, composed of 'Jubilee' 4-6-0 No 5728 *Defiance* and four coaches, reached Glenwhilly on time, but was then held awaiting arrival of a northbound freight. The freight, however, was unable to make it through the snow, although it set back successfully to New Luce, which was the next station south. A snowplough then cleared the section, travelling southwards, but while it was doing so snow was already accumulating again in the cuttings behind it. When the passenger train eventually set off, it got no more than half a mile before becoming stuck. There was light, heat and food on board, so the stranded passengers could have been worse off.

Left:
The final blizzard of the 1947 winter hit Northern Ireland, and on the 3ft-gauge Ballycastle branch the last train on 12 March became snowbound *en route* to Ballymoney. *National Museums and Galleries of Northern Ireland, Ulster Folk & Transport Museum, L4124/9*

Or so, at first, it seemed. But the following day the blizzard continued unabated. Pressure of snow on the windward side of the train cracked windows, and broke one of them. When the tender ran out of water, the locomotive could no longer provide steam heat; when the carriage batteries went flat, the lights flickered out. In these conditions the passengers had to spend a second night aboard. Only on the morning of the third day did the weather improve sufficiently for them to be evacuated to nearby houses. The locomotive and coaches spent six days in the snow.

Remarkably, snow problems in Galloway and County Antrim once again coincided to the day, as they had done long before in 1908. This time it was the turn of the 3ft-gauge Ballycastle branch of the Northern Counties Committee, which the snowstorm likewise reached on the evening of Wednesday 12 March. The last train from Ballycastle comprised 2-4-2T locomotive No 41 and two coaches. It failed to make the main-line junction at Ballymoney, for it had become embedded in a snowdrift on the way. The crew and the 16 passengers spent the night in the guard's van with its stove; they were rescued the following day, but it was Saturday before the line was operating normally again.

And then, as if to compensate, the weather turned mild. August 1947 was the hottest August for more than a century.

* * *

Over the next few years mild weather prevailed. There were some exceptions, of course. In 1950 a freak snowstorm as late as April brought down about 540 telegraph poles on British Railways' Southern Region, wrecked telegraphs and signals, and caused a great many delayed or cancelled trains. The following December a goods train became snowed up between Market Weighton and Driffield. In January 1955 the Stainmore route was again blocked near Barras; in February there was light snow across much of central England, and between Buxton and Ashbourne it was heavy enough for the snowploughs to be out.

Early in 1958 hard weather returned to the North of England and southern Scotland. More than 7in of snow fell on 22/23 January, and frozen and blocked points caused massive delays to trains in the Manchester area. On 24 February there was more snow, and the 10.45pm Blackpool-Manchester train became stuck in the snow overnight near Blackrod. A Ramsbottom-Colne train was stuck for 9 hours. The Woodhead route between Manchester and Sheffield was blocked by snowdrifts 18ft deep, and at least three trains became snowbound. There were drifts 5ft deep at Buxton station. In Yorkshire, Bridlington was cut off by rail from both Scarborough and Hull. Class D49/2 4-4-0 No 62741 was stuck in the snow with a passenger train between Scarborough and Bridlington.

In early 1959 the diesel locomotive of a King's Cross-Edinburgh express was derailed by frozen points at Arksey; a year later, on 9 January 1960, all the points at East Grinstead were jammed by snow. On 19 January the 4.27pm from Aberdeen to Glasgow became snowbound near Eassie; serious snow problems north of Aberdeen at the same time will be described in the next chapter. January 1961, though generally mild, produced enough snow in the North of England for two trains to become snowbound — one between Workington and Carlisle, and the other near Barnard Castle.

Above:
The frozen North: London Transport's
Northern Line near Finchley in January
1962. *London Transport Museum*

Left:
Snow-encrusted Underground stock at
Neasden in January 1962. *London
Transport Museum*

The turn of the year 1961/2 produced some harsh weather. The last trains on the former Midland line between Leicester and Rugby ran through snow on 30 December — we are into the sad era of railway closures now — and so did the last passenger trains on the Keighley-Oxenhope branch; it was to be 'abandoned completely' in June, noted *The Railway Magazine*. For once, happily, the magazine was to be proved wrong, by the Keighley & Worth Valley Railway Preservation Society.

Unusually heavy snow fell on the northern suburbs of London, producing a covering up to railhead level on New Year's Day and bringing problems both to British Railways and to the surface lines of London Transport. This winter is well within my own memory, with a mental picture of waiting on the Metropolitan Line platforms at King's Cross while trains from frozen Buckinghamshire passed through, still encrusted with ice and snow despite the warmer temperatures of their subterranean journey from Finchley Road.

I recollect, too, a journey by the up 'Cambrian Coast Express' on 30 December 1961, BR Mark 1 coaches in chocolate and cream, hauled by a 'Manor' through the snow from Machynlleth to Shrewsbury. Another mental picture: snow deep on the platform at Cemmes Road as we waited to cross a delayed down train — and the signalman running through the snow with the train staff, so that the express might not be delayed a second longer than necessary.

* * *

The winter of 1962/3 was one of the harshest that railways and railwaymen have ever experienced. What in retrospect seems to have been a foretaste of problems came as early as 19 November, when the overnight newspaper train from Manchester to Aberdeen became stuck in 10ft snowdrifts on the Waverley Route and a relief train sent to the rescue also became snowbound.

The real trouble started, however, during the last days of December when blizzards swept across the South of England. Bitter winds and hard frosts followed, with temperatures below freezing point throughout much of January. Snow fell in northeast England too, and soon covered most of Britain, and the North of Ireland as well. Central and southern Scotland were hard hit by blizzards early in February.

The freeze-up brought with it all the problems to be expected, from frozen couplings to snowed-up trains. Yet the railway system did not grind to a halt; rather, through great effort by all concerned, a great many trains kept moving, even when nearby roads were blocked. An exception, sadly, was where railways were due to be closed in any case, and the measure of their loss was re-emphasised by the conditions. The last passenger trains ran through the snow between Nottingham Victoria and Pinxton South on 5 January, and between Princes Risborough and Oxford on the 6th. On 5 January the Locomotive Club of Great Britain organised a special train of brake vans hauled by Class 8F No 48546 to mark the closure of the 1-in-27 Werneth Incline in Lancashire. The combined effects of the gradient and the snow were too much for the locomotive, which slipped to a stand.

Far more dramatic was closure of the former Great Western branch from Plymouth to Tavistock South and Launceston. The last trains were scheduled for 29 December, the 8.35pm Launceston-Plymouth and the 8.40pm Plymouth-Launceston. What actually happened was reported by M. L. Roach of Plymouth to *The Railway Magazine*, and appeared in the issue of March 1963. That morning snow had started to fall, and by evening had developed into a blizzard driven by 70mph winds. The 5.40pm from Launceston was prevented by frozen points from gaining the main line at Tavistock Junction for the final part of its run into Plymouth; after a delay of 2¼ hours it got through by rushing them. It was to become the last passenger train to make the full journey. Frozen points at Plymouth delayed the 6.20pm from Plymouth to Launceston, comprising 2-6-2T No 5568 and four

Below:
Cold-weather diesel failures resulted in steam, in the form of 'V2' No 60969, hauling the 11.12am Edinburgh Waverley-Perth on 3 January 1963; the train is seen here between Mawcarse Junction and Glenfarg on the direct line, now closed.
Rail Archive Stephenson, W. J. V. Anderson

coaches, which left at 7.32pm and was then obliged to wait for the 5.40 to clear the single line of the branch; it reached its first scheduled stop at Marsh Mills, just over 3 miles from Plymouth, at 10.14pm. Overcoming frozen brakes and frozen points, it continued to Bickleigh, where it crossed the 7.10pm from Tavistock to Plymouth. The latter train had been waiting for more than 3 hours, and during this enforced halt had become frozen to the rails. The 6.20 battled on into the teeth of the blizzard, its usual speed reduced by half. Passengers alighted at each halt. At first the crew insisted that they were going to Launceston and back come what may, but at Horrabridge it was announced that the train would make only the outward journey — the last trains in each direction had been cancelled. Then at Tavistock, reached at 12.23am, 5hr 20min late, the 6.20 could go no further. The wires were down over the next section to Lydford, and no train staff could be obtained; in any event, Lydford was already snowbound with drifts across the tracks to platform level.

The passengers, some of them locals, some of them railway enthusiasts, settled down for the rest of the night in the front two coaches, steam-heated by the locomotive and supplied with food by the stationmaster and signalman who remained on duty. The following morning passengers were evacuated to a church hall; their experiences, if my memory serves correctly, made national television news. Those who had wished to return to Plymouth by the former Southern Railway route from Tavistock North had been defeated, for this was equally blocked with the 7pm from Waterloo snowbound near Okehampton. A train did, however, come to their rescue by the Southern route from Plymouth later on the Sunday.

Meanwhile, at Bickleigh the three passengers in the 7.10pm Tavistock-Plymouth train had retreated to the signalbox after the locomotive had run out of water. A relief engine arrived on the Sunday afternoon to haul this train, with its locomotive and passengers, to Plymouth. Running 20 hours late, it became the final passenger train on the branch. A heroic end, but sad.

On 14 January 1963, despite the freeze-up, No 60103 *Flying Scotsman* triumphantly passes Potters Bar with the 1.15pm King's Cross-Leeds, her last official run in BR service before preservation by Alan Pegler. *Brian Stephenson*

All was not despair. On 14 January No 60103 *Flying Scotsman* made a triumphant last official run in BR service, hauling the 1.15pm King's Cross-Leeds as far as Doncaster, prior to completion of its purchase by Alan Pegler — the first locomotive to be preserved with the intention that it should run on the main line. *The Times* on 15 January carried a fine photograph of 60103 hurrying her train past snow-covered Potters Bar, exhaust enhanced by the cold.

Elsewhere, less spectacular trains were keeping going through the snow: to give a few examples, on the Southern line to Weymouth, on the Somerset & Dorset, on the Great Western lines in Gloucestershire and the main line out of Paddington. Even the little 2ft-gauge Leighton Buzzard Light Railway kept going through the snows of Bedfordshire, motive power for trains of sand-carrying skips being doubled up by the use of two Simplex locomotives, either double-headed or one at each end.

The surface lines of London Transport were hard hit. Snow started to fall on Boxing Day, which was a Wednesday, but the main blizzard built up over the following weekend. All surface lines were affected by snow; four of the branch lines — those to Chesham, Watford, Mill Hill and Ongar — were blocked by drifts up to 7ft deep. Temperatures went down to -7°C.

LT's railway control headquarters had been warned late on Christmas Day that heavy snow was on its way, and winter emergency organisation swung into action. Three hundred permanent way men were diverted to snow clearance, and worked night and day on 12-hour shifts to keep lines open and to clear those that were blocked. Track renewal gangs, unable to perform their usual tasks, went to depots where the many hand-worked points had to be dug out and kept clear of snow, so that trains could emerge from sidings into service. Extra staff came into depots overnight to keep trains free from ice and snow, operate brakes and doors at intervals, and keep a constant check to prevent snow from getting into the electrics. Where possible, tunnel sidings were used to stable trains. Signal engineering department men cleared snow and ice from train stops, colour-light signal lenses and points where these were unheated. Sleet locomotives, which are described further in Chapter 4, ran through the night to prevent the build-up of snow and ice on conductor rails. By the Sunday evening all lines were clear, and at the Monday morning rush-hour, despite the appalling conditions, as many as 91% of trains were running.

A brief thaw towards the end of January brought another problem to British Railways: large amounts of ice had formed on the damp and dripping walls of tunnels and their ventilating shafts, and this now fell on to tracks below. Half a ton of ice fell from a shaft in Chipping Sodbury Tunnel on to the main Paddington-South Wales line, and trains had to be diverted while it was removed; steam lances from locomotives were used to clear further overhanging ice. Other tunnels affected included Caerphilly, Gillingham (Dorset) and Sugar Loaf.

Further north, the Derby-Manchester line was blocked by snow at Chinley North and a two-car DMU was snowbound overnight. Snow blocked the Cromford & High Peak many times between January and March. The Settle & Carlisle line was blocked by snowdrifts between 20 and 25 January, and even when reopened there were only inches of clearance between snow banks and passing trains; Garsdale water troughs were frozen solid.

In North Yorkshire, snowfall was lighter than many places, but snowploughs were regularly needed to keep the Middlesbrough-Whitby line clear in conditions that had blocked local roads. Particularly bad drifts formed around Battersby, and were being tackled by snowploughs from both ends on 6 February when first one plough, or rather the tender of one of the locomotives powering it, became derailed, while the other plough became jammed in a drift with its wheels apparently supported not by the rails but by ice on top of them. It took 48 hours to clear the line.

In Scotland the Waverley Route was blocked by snow on three successive occasions in January; the problem section was between Steele Road, Riccarton and Whitrope. Two freight trains, up and down, were trapped in drifts on 1 January. The line was cleared, but both tracks were again blocked early on 6 January by avalanches of snow, presumably in cuttings, which took until 10 January to clear fully. They were then blocked again on 20 January, and although one track was reopened with single-line working on the following day, it was not until 24 January that things were back to normal.

Elsewhere in southern Scotland it was very cold. Then a blizzard struck the Lowlands on 5 February. Lines blocked as a result included the West Coast main line near Carstairs for a short time, the Muirkirk-Lanark branch for 24 hours, and the Carstairs-Edinburgh line for six days. The 5.10pm from Glasgow St Enoch to Stranraer — which by then had become a DMU — stuck in the snow near Barrhill and some passengers were eventually helicoptered to safety the following day. Others were taken back to Girvan by special train. The 7.25pm from Euston to Stranraer Harbour became snowbound only a couple of miles short of its destination; a snowplough-fitted locomotive with two coaches managed to get through from Stranraer to rescue the passengers. This line was reopened on 7 February, the line via Barrhill not until the 9th. It was then blocked again by a snowstorm on 13/14 February for several days. During this and the earlier blockage, special trains ran from Ayr to Stranraer via Dumfries.

The winter of 1964/5 saw some heavy falls of snow, but with comparatively little dislocation of train services. A blizzard that struck the line between Ayr and Stranraer on 3 March 1965 did leave snowdrifts too deep for DMUs to tackle, and steam trains replaced them for several days. The following winter was notable for snowfalls even later in the season, and trains in northwest England were delayed by snow at the beginning of April 1966. The South of England, by contrast, suffered heavy snow early in the winter of 1967/8, on 8 December. Trains generally seem to have got through, although the remaining, recently electrified, Ryde-Shanklin section of the Isle of Wight's railways was brought to a standstill.

February 1969 brought some heavy snow to the Midlands and the North West of England — sufficient for a Sheffield-Manchester train with around 70 passengers to become blocked in snowdrifts at Woodhead. It took 5 hours to clear the line.

On 3 January 1970 — a Saturday — a snowstorm accompanied the last trains to run on the Bangor-Caernarvon branch. On a positive note, on the next day the Worth Valley Railway, which had been reopened in 1968, was running its Sunday afternoon steam trains despite the snow. Such happenings became increasingly common over the next few years as more and more preserved railways were established near large centres of population, rather than in summer holiday districts. Subsequent Februarys in which Worth Valley steam trains ran through the snow included those of 1973 and 1978. On Boxing Day 1970 the Bluebell Railway's trains steamed through 9in of snow, while British Rail's electrified services nearby were descending into chaos. On 20 November 1971 a demonstration goods train hauled by 'P3' 0-8-0 No 2392 was operated over the snow-covered North Yorkshire Moors Railway by the North Eastern Locomotive Preservation Group, and there was snow on the ground when the Severn Valley Railway operated trains on New Year's Day 1977.

Generally, however, the winters of the late 1960s and early 1970s were mild. Indeed, in the July 1974 issue of *The Railway Magazine* D. E. Canning lamented in an article how since 1967 he had visited Shap winter after winter to photograph trains in the snow — to no avail until the previous March when, even then, only a sprinkling appeared.

* * *

Towards the end of the 1970s, truly wintry weather started to return. February 1978 saw a blizzard in the West Country that affected rail services over an area from Bristol to Exeter, and dumped enough snow on Taunton to render a DMU snowbound within the station itself. Fortunately Class 47 No 47030 was able to clear the snow sufficiently to come to its rescue.

The winter of 1978/9 was considered to be the worst for 16 years. Snow was widespread and snow scenes photographed between December and March, which appeared subsequently in the railway press, came from locations as far apart as Brockenhurst and Haltwhistle, with Newbury, Retford and Brinklow (for example) in between. Yet typically they show trains passing triumphantly through the snowbound countryside. Only the Southern Region seems to have been seriously disrupted, and there largely because problems with iced-up conductor rails were superimposed upon those already resulting from industrial disputes.

Among the success stories were a late instance of industrial steam still working hard among the snow at Bickershaw Colliery, Lancashire, and an early instance of first-generation diesel traction already preserved, with diesel-hydraulic No D1048 *Western Lady* hauling a tour train over the snow-covered North Yorkshire Moors Railway on 18 March. The winter of 1980/1 seems to have been relatively mild, although snowploughs were needed on the Settle & Carlisle line as late as 24/25 April. But December 1981 produced some of the worst early-December weather known for years. Blizzards accompanied by heavy snowfall and hard frost struck the South East, North and West of England and North Wales over 10-12 December, causing many difficulties, and one tragic accident.

Few railway accidents result from a single cause, and most from several in combination. But this heavy snowfall was the principal cause of a collision in unusual circumstances near Seer Green on 11 December, which regrettably had fatal consequences. Seer Green lies between Gerrards Cross and High Wycombe on what was formerly the Great Central & Great Western joint line, but by this date was part of the London Midland Region of British Rail. Passenger trains, which originated at Marylebone, were worked by diesel multiple-units. At Gerrards Cross itself trains were controlled by semaphore signals worked from a traditional mechanical signalbox; from Gerrards Cross past Seer Green to the next box at High Wycombe, absolute block working applied, but the line was track-circuited and broken up into additional sections worked automatically or semi-automatically by colour light signals. There was an illuminated track-circuit diagram in Gerrards Cross signalbox. In addition to this, Gerrards Cross box could be switched out when traffic was light, and trains were then worked by absolute block between West Ruislip (the next box towards Marylebone) and High Wycombe. That this complex blend of traditional and modern practices had grown up seems symptomatic of a railway that was underfunded.

A further and admitted symptom of underfunding was the lack of any systematic programme for clearing trees and vegetation, which had been allowed to spring up at the lineside since the withdrawal of spark-producing steam locomotives. The sum budgeted for clearance was sufficient to meet only specific priorities when, for instance, overgrowth started to interfere with sighting of signals. Between Gerrards Cross and Seer Green is a long cutting, the slopes of which had become covered by thick vegetation including many silver birch trees, which, though tall, were straight and well clear of the line. They presented no hazard to trains, or so at least it appeared until 8 December. According to the Inspecting Officer's eventual report into the collision (from which most of this account is drawn), snow then fell when it was already freezing; weighed down by accumulated snow, branches of trees started to brush against trains. This was reported by drivers, and permanent way staff did some trimming over the next two days.

In the early hours of 11 December there were more extremely heavy snowfalls. Gerrards Cross signalbox was switched out overnight. The signalman due to come on duty at 06.00 was young, keen and conscientious; although he was recently qualified, on his training course he had been regarded as an above-average student. But he still lacked experience. He lived 24 miles away in Aylesbury and travelled to work on his motorcycle. On this particular morning he set out soon after 04.30 and struggled as far as Wendover, some 5 miles, where the heavy snow defeated him. He returned to Aylesbury, but instead of giving up and going home, he arranged to travel on a freight train and to be set down at Gerrards Cross. There he arrived about 07.50, having taken nearly 3½ hours for a journey that normally took 40 minutes. It was still snowing, and blowing. He started to open the 'box, following the correct procedures; this included replacing the semaphore signals, which had been left in the 'clear' position overnight while the box was switched out, to 'danger'. The levers were stiff to move.

The position at Gerrards Cross that morning was complicated. The driver of the 06.03 Marylebone to High Wycombe had reported to the High Wycombe signalman that his cab had been struck, probably by a tree weighed down by snow (it was still dark) in the cutting approaching Seer Green. The High Wycombe signalman advised the signalman at West Ruislip by telephone to caution the drivers of all down trains. Thus the next two trains, the 06.33 and the 07.04 from Marylebone, passed safely from West Ruislip to High Wycombe.

There should have been a 06.50 Marylebone to Princes Risborough, but this did not run; its driver found the heating was not working and, in the prevailing weather, refused to take it. By the time a replacement DMU had been provided it was too late. This unit was, however, needed at Princes Risborough to work an up train, so it was arranged that it would leave Marylebone as empty stock at 07.25. At West Ruislip it was stopped by the signalman and the driver was warned of trees down beyond Gerrards Cross; he was to proceed with extreme caution.

It was at this point that the signalman at Gerrards Cross opened up his box. The West Ruislip signalman told him of the trees, and asked him to take over cautioning drivers; he offered him the 07.25, which was accepted. So the driver of this train was cautioned again at Gerrards Cross. In the cutting he was able to stop short of a tree which, he found, had been uprooted and was lying with its top 4 or 5ft across the track. Nearby was a signal. It controlled up trains, and was consequently equipped with a telephone to the signalbox at High Wycombe, but not to Gerrards Cross. The driver telephoned the signalman at High Wycombe, told him about the tree, said that he would be able to move it within about 5 minutes, and set off for the brake compartment to get an axe and a saw. He was to be rudely interrupted.

Back at Gerrards Cross the signalman, who had cleared his down starting signal for the 07.25, replaced it to 'danger' once the train had passed it; the lever was still stiff. The track circuiting then automatically locked the signal electrically for as long as the train occupied the section to which it controlled entry. The signalman gave 'train out of section' to West Ruislip on the telegraph, and was immediately offered another train. This was the 07.31 passenger, Marylebone to Banbury, which he accepted. Correctly the signalman brought it to a stand at his down platform signal, cleared the signal after the driver had sounded his horn, then stopped the train beside his open window by showing a red flag. He cautioned the driver about the trees and said he would clear his down starting signal. The lever would not move.

At this point inexperience and, probably, stress took their toll. Outside was a driver late and anxious to get on. In the box the signalman became confused. His hand still on the lever, he glanced at the track circuit diagram, where the lights indicating occupied sections were close together. He misunderstood them. He thought he saw one showing that the previous train had reached a section beyond Seer Green; the section through the cutting was also shown as occupied, but this he attributed to track circuit failure, and as for the lever, previously stiff, he assumed it was now frozen. He authorised the driver to pass the starting signal at danger, told him, in response to a query, that the empty train was running down towards Beaconsfield (and so was beyond Seer Green), and warned him to proceed with extreme caution. The driver replied something like, 'OK, mate, if you insist', and accelerated away into the snowstorm.

The signalman looked again at his diagram and, even before the train had finished passing his box, realised his mistake. He shouted urgently out of the window, trying to attract the attention of the guard. A railwayman waiting on the up platform heard the shouting, but not the words. The guard did not hear him at all.

The driver of the passenger train, travelling at a speed later calculated to have been some 35mph despite the conditions, evidently did not see the stationary train ahead of him until it was too late; although he applied the brakes, the passenger train collided violently with the rear of the stationary train. Sadly, the driver of the passenger train and three of the passengers were fatally injured.

Yet one cannot help but feel for the signalman, for, as the Inspecting Officer later commented in his inquiry report, a less conscientious man might have given up and returned home, in which case his signalbox would have remained switched out and the accident would probably not have happened.

Subsequently, overgrowth was removed from the sides of Seer Green cutting before the line was reopened; the track circuit diagram at Gerrards Cross box was made clearer, and the rules by which drivers might be instructed to pass signals at danger were tightened up. But the moral, I suppose, is never to relax vigilance for a moment.

* * *

There were other, less serious consequences of the snowfall. On 12 December a steam special hauled by No 34092 *City of Wells*, which was heading for Leeds, was obliged to turn back at Skipton lest passengers be unable to get home. The following day the weather proved more than appropriate for a train on the East Somerset Railway, which was carrying passengers to visit Santa in his grotto. Hauled by 'P' class 0-6-0T *Bluebell* (on loan from the Bluebell Railway) the train had scarcely left Cranmore when a blizzard swept down on it, quickly covering the track with drifting snow. A second locomotive, Andrew Barclay 0-4-0ST *Lord Fisher*, was coupled in front to assist, and Santa's grotto at Merryfield Lane was reached half an hour late. Children went to visit Santa, and their elders downed mince-pies and hot punch. On the return journey against the blizzard visibility was no more than a few yards; back at Cranmore, the passengers rapidly disappeared as they attempted to return home. Even while *Bluebell* was being disposed of in the shed yard, so much driven snow accumulated against the wheels that the locomotive had to be dug out before it could be moved into the shed. Roads became impassable; nine members of the railway's staff were marooned overnight (with a stock of brandy and mince-pies!) and even Santa himself, when he attempted to return to the North, became stranded in a pub not far away for 9 hours until the blizzard eased.

The snowstorms hit North Wales on two occasions, the first on 11 December 1981 and the second early in January; each time they were followed by a week or so of hard frost. On the branch from Llandudno Junction to Blaenau Ffestiniog and Trawsfynydd nuclear power station, BR had snowploughs out to clear the line, and a Class 25 diesel locomotive was coupled in front of the branch DMU to assist it through the snow. For the Festiniog Railway itself, the snow could scarcely have come at a worse time, for these were the final stages of reconstructing the line into Blaenau Ffestiniog for the long-planned reopening the following spring. Nevertheless the storm of 11 December did not prevent the first steam-hauled train for 35 years — a ballast train, hauled by 2-4-0 *Blanche* — from reaching Glanypwll, on the edge of Blaenau, in conditions re-creating those encountered by the *Scribner's* correspondent so long before — if not indeed worse. It did prevent car-borne working parties of volunteers from reaching the line, leaving the permanent staff to unload the train, then, on return, to get stuck in the blizzard at Tanygrisiau a couple of days later. Subsequently the frost made it impossible to use cement, and there was much snow to be shovelled off the track to enable works trains to take materials forward, while tracklaying went ahead with difficulty.

To the south, the effect of the snow on the Talyllyn Railway was even greater, the blizzard of 8/9 January 1982 resulting in deep drifts. The cutting between Wharf and Pendre had 3ft of snow in it, and at Pendre itself snow drifted against the engine shed doors to the height of the top hinges. Even within the doors gale-driven snow reached a depth of 2ft. Further up the line there were snowdrifts up to hedge-top level, and east of Abergynolwyn there was a drift 6ft

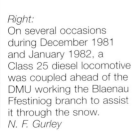

Right:
On several occasions during December 1981 and January 1982, a Class 25 diesel locomotive was coupled ahead of the DMU working the Blaenau Ffestiniog branch to assist it through the snow.
N. F. Gurley

deep. With the local road network snowbound, staff were unable to get to work and winter maintenance was interrupted. Despite clearance and a thaw, it was some weeks before the line was clear again throughout. On the Talyllyn, however, there was no interruption to traffic, for at that time of year there was no traffic to interrupt.

Quite otherwise was the effect of the storm on the nearby Cambrian Coast line of BR. Two two-car DMUs travelling in the up direction became snowbound and so did locomotives sent to rescue them. The 12.10 from Pwllheli to Dovey Junction on Friday 8 January left Barmouth about 14.00 with its train crew of driver and guard, a railway maintenance man, and four passengers. A little north of Tonfanau (that is, about 2½ miles short of Tywyn) it encountered a snowdrift in which it became stuck. Half a mile away was a lineside telephone; the train crew struggled through the blizzard to and fro between train and telephone several times over the next few hours, first to seek assistance, then to try to find out when it was coming. The second train was empty. It encountered a drift north of Barmouth, and the front car was derailed. The driver, however, was able to uncouple the rear car, and returned with this to Porthmadog, leaving the front car in the snow.

Meanwhile, diesel locomotive No 25201 was despatched from Machynlleth to the rescue of the train snowbound near Tonfanau, but was defeated by snowdrifts near Tywyn. A second Class 25, fitted with miniature snowploughs, was sent from Shrewsbury but was delayed by snowdrifts and frozen points. A helicopter was equally unable to reach the train. Finally, after the passengers and crew had spent the night on board the train, the helicopter was able to land close by on the Saturday morning and airlift them to Tywyn.

This DMU and the locomotive snowbound near Tywyn were both recovered the following day. Some local journeys were then made between Tywyn and Machynlleth, using a DMU with a locomotive coupled to it, but the drifts north of Tonfanau were so bad that locomotives attempting to get through became stuck twice more, and it was 17 January before the DMU car north of Barmouth was reached and replaced on the rails. The line was reopened fully on 18 January, ten days after the storm.

Nor was the Cambrian Coast the only district adjacent to the Irish Sea affected by the bad conditions on 8 January. On the Isle of Man, too, heavy snow was falling. The previous autumn, by way of experiment, a Fridays-only winter train had been introduced from Port Erin to Douglas and back, to carry people going shopping. As luck would have it, 8 January was, as we have seen, a Friday, and that morning No 12 *Hutchinson* set off from Port Erin with three coaches in falling snow and deteriorating weather. There were a few passengers despite the conditions, and a few more joined *en route*, but between Castletown and Ballasalla severe drifts were encountered. To get through one of them took five attempts — but the train did get through. Two of the coaches were detached at Ballasalla, and, with the one coach remaining, No 12 successfully reached Douglas.

* * *

SNOW
WAY
TO RUN
A RAILWAY

i
for ice
Why
ice and snow
disrupt
your trains

i
FOR INFORMATION
GETTING
YOU TO WORK
IN WINTER

≡ Southern

British Rail's Southern
Region keeps its
passengers informed.
*R. N. Forsythe
collection, courtesy
British Railways Board*

Subsequent winters during the 1980s produced some snow, but seldom sufficient to bring about any widespread dislocation of train services. Most regrettably, four railwaymen were killed at Severn Tunnel Junction on 11 February 1985, when hit by a train while they were clearing snow and frozen points.

It snowed hard during the celebrations on 24 March 1986 to mark the reopening of the Bathgate branch for passengers — one of an increasing number of reopenings of lines not in preservation but as part of the public railway network. Nonetheless, the Scottish Railway Preservation Society's 0-6-0 *Maude* was there to take part.

Early December 1990 saw some snow, enough for some railtours to be cancelled. But this was nothing compared with the difficulties experienced in February 1991. First it became exceptionally cold. By 7 February it was down to -15°C in the Midlands and -11°C in southeast England. By then it had started to snow, and it continued to snow through the following night. Most of Britain was affected, but worst affected was the South East. It was not, however, any great depth of snow that was the problem, but the nature of the snow itself combined with the low temperatures. Snowfall during that period of extreme cold came not as the usual wet lumpy flakes, but as flakes that were unusually dry, hard and tiny — no more than powder — that were swirled around by the wind or the slipstream of passing trains. Powdery snow was swept into the air intakes of new electric multiple-units with the cooling air in which it was suspended. Reaching the motors, it promptly melted and short-circuited them. That meant repair or replacement of damaged motors, with the train out of service meantime.

Similar problems had arisen as early as January 1985 with the new electric multiple-units of Class 317 just put into service on the Bedford-St Pancras line. Cold, powdery snow found its way into the electrical equipment, particularly chokes, and damaged them. They were subsequently modified, and coped with snowfall in 1987. But this experience was evidently not taken into account in the design of the Class 319 EMUs built during 1987-91 for the Thameslink service between Bedford and Brighton. Even in the snow of December 1990 they were in trouble; in February, far more. By the afternoon of 7 February, all Thameslink services south of the river had been cancelled. However, powdery snow in the electrics was far from the only problem. On these trains the pantographs used for current collection north of the river became frozen in the lowered position while running in the third-rail area south of it. Sliding doors, on these trains and many others, ceased to function; drain holes in the grooves froze up, so snow from boarding commuters' boots accumulated in the grooves and compacted into ice. There were widespread problems with frozen braking systems, frozen points and iced-up conductor rails. On the morning of 8 February, Waterloo station was closed from 09.00 to 10.00, and when it reopened only three platforms were in use. More and more trains were taken out of service, and commuters faced more and more cancellations and delays. There were problems, delays and cancellations also on the main lines to the North, the Midlands and the West.

The problems stemmed in part from the cheeseparing principles by which Government had been funding the nationalised railway system. Trains could have been built with ducts and filters to keep powdery snow out of the motors — but British Rail was provided with only so much funding to acquire trains to move so many passengers. If trains had been kept under cover overnight there would have been fewer frozen brakes and doors, but depots had been built with covered accommodation for maintenance only, and open-air sidings for stabling. Traction motor repairs were no longer undertaken locally by BR at Eastleigh, but put out to contract — in Glasgow — which meant days of delay.

In the public eye, however, it was British Rail that was to blame. During an interview on Radio 4's *Today* programme, Terry Worrall (Director of Operations, BRB) explained that it 'was not the volume of snow that was causing the problem, but the type of snow'. This was picked up by the *Evening Standard.* On 11 February, spread across the width of its front page, was the heading: 'BR warning as it blames "the wrong type of snow" '. Yet although Worrall was quoted in the story which followed, nowhere in it was the word 'wrong' attributed to him or to BR. It appears to be journalistic licence.

But the damage was done. Somehow the word 'type' became transformed into 'kind', and, as BR's supposed excuse, the phrase 'the wrong kind of snow'gained instant notoriety — it was quoted almost immediately in Parliament — and the industry has been pilloried for it ever since.

* * *

Little snow of any kind was in evidence over the next few winters, and it was not until the winter of 1995/6 that it reappeared in quantity. At Christmas-time, snow on the ground provided a seasonal background for Santa Specials at Bo'ness and Alston. Its effect on the North Yorkshire Moors Railway was more serious. With a foot of snow at Grosmont and use of roads in the district discouraged by police, few staff could get there and train services had to be much restricted or cancelled. Those cancelled at first included the 'Moorlander' Pullman lunch train. On 28 December, however, at the third attempt, a few of the train's staff did successfully struggle through the snow to Grosmont. Passengers were telephoned to join the train at Pickering, and the train of six (or more) Pullman cars, headed by 'S160' 2-8-0 No 2253 and propelled at the rear by Class 5 4-6-0 No 45428 *Eric Treacy*, set out through the snowy wastes under a clear blue sky. It must have been a magnificent sight. At Pickering there were plenty of passengers waiting, but very few train crew. I gather that any volunteer who looked as if he wasn't doing much was promptly grabbed, then, despite frozen steam heating pipes in one of the Pullmans, a good time was had by all. The train became known as the 'Arctic Pullman'.

Towards the end of January 1996 there was widespread snow in the Midlands, the West of England and the North of England. In places it was heavy. On 27 January, for instance, heavy snow in Yorkshire disrupted East Coast main line train services to the extent that the timetable was withdrawn and an emergency service substituted. The Settle & Carlisle line was blocked by drifts. On 5 February snow blocked the Cumbrian Coast line at Whitehaven for two days; near Stranraer snowdrifts were so bad at this time that passengers and crew had to be airlifted from a train.

On 20 February snowy weather even managed to bring trains to a stand within the Channel Tunnel. The 08.27 Eurostar from London to Brussels stalled 4 miles short of the French portal; the trouble was that snow and low temperatures in the open, and comparative warmth within the tunnel, coupled with high humidity, had caused damp to affect the train's electronics. It was rescued by a pair of diesels, then the whole performance was repeated by the 12.53 London-Paris. Shuttle services for road vehicles were affected too, by drifts at the French terminal and by snow on the tops of lorries, which thawed, ran down on to the track, and caused track-circuit failures.

Subsequent winters in the 1990s produced little snow, but in 1998 as late as 14 April a blizzard struck the Isle of Man. The Isle of Man Railway, having already opened for the summer season, found its trains puffing photogenically through the snow.

Such scenes were repeated on heritage railways throughout England and Wales at the end of December 2000 when snow, which fell several inches deep in places, was followed by clear sunny days at the height of the Christmas/New Year holiday season. Steam trains were running through the snow on railways as far apart as Romney and Ravenglass, West Somerset and the North Yorkshire Moors. On the Ffestiniog, snow cover extended as low down as Minffordd; on the Great Central's newly completed double track, scenes from the snows of 40 years earlier were being convincingly re-created.

All this seemed to happen with conditions having little adverse effect on operation. On the national network it was otherwise — there were numerous delays, particularly on the West Coast main line. A steam special to be hauled by No 60800 *Green Arrow* from Crewe to Carlisle via the Settle & Carlisle line on 28 December was caught up in these. The train, which had originated at Milton Keynes, left Crewe 2½ hours late. On the Clitheroe-Hellifield section, used only by diverted trains and specials, *Green Arrow* had the greatest difficulty keeping moving with 2in of snow on the rails, and on the 'Long Drag' beyond Settle eventually slipped to a stand. Sand was placed on the rails manually to provide the cure, and the train was eventually on its way again. Since it was loaded to 13 coaches, and even 'A3' Pacifics are said to have been limited to eight coaches on the S&C, locomotive performance was in truth very creditable.

On 27 February 2001 it was the turn of Scotland, when a fierce blizzard from the North covered much of the southern part of the country in snow. The West Coast main line and the East Coast main line were both hit, with train services cancelled; so were services between Carlisle and Kilmarnock, Motherwell and Cumbernauld, and Glasgow and Edinburgh via Shotts and via Carstairs — yet so typically capricious in its arrival was even this heavy snow that the main Glasgow Queen Street-Edinburgh line was running almost normally.

The worst experience was that of the 06.32 from Kilmarnock to Glasgow Central, formed of DMU No 156467 with 97 passengers. Blinding driven snow was too much for the windscreen wiper, and forced the driver to slow down from the usual 60mph to around 15mph, which was as well, for near Stewarton at about 07.30 the train ran into an unseen drift and became embedded. The drift was reported as being as much as 10ft deep.

Rescue took most of the day and included the use of a snowplough to clear the line. But eventually the train was dug out around 16.00 and resumed its journey. It brought its passengers to Glasgow, at about 16.30 instead of 07.18; strangely, commuters aboard, while appreciating their rescue, seemed only to want to go straight home again!

48

Chapter 3

Snow in the Highlands of Scotland

The precise extent of the Scottish Highlands is something about which geographers, bureaucrats and others have differed markedly. For the purpose of this book, however, we will take it as being the district served by the Great North of Scotland Railway (GNSR) and Highland Railway (HR), and the Callander & Oban and West Highland lines. It includes therefore some of the wildest and most remote regions traversed by railways in Britain, and the highest summit reached by a main line at Druimuachdar (1,484ft above sea level). Motorists on the adjoining road know it by the alternative, and more usual, spelling of Drumochter. Since the region lies further north and, over much of its area, at higher altitudes than the rest of Britain, its climate tends to be more severe. Precipitation, which comes as rain at low altitudes, falls as snow higher up. The average number of days per year during which snow is lying at Druimuachdar is 70, compared with 5-10 throughout most of England and Wales. Gales, too, often accompany snowfall. A gust with a wind speed as high as 173mph was recorded near the summit of Cairngorm in March 1986, while at low-level Fraserburgh a gust of 142mph was recorded in February 1989. When gales accompany snowfall they tend to sweep exposed ground clear of snow; the snow then falls in places where the air is relatively still, such as railway cuttings. There it forms drifts, and 'wreaths' — wave-like accumulations of snow just below the top edge of the cutting side. Furthermore, conditions are rarely the same throughout the Highlands — heavy snow may be falling in one part while another gets off lightly.

In my experience, having lived in the area for many years, the overriding characteristic of its weather is not severity but unreliability. Snow may arrive at any time from October to May; the worst snow is to be expected in January and February, yet we can go right through those months without any snowfall. A sudden heatwave at midsummer can render Highland glens the hottest places in Britain, yet I have walked in those conditions on the hills high above the West Highland line to encounter, with relief, the snowfields that were still present.

The first railway in these parts was a small concern, at low level: the Morayshire Railway opened for 5½ miles from Lossiemouth to Elgin in 1852. It suffered, nonetheless, from a severe snowstorm early in 1854, with snow lying on the track to a depth of 5 or 6ft. To clear the line the Locomotive Superintendent designed an early snowplough for attachment to the front of a locomotive.

The Morayshire Railway eventually became part of the Great North of Scotland Railway. This, too, was an early user of snowploughs, although during most of the late 1860s any snow that fell was removed by digging. On 25 and 26 December 1869, however, a snowstorm resulted in drifts 3 or 4ft deep. The plough train was therefore sent out on the morning of Monday 27 December; it cleared the line from Aberdeen to Keith satisfactorily, but by evening snow was drifting again in the cuttings and the last up train was held overnight at Huntly. The plough train was therefore sent out again at 1.45am on 28 December. This second expedition resulted in a tragic accident in which four of the crew were killed, but since its causes related closely to the construction of the plough and, more particularly, its method of use, I will defer further consideration to the next chapter.

The GNSR's system was to be badly affected by snow down the years, particularly the lines in gale-swept Buchan and in the Grampian glens, and the upper part of the Deeside line. We will return to them. In the meantime a railway system that was to be even more at the mercy of snow was being built — the Highland Railway.

The earliest sections were also at low level, and it was after the main line — the Inverness & Perth Junction — was opened throughout from Forres to Dunkeld in 1863 that difficulties became apparent. This included two summits: on the moor of Dava, 1,052ft, and at Druimuachdar itself. That the latter summit would give trouble was doubtless foreseen; the coach road that took the same pass through the mountains had been blocked by snow in 1808, 1823 and 1841, and probably on other occasions. In 1841 it was blocked for six weeks.

The Highland's main line got off lightly in its first winter, but in February 1865 there was a heavy snowstorm and the line was blocked, taking five days to clear. Construction of snow fences commenced, to protect the line from wind-blown snow. February 1866 was worse; the line was blocked at Dava and Dalwhinnie, at the latter point (on the approach to Druimuachdar) by drifts more than 8ft deep. Traffic was interrupted for almost a week. Dalwhinnie was cleared by a small snowplough assisted by men with shovels when the drifts were too deep. Locomotive Superintendent William Stroudley set about designing larger ploughs, and these were to see plenty of use: there was heavy snow in the Highlands each subsequent winter until 1870/1, and again in 1875.

Dava was approached from the north by an uphill slog of some 18 miles from Forres, much of it at 1 in 70 and 1 in 75. This presented problems when conditions were bad, which led to unusual operating practices. Niall Ferguson in 'Snow in the Highlands' records how on 9 November 1871 the up Mail of 14 vehicles left Forres double-headed; the pilot engine was to be detached at Dava station, short of the summit by a couple of miles of easier gradients. In snow and a gale, however, the driver of the train engine decided he would need assistance to the summit proper. Rather than be double-headed as far as Grantown, however, the next place beyond at which the pilot engine could be detached, he sent his fireman forward along the footplate to make these arrangements with its driver: shortly before Dava station, they would slow to about 10mph; the pilot engine would be uncoupled and run ahead to the station; the train, keeping on the move, would overtake it through the loop; and the pilot engine would catch it up and bank the rest of the way to the summit. This they did, and all might have gone well had not the train had to punch its way through a drift, which checked its speed just at the moment the pilot engine caught up with it. So the pilot engine hit the main train with considerably more force than intended, and there were injuries to passengers.

On a later occasion, a banking engine was returning downhill from Dava in a blizzard from which the crew on the footplate had no protection. So they retreated to the front footplate to shelter in the lee of the warm smokebox. A knife was used to prise the vacuum brake hose coupling slightly off its dummy, and so to allow air into the pipe and operate the brakes, whenever they judged speed should be reduced. Unfortunately from this position they failed to see a snowdrift — the tender struck it, and was derailed.

On the GNSR on 21 December 1878 the last train from Aberdeen was heading for Ballater on a wild and snowy night. Aboyne was left half an hour late, but Dinnet was reached without apparent difficulty. Then there was a long delay; when passengers asked why, they were told that the engine had gone ahead to clear a way through the snow. It returned, but after the train had travelled a further mile it came to a stand. The engine was again detached in an attempt to clear the way — but became snowed up only a few yards up the line.

The train was now some 5 miles short of the terminus, and a dozen hardy spirits among the passengers decided to set out on foot; they included three young ladies. Since this story (which appeared in the *Dundee Advertiser* for 24 December 1878, and was repeated in *Great North Review* in April 1993) does not end in tragedy, one feels that they must have been locals who knew what they were doing. Nevertheless, the ladies were glad enough to take refuge with a railwayman and his wife at Cambus o'May, the next station; three of the men also found refuge between there and Ballater, but the remainder reached their destination safely. The young ladies were brought in the following morning, by sleigh. The train was still snowed up two days later.

The winter of 1880/1 was particularly hard, with successive snow blockages on the Highland main line from December until March. During a blizzard on 17 December two trains — one up, one down — became snowbound, one on either side of Dava station. Passengers from both managed to reach the station before conditions deteriorated too much; it was as well they did, for both trains became buried, the down train with, eventually, its coaches beneath deep snow. The up train was mixed, and included five loaded cattle wagons. Although the doors were opened and attempts made to get the cattle out, they could not be persuaded to leave their apparent shelter. Regrettably, they were suffocated. The line was blocked again at Dava and Druimuachdar in mid-January, and at Dava yet again in early March. On both these occasions telegraph communication was broken, which was particularly serious on a line then operated by telegraph and train order.

By now other lines were open in the Highlands. The line to the Far North, to Wick and Thurso, had been completed in 1874 with its summit at County March between Forsinard and Altnabreac — only 707ft, but very exposed. On 24 December 1880 an up train from Wick became snowbound about a mile south of Scotscalder. A large plough powered by no fewer than four locomotives was sent to the rescue from the south, but itself became snowed up near Altnabreac. The passengers on the up train were rescued on 27 December, but the line was not cleared until the 29th. As on the line to the south of Inverness, however, this proved to be no more than a start. The mid-January blizzards left two trains buried in snow near Helmsdale by the 21st; the line was reopened on the 24th, but blocked again for 24 hours on 7 February. Yet another blizzard blocked the line again on 13 February.

The Callander & Oban line had been completed through to Oban in 1880 after many years of struggle. It seems to have got through most of the winter of 1880/1 without too much trouble, then, in the small hours of 4 March, the down Mail ran into deep snow near the line's 914ft summit at Glenoglehead, or Killin as the station at that point was then called. The train became stuck, and although the passengers were eventually able to make their own way through the drifts to the station, the line was blocked for several days.

On 3 March 1883, after a winter that had generally been mild, a severe blizzard blew up and marooned a double-headed goods train in drifts at Dava for the best part of a week. Once again it included some livestock in its cargo, but on this occasion, although some animals perished, the train crew were able during a lull in the storm to release the rest into the shelter of a wood beside the line. In January 1884 the Dingwall & Skye line (completed from Dingwall as far as Strome Ferry in 1870) was blocked at several locations by a severe snowstorm.

In the Scottish Record Office there survives a letter (ref GD.374/14/15) that describes the plight of passengers on a snowed-up train. Short of food and drink, they were reduced to eating herrings, cooked on the fireman's shovel. They were able to quench their thirst — which perhaps resulted from their diet — to a limited extent by drinking water from the footwarmers. The letter is dated March 1886, but there seem to have been no serious snow problems in the Highlands that year so it may refer to an earlier year — I have not had an opportunity to study the original document. The mention of herrings suggests a train from Wick, perhaps one of those snowbound in 1880/1. Alternatively the letter might refer to one of the up East Coast expresses that became snowbound north of Newcastle in March 1886, as described in the previous chapter.

For a few years in the late 1880s and the early 1890s the winters continued mild. Early in 1892, however, there was a sharp reminder of what winter could do. Overnight on 7/8 January there was an exceptionally heavy snowstorm across much of the northern Highlands. In Strathspey by morning snow as deep as 2ft 6in to 3ft was measured in sheltered places at

Kingussie, with drifts up to 10ft deep. Five trains were snowed up between Grantown and Dalnaspidal. There were several blocks on the line north from Inverness. The passengers from one train, after an uncomfortable night in the coaches, managed to struggle through the snow to the shelter of the hotel at Forsinard, where they arrived exhausted.

Travelling on the Skye line were 250 volunteer militiamen from Lewis in the Outer Hebrides, *en route* to Fort George near Inverness for their annual training. They had already been delayed by gales at Stornoway for three days before a steamer could make the crossing. A special train carrying the mails and the militia then set out from Strome at 10.25pm on Saturday 9 January. All went well at first, then, between Garve and Achterneed, the train struck a large snowdrift and became embedded.

Early the following day, although it was Sunday, a double-headed train set out from Dingwall with a large crew of men ready to dig out the stranded train. But the rescue train itself became stuck in a snowdrift before it reached Achterneed, and the men had to dig their own train out first, then gradually work it forward through further blocks. A second train brought up food and supplies on Monday; since the line was still blocked, the militiamen struggled through the snow past the blockage to reach this train. One of the engines returned to Dingwall for coaches, which then formed a train to carry the militia to their destination. All were at least six days on the journey; some of them, who came from remote parts of the islands, as much as ten days. The line was finally cleared late on the Monday.

Though January 1892 was bad, the winter of 1894/5 was far worse. A severe blizzard came on 29 December and covered much of the Highlands with snow. There were further heavy snowfalls on 13/14 January, 25-28 January, 5-7 February and 13-15 February. The consequence was that from 29 December until 4 March some part or parts of the Highland Railway were blocked by snow. Between Perth and Wick, the only substantial length that remained clear was that from Inverness to Helmsdale. Furthermore the snow was accompanied by severe frosts, which commenced on New Year's Day. For the whole of January and much of February the temperature in Inverness never rose above freezing; on 7 February it was as low as -6°F.

One of the first trains affected was an up fish special from Wick, which became snowbound at Fairy Hillocks near Forsinard; in the prevailing conditions it is scarcely surprising to learn that, when it was eventually released ten days later, the herrings that it carried, having been well refrigerated, were in good condition and were eventually delivered to their consignees.

The length of line blocked by snow was long but, by much hard work on the part of those clearing it, it was in due course reduced to about a mile. The decision was then taken that the mails should be carried across the blockage, between trains either side, by men walking through the snow. Vallance, in *The Highland Railway*, quotes a letter written soon afterwards by a passenger, one of six held up in Thurso who obtained permission to accompany the mails party at their own risk. While they were travelling out in the van in the early morning, they were advised by platelayers and Post Office staff to tie their trousers tightly round their boots with stout string, taking it under the boots like stirrups. Once on foot he found that so long as the frozen crust of snow bore his weight he was all right; as soon as the crust was broken, he was floundering in snow to a depth of 3 or 4ft.

A first-hand account of an encounter with another snow blockage at this period, from the point of view of the postal sorter in the Travelling Post Office, was provided by 'Caberfeidh' in 'Reminiscences of the TPO Services in the Highlands, 1873-1923' and reproduced in *Railway Philately*, the magazine of the Railway Philatelic Group, in June 1996. Although phrased in the flowery manner of the time, it is reproduced again here, by permission of the Communication Managers' Association. 'Caberfeidh' was the *nom de plume* of Charles

MacKenzie, later head postmaster at Inverness; the train is travelling from Perth towards Druimuachdar:

'Leaving the … shelter of the covered-in platform of the terminus those who, on business or under necessity, were obliged to face the howling wind and blinding snow, were borne onwards and upwards from the plains, with their comparative immunity from drift, through glens and the corries of the majestic hills, where the white feathered flakes were piled in countless myriads in every gully which could afford them a cover and resting place from the sweeping winds. Every railway cutting formed an ideal home for a snow drift, and though every modern device of man's ingenuity was pitted against the tiny snowflake it soon defied them all, blotting out the topographical features of the landscape in its irresistible embrace. So long as the warfare was maintained on level ground progress was possible, and the first stretch of forty odd miles was passed uneventfully. After a pause for replenishing the water tank the second stage of the journey was entered upon. Here the line is formed on an incline rising to almost 1500ft above sea level. Steadily the driver puts his iron steed to the brae holding in reserve, as indicated by the escaping steam from the safety valve, a store of as yet latent power to meet the approaching strife. After the first mile over a comparatively clear road the train gradually gathers speed until it appears to have overcome the opposing forces, which are scattered to left and right by the oncoming plough. Well does the driver know that these are merely the outpost wreaths guarding and warning what is hidden beyond. Anon the fireman opens the stoke hole and replenishes the greedy furnace. A series of feint and guard passes, becoming ever more frequent, are noticeable, and the spent drift, at first falling in showers on the mail van, becomes one continuous cloud of increasing density. As the train approaches the cuttings the noise is as an avalanche had engulfed it, but, with titanic efforts, it frees itself and emerges on succeeding embankments, mercifully clear of drift, where, within a few brief seconds, a further charge can be given to the glowing volcano which alone can prove our salvation. We dare not pause or lose momentum, and so the struggle is maintained until the summit appears in the near distance. But, ere it is attained, the foe descends in unabated fury upon the challenge of its omnipotence, and slowly, yet surely, first enshrouds, then overcomes, with its density all the efforts of the iron steed. In vain the driver urges it to one last effort, while the stoker, midst the ice and snow, appears as first assistant in the hellish scene. Meanwhile the Mail Sorters and the train guards merely play the role of supercargo within the inky darkness of their several cells. There follow a succession of shocks and recoils, a screeching of revolving wheels no longer able to hold on the rails, the noise of escaping steam, which has lost its power of attack, and then a deadly lull marks the beginning of the end of the struggle. In a short time the smoke emitted from the engine funnel forms a blow hole in the snow to indicate the position of the buried train, while sheltering within the cab are driver, stoker, sorters and guards. Nor are the conditions altogether unendurable. With a wagon cover stretched from the roof of the cab to the rear of the tender, an almost unlimited supply of coal, the stoker's shovel for a grid iron, and a box of kippers, there we wait the passing of the storm and the arrival of the relief gang. Day passes and night brings no abatement of the storm, but with the dawn the wind ceases, and there is a great calm. One cannot adequately describe the early morning scene of snow-clad glen and hillside corry, with the mountain peaks standing out in bare and rugged relief, and not a sound to disturb the awful silence of the wilds at rest. After hours of weary waiting, the welcome arrival of the relief gang enables us to damp down the engine fire and abandon our refuge of safety for a more congenial shelter. Two days later, on return to the starting terminus, we presented, I venture to state, a unique spectacle to the wondering gaze of the curious. Exhausted to the last degree, and chilled to the bone with the intense cold, the vanquished heroes stepped on to the platform, using, for a smock-frock, a mailbag pierced on the sides and bottom with holes for arms and head, and, for puttees, two more bags wrapped from ankle to thigh.'

Blockages such as this played havoc with the disposition of the sorting carriages, and the same writer later records how, when urgent mails were to be transmitted and all sorting carriages stranded elsewhere, he successfully completed a journey in an ordinary van, using an orange box for a letter sorting frame and a GPO button for a date stamp, smeared with soot from the sealing-wax pot.

The main effort had to be concentrated on clearing snow blockages from the main line, and at one stage the Skye line, also blocked, remained so for a week. This in turn delayed work in progress on building the extension from Strome to Kyle of Lochalsh.

* * *

Construction of this extension had been prompted by the threat of competition from another railway to the western seaboard. This, the West Highland line, was opened from Craigendoran to Fort William in 1894, just in time for the hardest winter for years. Its summit at Corrour is 1,347ft above sea level, while for many miles on either side of the summit the line crosses remote and exposed moorland that lies above the 1,000ft contour.

In this part of the Highlands, according to John Thomas in *The West Highland Railway*, the hard weather of 1894/5 came in three phases. The principal snowstorms occurred on 29 December, 29 January and, the worst of all, 5/6 February. There were lesser blizzards in between, and for most of the time it was, as elsewhere, exceptionally cold. The first big storm submerged most of the line under snow, and for weeks on end up trains could seldom travel beyond Tulloch, while down trains struggled as far as Bridge of Orchy. In between, snowploughs and gangs of men battled to reopen the line, and as soon as they had cleared any of it, it seemed, another blizzard came to fill up the cuttings again with snow. The management, meanwhile, was faced with escalating costs of snow clearance, and a simultaneous collapse in takings at the booking offices.

On 6 February the line had been cleared sufficiently for an up train to run. From it at Rannoch (the first station south of Corrour) there disembarked the Fort William curling team. They were keen to take advantage of the conditions, and the railway, to hold a match with their rivals from the Rannoch area, which to this day is more easily reached from Fort William by rail than by road. But scarcely had the match started when the weather closed in again with the worst storm of all. The curlers retreated to the station, but the line was already blocked. Fortunately huts used by the contractors who had built the railway had yet to be dismantled and in one of these, which still contained supplies of food and fuel, the curlers took refuge. The following day a relief train with a gang of men arrived from the south, but conditions were still bad beyond Rannoch and three more trains arrived successively, none of them able to proceed. Their occupants joined the curling party. Only on the day after that did conditions improve sufficiently for work to start on digging out the frozen snow and ice that blocked Cruach Cutting to the north of the station. By the end of the day the line was open again, but for weeks afterwards trains passed through narrow clefts between high walls of snow.

That first winter on the West Highland did, however, provide valuable experience for tackling snow in subsequent years — which was as well, for the line experienced heavy snow again in 1902, 1906, 1908, 1909 and many more recent winters. Indeed, one is left with the impression that snow problems on the West Highland have been so endemic as not always to have been found newsworthy.

* * *

The Highland Railway installed double track from Blair Atholl over Druimuachdar as far as Dalwhinnie between 1897 and 1909. Doubling brought the incidental advantage that the cuttings, wider than before, were much less liable to become blocked by snowdrifts.

The widespread snows of December 1906, which led to the disaster at Elliot Junction, affected the Highland worst in the vicinity of Dingwall. The mail train to the north was snowed up near Foulis, and the Skye line was blocked by drifts near Achterneed, which took three days to clear. The Great North of Scotland was also badly affected, with more than 1,000 men drafted in to help clear the drifts. Nonetheless, it took two days to clear the main line, which was blocked with 15 to 20ft of snow in the cuttings between Gartly and Kennethmont.

The GNSR had to cope with more heavy snowfalls two years later, at the end of December 1908, when in some places a fall as deep as 4ft on the level was recorded, and the Deeside line was blocked not far out of Aberdeen. A report dating from 1933, which was quoted in *Great North Review* for Spring 1990, records yet more heavy snowfalls that affected that system in the early parts of the years 1916, 1918, 1922, 1924 and 1933. Snowploughs, supported by large gangs of men to cast the snow (ie to shovel it away), seem to have kept trains on the move.

The snow of early 1918 also hit the Highland Railway in Caithness. A 'Jellicoe Special', carrying Naval personnel from Euston to Thurso for the fleet based on Scapa Flow, became snowed up soon after entering the county; a snowplough locomotive sent out earlier to clear the way for it had already become stuck itself near Scotscalder. It was a week before the line was cleared sufficiently for a full service to resume.

* * *

The winters of the 1930s seem to have been as mild in the north as in the south; then hard winters returned in the 1940s. The railways of the Highlands, however, appear to have got off lightly in January 1940 when snow was causing so much trouble further south. There was one exception — the West Highland line — not, however, around Rannoch, where problems might have been expected, but at the southern end of the line between Garelochhead and Arrochar.

In this case there was a severe snowstorm on Sunday 28 January, and by Monday morning a 6-mile length of line was snowed up, most of it under at least 4ft of snow and with 10ft drifts in cuttings. Also snowed up about halfway along were a plough with two locomotives, which had been attempting to keep the line clear, and another locomotive that had been sent from Arrochar with a gang to help clear the snowed-up plough. The task of clearing the line recommenced — a thankless task, for once again it seemed that progress had scarcely been made when another storm brought more snow. On 31 January a train of empty stock became stuck in a drift near Helensburgh, preventing the line-clearing gang from reaching the main scene of operations, and on 3/4 February a 70mph blizzard undid all the work so far. A further plough attempting to clear the line had the narrowest of escapes, and after the storm a cutting to the north of Glen Douglas now had some 20ft of snow in it. Late on 6 February, however, the snowbound locomotives were reached from the south and the following day they were lit up amid the snow and ice, and moved away under their own steam. The remaining deeply blocked cutting was cleared in time for goods traffic to resume on 9 February and passenger traffic on Monday 12 February.

The following winter, that of early 1941, brought a succession of snow problems to Sutherland and Caithness, where the lines of the former Highland Railway were now part of the London Midland & Scottish. From the second week of January there was snow and frost, and on Tuesday 21 January, despite the efforts of snowploughs, a down goods train became snowbound at Forsinard. A passenger train following was therefore held at Kinbrace, where it too became snowbound. Early the following morning a permanent way train set out to the rescue from Wick, with an inspector and a gang of 16 men, but this too became embedded in a drift near County March Summit. So the following day, Thursday 23 January, a second rescue train set out from Wick, and this in turn stuck in the snow near Altnabreac.

The lineside telephone was still working, and the crews of the rescue trains were able to report their positions and, indeed, to attempt to dig their way out. On the Thursday, despite appalling weather, an aeroplane flew out from Wick and made an air-drop of food to the train stuck near County March, but not without difficulty in finding it, for it was now so deeply buried that it was necessary to relight the locomotive's fire so that its smoke might act as a marker. The same aeroplane air-dropped food at Altnabreac.

Meanwhile the crew of the snowbound goods had been able to take refuge in the hotel at Forsinard, but the passengers at Kinbrace were marooned on an unheated train with very little food. A locomotive managed to bring a dining car from Helmsdale close enough to provide more food, then on the Thursday the train was released and taken back to Helmsdale. Even there, however, there was no accommodation to be had and passengers had to remain on board until Saturday 25 January, when the line was reopened throughout and they resumed their journey.

That was just the first act. On Thursday 4 February there came a second blizzard. The 11.15am from Inverness became snowbound a little north of Forsinard, despite having had the locomotive from a following goods train attached in front of its own locomotive as pilot. The locomotives were able to steam-heat the train overnight, until their water supplies ran out; the 89 passengers then succeeded in making their way on foot back to Forsinard where, not surprisingly, they overflowed the hotel and were accommodated also in the station and the school. Another air-drop brought food.

Meanwhile a snowplough train with a gang of men was endeavouring to fight its way through deep drifts from the north. It released a freight train, also snowbound, from Altnabreac, but itself became snowbound for a while. A second snow-clearing gang from the south reached Forsinard and the two gangs met, clearing the blockage, on 8 February.

Yet another severe snowstorm struck the Far North on Wednesday 26 March, interrupting communications by rail, road and telephone. The 11.15 from Inverness, with more than 100 passengers, reached Helmsdale, but the line was already blocked at Kinbrace, where a snowplough became stuck. It was decided that the train should return to Inverness, but it got no farther than Rogart, for by then the line was blocked in several places to the south, and a train was stranded at Lairg. After a night at Rogart, with passengers eating at a hotel, the train went back to Helmsdale. There, however, its locomotive was taken off to assist the snowploughing; passengers had two more nights in the train, unheated presumably, although meals were provided by a nearby hotel. A snowplough with a gang from Wick eventually reached the stranded plough at Kinbrace, having itself got stuck several times in the attempt, and reached Helmsdale on the Friday night. The train service was resumed on the Monday.

* * *

As seems so often to happen, these events proved to be a climax, and for a few years winters in the North of Scotland were comparatively mild. January 1942, however, was hard enough for the former GNSR Buchan line to become blocked by snow in at least two places. The winter of 1947, though harsh in the South, was less severe in the North, although an up goods train, which included some vans of sheep, became trapped in the snow near Dalwhinnie. The circumstances were sadly reminiscent of the snow blockage at Dava long before. On this occasion, however, when a relief driver and fireman arrived from Perth, struggling along the line through the blizzard, they found it impossible to open the van doors, for snow was drifted high against them, and whenever the snowplough passed on the other road, attempting to keep it clear, it threw a whole lot more snow over the goods train. This train was eventually released and taken forward to Perth Cattle Bank Sidings, but on arrival all the sheep were found to be dead, frozen to the floors of the vans. This distressing occurrence was recalled by the relief locomotive fireman in *The Courier* as recently as 16 March 2001.

Snowdrifts also caused problems on the Callander & Oban line in 1947. Early in 1951 snowploughs were at work on the Highland main line, and the weather was bad enough for a West Highland train to become snowbound. This was the 3.46pm Glasgow-Mallaig on 17 February, five coaches double-headed by two 'K2' class 2-6-0s, which became trapped overnight in deep drifts near Corrour. Snow caused problems on lines both north and south of Inverness in February 1955. Early in 1958 three trains and a snowplough were stuck on the Aberdeen-Fraserburgh line, and early in 1959 the Wick line was once again blocked by drifts near Forsinard.

The lines of the former GNSR were seriously affected by snow early in 1960. In the early part of January there was snow, but no more than to be expected. Then on the morning of Wednesday 18 January there was a heavy snowfall. In the afternoon it eased, but a severe frost set in; in the evening the wind rose to a gale and brought down innumerable telegraph poles. On the main line from Aberdeen to Inverness the 6.30pm was the first train to run that day, and it did not reach its destination until 1.48am. An up train was stuck overnight at Insch. All the branch lines were affected to a greater or lesser extent. The Deeside line, for instance, was cleared by stages, with trains as far as Banchory by Thursday and Torphins by the same evening; a Class 5 4-6-0 fitted with a large snowplough and accompanied by a gang of workmen with shovels managed to get through to Ballater in time for train services to resume on the Friday evening.

On the Buchan line, under the modernisation plan of the period, passenger trains were now worked by diesel multiple-units. At about 11am on 19 January, during a blizzard, a train comprised of two two-car DMUs — the 9.17am from Fraserburgh attached to the 9.30am from Peterhead — was a few hundred yards north of Newmachar when it ran into a deep drift in a cutting and became snowbound. What happened then, seen from the railwaymen's point of view, was described in an article in *Great North Review* for February 1995. Roads were blocked and a relief train carrying the Assistant District Engineer Mr Graham, Chief

Left:
Two ex-GNSR 4-4-0s were in action on 27 January 1942, ploughing snow on the Buchan line.
Aberdeen Journals Ltd

58

Permanent Way Inspector Ogilvie and about 25 men (who had been on duty since early morning), hauled by a Type 2 diesel, left Aberdeen at 3.30pm. But there were numerous halts to clear telegraph poles foul of the line, and wires wrapped around the engine, and it was 7.30 before it reached the junction at Dyce, 6¼ miles from Aberdeen. There it had to await arrival of a large snowplough. This left Dyce for Newmachar, 5¼ miles away, at 8.35pm, with the relief train following 15 minutes later.

There was now no telephone communication to Newmachar, and by midnight Aberdeen Control had heard nothing of what might have happened to the two trains. An attempt was made to reach them using the District Engineer's Land Rover, but this was frustrated as roads were blocked by snowdrifts and stranded vehicles. At 1am a further locomotive was sent into the section, and at 3.45am this did return with the news that the snowplough was working its way through deep drifts south of Newmachar.

In this way the relief train managed to reach a point within a quarter of a mile of the stranded DMU. The Assistant Engineer and some of the men then set out through the drifts with food and tea for the passengers. It took almost half an hour to reach the DMU and, when they did reach it, a snowdrift prevented the driver's door from being opened and access had to be gained through the window. The passengers, however, were comfortable, for heating and lighting were still working. The guard had been able to heat up some cans of soup, provided by a passenger, on the electric grill with which his accommodation was equipped — no more kippers off the fireman's shovel! But there were far more passengers than anticipated, so not enough food had been brought; the

59

Left:
The DMUs from
Fraserburgh and
Peterhead that became
snowbound near
Newmachar are dug out
on 20 January 1960.
Aberdeen Journals Ltd

Engineer and some volunteers then struggled through the snow for over half a mile to Newmachar village, where tradespeople were happy to provide more food despite the fact that it was the middle of the night.

What was clear was that it would take half a day or more to release the train. The passengers all agreed to be transferred to the relief train, with its single coach and brake van; they were escorted to it though the snow during lulls in the storm, and one who was lame was carried on a railwayman's back. The relief train was eventually propelled back to Aberdeen, where it arrived at about 6am on 20 January.

This day turned out to be bright, clear and windless, but it was still 5.30pm before the DMU could be extracted from the snow. It was only then that work could begin clearing the line further north, where two fish trains were stranded. The Assistant Engineer was instructed to return home that night; he had been on duty continuously for some 37 hours. It was another two days before the first passenger train could run.

Sadly, neither modernisation nor railwaymen's devotion to duty were sufficient to make this line seem an economic proposition in the climate of the 1960s. It and many others like it on the GNSR system were closed to passengers a few years later.

* * *

Like the railways of other parts of Britain, those of the Highlands were affected by the great snow of early 1963, although to a lesser extent than might have been expected. Lines generally seem to have been kept clear, and trains moving. Snow lay deep on Rannoch Moor, for instance, but I have found no reference to the West Highland having become blocked. However, early in February the former Highland Railway line was blocked by drifts near Dava, scene of famous blockages in days gone by. This route was no longer the main line, and had not been since opening of the direct line between Aviemore and Inverness via Carrbridge in the 1890s, but remained open as a secondary line. First of all an up passenger train became snowbound near Dunphail, then, while it was being released, more drifts built up near Dava itself, and snowploughs had to be sent in from the Forres direction to clear them.

By now dieselisation had set in. The Highland, and the LMS after it, had cleared snow by large ploughs constructed upon the fronts of steam locomotives. This form of construction did not lend itself to adaptation to diesel locomotives, and two independent ploughs, for propulsion by diesels, had been provided. The intended method of operation was for two diesel locomotives to be used, sandwiched between the ploughs, which faced in opposite directions; there is more about these in the next chapter. However, this, the first occasion upon which they saw serious use in the Highlands, proved disastrous. The leading plough became not merely derailed but overturned on to its side; both the Sulzer Type 2 locomotives propelling it were

also derailed. The cause seems to have been that the blade had encountered an obstruction with such force that it had been bent right back beneath the chassis of the plough.

Once the snow surrounding them had been shovelled clear and the diesels re-railed, this snowplough was, for the time being, shifted clear of the track by a breakdown crane. The remaining plough was taken to the south end of the blockage by an alternative route and, propelled by two diesels, tackled the drifts from that end; a mechanical excavator was brought in to the north end of the blockage to clear the drifts there.

Only a week or so after the line had been cleared, it became blocked again. This time two diesels fitted with nose ploughs, which had been patrolling the line, became stuck in a drift during a blizzard, and remained there for a couple of weeks. During the same blizzard a freight train became snowbound on the main line near Dalwhinnie; once the blizzard had abated enough to make a start, all efforts had to go into clearing this blockage first.

On the Dava route, sadly, all the hard work and frustration experienced by railwaymen attempting to keep it clear of snow were rewarded by the threat of closure under the Beeching Plan, which was made public a couple of months later — a threat that was in due course carried out.

It was, however, at this time of rapid change that the Scottish Region of British Railways restored certain historic locomotives and operated them for a few years on special trains. One such, which comprised the famous Caledonian Railway 4-2-2 No 123 and Caledonian coaches, was traversing the Callander & Oban line as late in the winter as Good Friday, 12 April 1963, when it encountered a raging blizzard around Glen Ogle and Killin Junction. The blizzard does not, however, seem to have affected the running of the train, despite the gradients and the 'single-wheeler' locomotive.

* * *

The next severe winters in the Highlands were those of the late 1970s and early 1980s. On the evening of 28 January 1978 heavy snow was falling in Caithness and Sutherland, and in these conditions Inverness Control decided that the 17.15 from Inverness to Wick and Thurso should be double-headed north of Helmsdale. The Type 2 diesel working the Thurso branch was therefore sent south to Helmsdale through the increasing storm to meet it and assist the train engine north again. Conditions had been bad going down, but coming back north with the double-headed train they were atrocious. Driving snow made the windscreen wipers and the headlight almost useless, the driver later told *Rail News*; most of the time the crew could see nothing, but every so often there would be a jolt as the nose plough hit a drift.

Soon after Forsinard they encountered a deep drift, and all coaches but the front one left the rails. The guard, assisted by the crew of the train locomotive, then moved all the 70 passengers

Above and left:
Despite any impression to the contrary given by the illustrations earlier in this chapter, trains regularly ran through snow in the Highlands without trouble. Here they cross at Achnasheen on the Kyle line in February 1970. Evidently nothing has run on the up line since the snow fell. After the trains have gone, the snow does not prevent the connecting bus for Gairloch from backing across the tracks to load parcels from the down platform. *(both) Author*

into the front carriage, and the two locomotives and single coach set off again. They got only 2 miles before encountering an even deeper drift and became snowbound, with snow up to roof level. This had accumulated since the locomotive went south a few hours before, an indication of the severity of the storm. White-out conditions made it pointless to attempt to reach the next lineside telephone, at Altnabreac, on foot, and train crew and passengers settled down for the night.

But as time went by the signalman at Georgemas Junction became concerned at the train's non-arrival. He contacted Control, and the one remaining locomotive at that end of the line, No 26031, which had been working the Wick branch, was brought to Georgemas ready to assist if needed. It was ready by 01.00. The thinking was that, if the down train were stranded, an additional locomotive might just be sufficient to haul it clear.

A modification to block regulations allowed for train failures north of Forsinard, but depended on the driver making contact with Georgemas signalbox. That he had neither done so, nor arrived, made it seem clear that the train was stuck. The locomotive at Georgemas was given dispensation, by Control, to enter the section, running towards the train with extreme caution, the headlight on, and the whistle sounding continuously. Thus it disappeared into the blizzard.

For some hours no further word reached Control. There were, however, other problems demanding attention. The Kyle line was blocked by snow at Garve, and the main line south at Carrbridge, and traffic had to be diverted via Aberdeen. About 08.00 there was a message: No 26031 had become stuck in a drift a mile short of Altnabreac, the crew had dug it out and returned, without any sight of the missing train. Then at about 09.30 came a telephone call from Altnabreac to Georgemas: the locomotive crew from the Inverness train had successfully struggled through 9ft drifts to the telephone. No 26031 went back into the section carrying a permanent way inspector and several men equipped with shovels, and cans of soup for the stranded passengers. It reached Altnabreac and the locomotive crew from the down train. Then, attempting to reach the train, it too became derailed in the snow. The soup was delivered on foot.

There were now no more locomotives north of the snow blockage, and to the south of the coach containing the passengers were several more coaches, snowbound and derailed on damaged track. Scottish Region approached the police, to request helicopter assistance. Even then, with people marooned in buses and cars across the North of Scotland, it was 6 hours before two helicopters arrived. Despite the continuing blizzard and gathering darkness, they were able to land and to shuttle everyone to safety. The line was not reopened until 6 February.

A year later, in February 1979, blizzards blocked the main line south of Inverness. On the Strathspey Railway — reopened from Aviemore to Boat of Garten the previous summer — volunteers who managed to make their way to Boat of Garten, to continue the work of restoration, found everything buried beneath deep snow. Early in 1982 the Far North line was again blocked for a week by snow at Fairy Hillocks.

* * *

In January 1984 conditions were severe enough to block not only the West Highland but also the Callander & Oban, or rather its surviving section operated as a branch from the WHR at Crianlarich. On Saturday 21 January it snowed heavily with extensive drifts. The last Oban-Glasgow train of the day, comprising Class 37 No 37188 and three coaches, encountered a drift near Tyndrum Lower. The locomotive was fitted with a miniature plough and, despite the crew's attempts to reverse and charge the drift, the train became embedded in the snow. The passengers took refuge in a house close by.

The following day a snowplough managed to clear the line from Crianlarich. The locomotive was recovered but the train was impossible to move. The evening after that, when platelayers eventually succeeded in digging away the snow from it, it was found that apart from one bogie all wheels of the coaches were derailed. In cramped conditions, for snow had now turned to ice, it was an all-day task to re-rail them.

Meanwhile the West Highland line proper had been blocked by snowdrifts north of Bridge of Orchy and by a snowplough-fitted locomotive from Fort William, which had itself become snowbound at Rannoch while attempting to clear them. Although the blocks were tackled by snowploughs from both ends, it nonetheless took until the Thursday to clear the line throughout and enable a freight train to reach Fort William. This carried bauxite urgently needed by Fort William's aluminium works — without it the furnaces would have had to have been shut down.

So to the winter of 2000/1. Even while I was writing this book, the winter was appropriately hard. On 6 February 2001, after a couple of days of snowstorms, a blizzard of traditional proportions raged across the Highlands. The accompanying gale brought a massive oak tree down on to the Perth-Inverness line, and the consequences are described in Chapter 11. On the Sutherland/Caithness border the blizzard brought snow to a depth of 2-3ft. Through this

ScotRail's 11.29 from Inverness to Wick was heading northwards from Helmsdale; it was composed of two-car 'Sprinter' unit No 158721, and it had on board 15 passengers (some of whom were on their way home from hospital visits), driver, guard and refreshment trolley attendant. It had already been held at Ardgay for some 3 hours while a snowplough cleared the line, and it was now about 5 hours late. The snowplough preceded it north of Helmsdale to clear the way, but had of course to emerge from the section before the train could follow. In the interval it seems that more snow accumulated, perhaps blown by the wind. At any rate, around 19.30 and a little short of Kinbrace, the train became embedded in a snowdrift 4ft deep, unable to move.

A rescue operation was mounted by the police. The road nearby was passable, once ploughed, but the snow between it and the train was not, being too deep for pedestrians. At midnight the police alerted the staff of the Borrobol Estate nearby, which possessed a 35-year-old Sno-cat tracked vehicle. This was driven across the snow to the train, and by it passengers and crew were evacuated about 02.00.

Meanwhile the 16.16 train from Wick to Inverness had been terminated at Thurso when conditions worsened. Endeavouring to return to Wick, it too became snowbound at Lynegar near Watten soon after 17.00; its three passengers were rescued by emergency services. Yet a third train was affected, the 17.30 Inverness-Wick, which was terminated at Brora, where ScotRail put up the passengers in a hotel.

And so the saga of snow in the Highlands continues…

Chapter 4

Snow and Ice: Cures

The easiest way to dispose of snow and ice is of course to wait for the thaw. Regrettably this, unless the thaw is almost immediate, is seldom practicable in railway operation.

One means to alleviate the effect of snow has been to reduce the loading of trains, particularly freight trains, or to increase the motive power by double-heading. But almost as soon as snow starts to fall, it has always been necessary to start clearing it away; for permanent way gangs, manual clearance of snow from around signal wires and point rodding, detectors, switches and locking bars has been routine, as has clearance of flangeways at points, crossings and level crossings. Then, as snow falls more and more heavily, a line that despite all efforts becomes blocked by snow has to be cleared.

A particular problem that has arisen in the Highlands is that lineside fences become buried in wind-blown snow while an adjoining embankment, say, remains bare; the exposed grass then tempts sheep on to the line, so that fences have to be cleared to maintain a barrier.

Throughout most of the railway era all the tasks just mentioned have been the work of manual labour. Certainly, snowploughs were available from early on to assist — and later the roles were reversed, with men assisting the snowploughs. Nevertheless, there have been times, notably during the 1960s, when lack of adequate railway snow-fighting equipment has become a matter of controversy — a question of how much capital should be expended on equipment which would see only limited use.

Right:
Snow clearance by shovel, at Tow Law, LNER, in February 1941. But the snowplough was present too. *National Railway Museum*

Above:
Railwaymen in four tiers excavate the snow from a blocked cutting on the Highland Railway, shovelling it up from one tier to the next. *The Wick Society*

Right:
The Army has arrived to help clear the LNER Woodhead route at Hadfield in 1940. *National Railway Museum*

Let us consider how snow clearance by manual labour has fared down the years. Some early attempts seem to have involved sweeping it away. When the Liverpool & Manchester Railway experienced its first snowfall on 12 December 1830, the snow was swept by railway employees and hired labourers; subsequently the railway company arranged for a force of labourers to be available, and when heavy snow fell in February 1831 fewer delays occurred. The 1881 experiences of the LSWR guard, quoted in Chapter 2, came despite attempts to sweep the snow away — the wind blew it back again almost as quick as the men could brush it, commented F. S. Williams. But they were digging, too, for the snow came out in square blocks like sugar, or starch.

Earlier, on the Cromford & High Peak in January 1842, from 90 to 100 men laboured to clear the snow that blocked the summit level. A year later, as many as 300 men were needed to clear the line after an exceptionally heavy snowfall.

Left:
Railwaymen and soldiers cast snow near Maud on the GNSR section of the LNER on 23 January 1942.
Aberdeen Journals Ltd

On the Highland Railway, gangs of men with shovels became a regular feature, assembled winter by winter as circumstances dictated. Where a deep cutting was blocked, they worked in tiers: men at the bottom threw the snow part of the way up the slope, and a second and sometimes a third or even a fourth gang of men shovelled it higher still until it was clear. The passenger of 1895 quoted by Vallance in *The Highland Railway*, who accompanied the mails party on foot over the snow near Fairy Hillocks, described the scene as picturesque — a hundred men working in the snow at that remote spot, looking like silhouettes. They were working in triple tier, each spadeful of snow being handled three times.

During both world wars servicemen came to the aid of railwaymen in clearing snow-blocked lines. The party of men dispatched to rescue the 'Jellicoe Special' that became snowbound early in 1918 included 50 naval ratings. The far worse weather experienced during World War 2 required far greater numbers of troops. In January 1940 the 200 LNER employees struggling to clear the West Highland were assisted by an equal number of soldiers. Early in 1941 the LNER was assisted by some 1,000 troops, as mentioned earlier, when the February blizzard brought the railways of northeast England to a stand. Earlier that winter, as many as 5,000 troops had been helping the LMS to clear its many snow blocks.

In March 1947 National Service soldiers were employed in clearing snow from lines of both the LMS and the LNER in central Scotland. At the same period the railwaymen attempting to clear the Settle & Carlisle line had the assistance not only of British troops but of also Polish troops who had not returned home, and of German and Italian ex-prisoners of war who awaited repatriation. Italian ex-prisoners were also employed in large numbers in March 1947 to clear the Cromford & High Peak. In 1960 troops were called out to clear the blockage on the Buchan line at Newmachar described in Chapter 3, and as late as 1963 it was stated that in the event of serious snow blockage arrangements were made for military assistance, although I have not traced any instance in the snows of that year when the military were in fact used.

By the 1950s railway management at Inverness had got the arrangements for assembling and despatching snow-clearing gangs down to a fine art, to judge from M. Harbottle's article in January 1960. When conditions seemed likely to deteriorate, a special train of mess van and steam-heated coaches was kept ready. Once it was decided to call out men, their tools, equipment, blankets and so on were loaded from an emergency store, while supplies of food — nourishing soups and hot dishes — were provided by the nearby British Transport hotel. Meanwhile, locomotives and train crews were being made available, and a priority path prepared for the special by the duty controller. Before long the train was on its way with a gang of perhaps 50 men, picking up more *en route* following emergency calls to permanent way inspectors. If all went well, a large gang would arrive on site at daybreak. Experience showed that unless passengers or staff were actually marooned on a snowbound train, attempts to clear the blocked line while a blizzard raged simply tired men out with little result; it was more effective in the long run to wait until conditions improved, then tackle the blockage with men who were fresh.

Sometimes snow excavated from lineside drifts has to be loaded into wagons, taken away and dumped where the lineside is clear. This was done on the Settle & Carlisle in 1947, at Dava and on the Waverley Route at Whitrope in 1963, and doubtless in other places. At Whitrope at this date it was necessary to use explosives to bring down snow cornices, which had built up along the top edge of the cutting.

Remarkably, mechanical plant (other than snowploughs and the like) seems to have been used to excavate snow blockages only to a limited extent. A mechanical excavator was, however, used at Dent on the Settle & Carlisle in March 1947. Another cleared part of the blockage at Dava on the Highland line in February 1963, and yet another, mounted on a bogie wagon, was used at Forsinard in January 1978.

During the spring of 1986, after a hard winter, a small skid-steer loader was used to clear the Snowdon Mountain Railway's track of snow and loose rock prior to opening for the season; it was taken up the mountain daily on the works train. One of these machines is

normally based at Llanberis where its tasks are to load coal into locomotive bunkers and ballast into wagons. It is used for snow clearance perhaps three or four times in ten years. It was not used in 2001, for instance, although the line had to be dug out manually before reopening to Clogwyn on 23 March.

* * *

Let us turn now to the development of snowploughs. Initially when — or rather, perhaps, where — they were not available, light engines were sometimes employed to charge their way through snowdrifts. F. S. Williams recorded the locomotive of a train being detached for this purpose on the LSWR in 1881, in the passage quoted in Chapter 2. In one incident in the 1891 West Country blizzard, this practice was over-successful: when a light engine was brought to the rescue of a snowbound locomotive near Chacewater, it charged the drifts so effectively that it collided with the stranded locomotive, and the light engine's brakesman was thrown to the ground and injured.

London Transport used this technique as recently as New Year 1963, when Neasden-based steam locomotives were used to push their way through the drifts on the snowbound Metropolitan Line branches to Watford and Chesham.

When the Cromford & High Peak Railway considered a machine for clearing snow back in 1832, it seems to have sought advice from the Stockton & Darlington Railway, but without success. W. W. Tomlinson's *The North Eastern Railway* offers no enlightenment on this, but does note that an engine on the Newcastle & Carlisle Railway was said to have had two besoms tied to it to sweep snow from the rails; Tomlinson even gives the date, 29 October 1836. The Newcastle & Carlisle was not alone: the same principle, of attaching besoms to the guard irons, was known on the British-influenced 3ft 6in-gauge railways in Norway, where it could still be seen in 1920. W. H. Bishop, too, during his 1878 visit to the Festiniog Railway for *Scribner's*, reported the deficiency of the line in snowploughs other than 'old brooms tied to the engine's head'.

Maybe, however, besoms were found wanting on the Newcastle & Carlisle. Tomlinson states that in 1837 William Hawthorn brought out his 'railway engine protector' to clear the rails from obstructions. He was, presumably, the W. Hawthorn of R. & W. Hawthorn, the locomotive builder whose customers included the Newcastle & Carlisle. Certainly Francis Whishaw in *The Railways of Great Britain and Ireland* (1842) states of the Newcastle & Carlisle locomotives that 'all … have ploughs in front of the fore-wheels, to clear the snow and other impediments which may present themselves'.

In considering the further development of snowploughs, one is hampered by the imprecise manner in which railwaymen have used the term. It is used for the fitment attached to the front of a locomotive or railcar to clear snow off the line. It is also used of a locomotive or locomotives so fitted, when they are working to clear a line of snow. And it is used of independent snowploughs, that is snow-clearing vehicles propelled by separate locomotives. As railwaymen have tended to use the term indiscriminately between these three, it is sometimes difficult, when reading of snowploughs in days gone by, to establish exactly which meaning is intended.

Of the Morayshire Railway's snowplough of 1854, however, we do have a detailed description. It appeared in the *Elgin & Morayshire Courier* for 10 March of that year, and was quoted in *Great North Review* for November 1994. The plough, the newspaper said, was made in the form of a wedge about 6ft long and 2ft deep, which was attached to the front of the engine where it projected about 12in beyond the rails — on either side, presumably. This threw snow off the wheels of the engine. The plough stood about 7in above the rails lest it came into contact with anything on the line, but was fitted with two iron plates standing about 1in above the rails and 10in on each side; these were at the same angle as the plough and acted as

Above:
A Highland Railway 2-4-0 fitted with
Stroudley's large snowplough, with its
tender protected from flying snow, is ready
to tackle the next winter's snow blocks
with the assistance of three further
locomotives. *Highland Railway Society*

scrapers. Immediately behind them and fixed to the guard rails of the engine were two brushes to sweep the rails and leave the path of the engine clear. From the buffer-beam to the point of the plough, vacant space was covered with canvas like a roof, which prevented snow from getting at the machinery. It all worked, apparently, extremely well, and the credit for 'this excellent and useful' invention was due to Joseph Taylor, Locomotive Superintendent.

While the Morayshire Railway's snowplough had been demolishing the drifts that lay in its way early in 1854, snow was bringing the far more important Great Northern Railway to a stand. In consequence, Archibald Sturrock, Locomotive Superintendent, had snowploughs built at Doncaster, which were ready for the following winter. Whether there was any link between the two developments I do not know, but the Morayshire Railway had been engineered by James Samuel of the Eastern Counties Railway, so it is just possible that there may have been. It may also be relevant that R. & W. Hawthorn was favoured as builder of locomotives for the Great Northern. The engineering world of those days was a small one.

There was, however, a definite link between the Great Northern and the next set of snowploughs designed for use in the Highlands. William Stroudley, Locomotive Superintendent of the Highland Railway, had them designed and built during 1865-9. He had been Running Foreman for the GNR at Peterborough in 1854, where he must at least have been aware of construction of Sturrock's snowploughs and of the need for them. Indeed, one authority (John Thomas & David Turnock, *A Regional History of the Railways of Great Britain, Vol 15: North of Scotland*) states that he designed a snowplough himself while at Peterborough. This is surprising, for he was not yet in a senior position — his immediate superior was Charles Sacré, who was in turn responsible to Sturrock — yet it is not inconceivable that in the circumstances a running foreman might have a go at producing something himself.

For the Highland, Stroudley developed a range of three sizes of snowplough. The smallest type, which could cope with drifts up to 2ft deep, was attached to many of the locomotives at the beginning of each winter as a matter of routine. These ploughs were an aid to locomotives as they hauled trains, and locomotives fitted with them could be coupled together, double-headed. A larger plough, built up on the front of a locomotive — it reached about halfway up the smokebox — could deal with drifts up to 5ft deep; locomotives equipped with such ploughs were coupled ahead of the train locomotives as pilot engines.

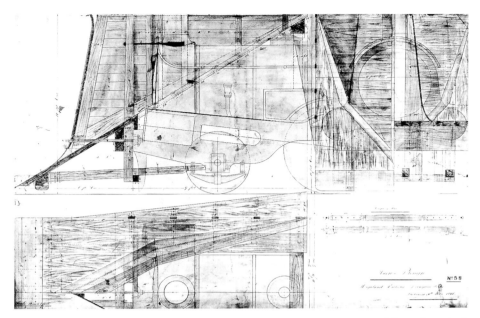

Ploughs of the largest type of all could deal with drifts of 10 or 12ft, and worked independently of trains to clear blocked lines. They were built up around the front of Crewe-type 2-4-0 goods engines so that only the top of the chimney showed; cab and tender were covered in to protect them from falling snow. In later years David Jones's 4-6-0 goods locomotives were favoured motive power. Propelled additionally by two, three or more further locomotives, this rail-borne battering ram would take a run of half a mile to charge into a snowdrift. Snow flew up to an astonishing height and all around; the plough and its own locomotive were temporarily obliterated within it, and bystanders had to stand well back to escape being stunned by flying lumps of snow, or even buried and perhaps suffocated.

Ploughs of these three sizes became known respectively as third-, second- and first-class ploughs. The small, third-class plough was a wedge plough attached below the buffer-beam. The other two comprised a blade in the shape of an inclined plane reaching almost to rail level, with a prominent V-shaped divider to throw the snow off to the sides. On at least some of the

Above:
Construction of Stroudley's large snowplough is clearly shown in this drawing prepared at Lochgorm Works and dated 30 November 1866. *National Railway Museum*

Right:
The cab has been protected too in this later photograph of a locomotive fitted with a first-class snowplough in action. *Highland Railway Society*

first-class ploughs, there were on either side of the inclined blade hinged extensions to ensure that the passageway cleared through a drift was substantially wider than the rolling stock. The hinges enabled the extensions to be folded back within the loading gauge when not at work.

The divisions between the usages of the three sizes of snowplough were not rigid. Locomotives equipped with second-class ploughs were sometimes operated singly, between scheduled trains, to keep lines clear, and they were also used to clear drifts, in which case they were propelled additionally by further locomotives and used as described above. No doubt much depended upon when, where and in what quantity the snow came, and where the ploughs were based at the time. W. M. Acworth, in *The Railways of Scotland*, notes that a batch of snowploughs was often to be observed at Blair Atholl. Unfortunately the winters immediately preceding publication of his book in 1890 were mild, and it contains no description of ploughs in operation, although his forecast that the extreme north was unlikely to escape snow for much longer was remarkably prescient.

The snowploughs' task in clearing drifts was made easier and quicker by cutting, manually, a series of trenches in the snow across the track; these greatly reduced the build-up of compressed snow and so reduced resistance. Once a snowplough-fitted locomotive had forced its way through a snowdrift, it was not the practice on the Highland Railway for it to return tender-first through the ploughed drift; this was, presumably, a precaution against derailment. The locomotive, or locomotives, had to go forward to the nearest turntable for turning, notwithstanding that this was sometimes inconvenient. Once, when a blockage between Dingwall and Ravens Rock summit had been cleared, the plough locomotives had to go right through to Kyle of Lochalsh, nearly 60 miles, to be turned.

This basic range of ploughs in three sizes, or something like it, lasted until the end of steam, although there were detailed developments over the years. The LMS, typically, attempted to standardise on a very similar (though more extensive) range of ploughs developed by the

Caledonian Railway. But ploughs of any sort saw little use in the winters immediately following the Grouping of 1923. By the time heavy snows again arrived, so had the Class 5 4-6-0, which the smallest Caledonian plough would not fit. St Rollox Works produced ploughs to a new design that did, and Class 5 locomotives fitted with them became a familiar sight throughout the Highland winter. Forty new ploughs, in the same basic range of three sizes, were built at St Rollox in about 1956. By then they had become known as (in ascending order of size) the No 6 nose plough, the No 3 heavy-duty plough, and the No 2 heavy-duty plough complete with cab and tender protection.

The snowploughs were originally constructed from timber with iron reinforcements, but developed over the years and eventually became welded steel. With increasing use of iron and steel, it seems that increasingly graceful curves could be incorporated into the ploughs' design as aids to penetrating the snow and throwing it off.

* * *

Tracing the origins and development of the Highland Railway's snowploughs and snowploughing practices has taken us far ahead in terms of time, and it is now necessary to return to an earlier period and to other companies — indeed, to an earlier snowplough. I mentioned in the last chapter that the Great North of Scotland Railway's snowplough train had been involved in a serious accident in the small hours of 28 December 1869. The accident was investigated by the Board of Trade's inspecting officer, Lt-Col C. S. Hutchinson, and we therefore have in his report a detailed description of both the snowplough itself and snowploughing practices of the time.

The plough, which was attached to the buffer-beam of an engine, comprised two faces of 2in planking that met at an angle of 90°; the pointed end was 2ft 6in in front of the front face of the buffer-beam, and the top was level with the bottom of the buffer-beam, 2ft 8in above the top of the rails; the triangular space thus formed was planked over. The faces were 2ft 4in high, but only the central 1ft 6in was vertical; above and below this the faces were inclined forwards at 45°. The faces ran back to 2ft behind the buffer-beam, and had an extreme overall width of 8ft 6in. The whole structure was strengthened by horizontal timbers, and wrought-iron straps and ties; a small iron shoe was fastened to the bottom of the front angle. The plough weighed nearly 500lb; to prevent it from dipping downwards, it was supported by a chain from the chimney.

This plough was mounted upon a six-wheeled tender engine, 'with the driving and trailing wheels coupled', ie a 2-4-0. Coupled behind this was a second locomotive, 'an eight-wheeled one, with the front four wheels on a bogie frame, and a four-wheeled tender' — in other words a 4-4-0, the GNSR being an early user of this wheel arrangement. Bringing up the rear was a brake van carrying two guards and 15 platelayers. The front locomotive was driven by the most experienced driver in the company's service — he had 16 years' experience. On board also was the company's 'chief inspector of permanent way', who likewise had 16 years' service, and 31 altogether on railway work. The driver of the second locomotive had 12 years' service. It had been found that the plough would clear drifts from 3 to 4ft deep; deeper drifts were cleared by digging.

During 27 December, it will be recalled, the plough train had successfully cleared the line from Aberdeen to Keith, but drifts had accumulated again and the last up train had got no further than Huntly. The plough train was therefore sent out again from Kittybrewster at 1.40am on a clear night with a very sharp frost. As far as Gartly, 34 miles from Aberdeen and the last station before Huntly, all went well; the train arrived at 3.28am, and the plough was carefully examined and found in order. At 3.35am it set off again. Three miles further on the driver of the second engine felt a check to its speed while running through a cutting, and when his engine emerged it was going down the side of an embankment. He remembered nothing more until he came to, lying in a heap of coal near the foot of the embankment with his leg bruised. Among those on the footplates, he was the lucky one — the only survivor. The body of his fireman was found halfway down the embankment, which was about 18ft high. Their locomotive and tender were at the bottom of the bank, outside the boundary fence on the west side of the line, still coupled together and pointing in the correct direction but having, it appeared, turned completely over twice during their descent. They were some 40yd from the point at which, it was established, they had first left the rails.

The leading engine was at the bottom of embankment on the opposite side of the line: standing on its wheels, and about 25yd short of the other. Its tender had become uncoupled and was lying, upside down, about 10yd ahead of its engine. Driver, fireman, and permanent way inspector were all found dead; the inspector's watch had stopped at 3.41. The coupling between the second tender and the brake van had, mercifully, given way; the van was derailed but its occupants were uninjured.

Of witnesses to the entire sequence of events sadly there were none. What Col Hutchinson deduced had probably happened was this. Through the cutting the line curved to the west, and at its north end the previous night's ploughing had left a vertical wall of snow on the west side of the line, which (one may assume) was only just outside the reach of the plough. This had become frozen with a roughened face, and more snow had drifted into the angle between it and the track. The plough train must have been travelling at what he considered a very injudicious speed, averaging more than 30mph from Gartly. Possibly the plough had been damaged in the drifts further back in the cutting; at any rate, for some reason or other, perhaps a lurch by the engine, it came into violent contact with the frozen snow and started to break up. Fragments, found later, appeared to have gone under the wheels causing the leading wheels to derail. Damaged keys showed that the flange of the right-hand wheel had run along outside the rail. Col Hutchinson observed no wheel marks in the ballast, which he attributed to its having been frozen hard and covered with frozen snow. In view of this, one wonders whether broken snow from the earlier ploughing had frozen in the flangeways and contributed to raising the wheel on to the railhead. At any rate, at the end of the cutting the curve ended and the line became straight; the engine clearly became wholly derailed and went down the bank.

Col Hutchinson considered that although 'injudicious speed' was the main cause of the accident, the form of the plough could have been improved. With a sharper point, the shock on entering a bed of snow could be made as gentle as possible.

In later years the GNSR used ploughs comparable to those of the Highland Railway. The report of 1933, mentioned in the last chapter, records that up to seven ploughs were at work during the heavy snow of December 1908 and cleared about 50 miles of line. In January 1918 the ploughs ran 5,672 miles on 144 separate journeys.

January 1922 saw snowploughs deployed thus: Kittybrewster had two locomotives fitted with heavy ploughs, three with medium ploughs and one or more with light ploughs; at Keith was a locomotive with a heavy plough; and at Elgin one with a medium plough. Engines with snowboards were specified for the lines to Alford, Ballater, Boddam and Peterhead; the term 'snowboard' does not seem to be defined, but I deduce some sort of light plough or snow deflector. In 1924 there were five engines fitted with ploughs stationed at Kittybrewster, one at Keith and one at Elgin.

In 1933 there were four engines stationed at Kittybrewster with ploughs attached, and one plough van. At Keith was another plough van, and an engine with plough attached was at Elgin. These two plough vans were doubtless the independent snowploughs of North Eastern Railway build, which the LNER had transferred from Yorkshire; they form part of another line of snowplough development they will be described shortly. Although they were present on the GNSR for some years, just how much use they saw I do not know. Certainly in January 1960, on the occasion when the DMU became snowed up on the Buchan line, ploughing was being done by a Class 5 fitted with a large plough and assisted by another engine.

Another Scottish railway, the Glasgow & South Western (GSWR), was employing in about 1908 a snowplough similar to a Highland Railway second-class plough. It was mounted upon a domeless 0-4-2, which was assisted from the rear by two further locomotives of the same type.

* * *

The Midland Railway employed snowploughs mounted upon locomotives, or so it appears, for F. S. Williams on the title page of the 1883 edition of *Our Iron Roads* illustrates what looks like a Johnson 2-4-0 equipped with a medium-sized plough. This is forcing its way through a drift with the assistance of two more locomotives of the same type to propel it. By the 1920s, however, the Midland was employing independent ploughs on the Settle & Carlisle. Then in the 1930s these in turn were replaced by the LMS with steel ploughs mounted upon locomotives. How these were used in 1947 was recalled by Inspector F. Slindon in his article in *Railway World* of February 1981, from which the following is quoted by permission of the editor:

'Precautions were taken to cope with emergencies created by snowstorms. A number of '4F' 0-6-0s were adapted for the fitting of steel snowploughs at the chimney end by Skipton and Hellifield motive power depots. In the autumn, several of these engines had the ploughs fitted ready for use and during winter months they were not allowed out of the district. Several goods brake vans were converted into mess vans with accommodation for six men and were equipped with the necessary tools as well as a portable telephone to help communicate with signalboxes when necessary. When in action each snowplough was in the charge of an operating inspector, a stationmaster or relief signalman, a loco inspector and fitter, and a permanent way inspector. The ploughs ran back to back with the plough brake between, thereby allowing movement in either direction.

'Being in the centre of the area, a small loco depot was set up at Dent. This included accommodation for ten men with bunking and messing facilities and when necessary a loco inspector and fitter also attended. A wagon of coal was placed in position in the late autumn to provide a stock of fuel. Plug points were installed in each platelayer's cabin and on walls at various locations so that the plough crews could contact the signalmen on their portable telephones. All equipment was tested in the autumn to make sure it was working properly.

'On Sunday 3 February 1947 a slight fall of snow had been reported in the area. Several snowploughs were fitted to engines which were steamed and made ready for manning. During the night snow fell again, accompanied by rising winds, so two sets of ploughs were turned out in the charge of relief signalmen. The night trains got through but the snowploughs experienced difficulty in keeping the lines clear. Shortly after I arrived on duty we were told that one of the ploughs had derailed at Blea Moor and the other one was coming into Hellifield for servicing and to raise steam.

'It was agreed I should take charge of this plough when it was ready to leave Hellifield shed. Once under way we had little difficulty in reaching Horton where we were told that the down express which had been doing badly when passing that point had come to a stand about a mile from Ribblehead. I immediately contacted the operating manager at Leeds and advised him of the circumstances. We both realised the importance of moving the express as quickly as possible and he agreed that once the express was clear of the area the line should be closed to traffic and handed over to the snowploughs. The stationmaster and early-turn signalman volunteered to accompany us and help to free the express. We set off towards Ribblehead over the up line and drew alongside the train and I advised its driver that we intended crossing over to the down line at Ribblehead. Then we would plough back towards the front of his train. He agreed to look out for us and guide us back to the express. Arriving at Ribblehead, we cleared the snow from the crossover road and crossed to the down line. Our next job was to find a set of catch-points about half a mile to the south. Having located them we cleared them of snow, clipped them up, and proceeded towards the train, stopping about fifty yards short, at which point its driver was waiting for us. We cleared snow from under the locomotive and a short distance ahead, and threw some sand under the locomotive's wheels and on the rails ahead. The driver agreed that he should be able to move. I asked him to send his fireman back to Selside signalbox and to stay there until I had spoken to him from Ribblehead. Then he was to return to the train and tell the driver to proceed to Ribblehead. The ploughs moved forward to Blea Moor. I spoke to the driver again from there and we agreed that we should carry on in this manner moving from box to box. We did very well until approaching Mallerstang where the signals were against us and a freight train was standing on the up line. I went to the signalbox there and asked why we were being held up, to be told that at the south end of Birkett Tunnel, about half a mile ahead, the line was blocked by snow; according to the local ganger snow completely filled the tunnel mouth. The plough drivers, well experienced in this type of thing, reckoned that as the snow was freshly fallen, and the plough was on a falling gradient, we should be able to force our way through. All the time the weather continued to worsen. I spoke to the driver of the express which was now standing at Ais Gill and told him not to move the train until I contacted him from Kirkby Stephen. So we forced our way through Birkett Tunnel and on arrival at Kirkby Stephen I informed the driver of the express of the conditions at the tunnel, warning him that he could expect a lot of the snow to have fallen back on to the track due to the very confined space at the mouth of the tunnel. He should approach the tunnel at reduced speed to avoid any undue shock to the passengers, relying on the falling gradient and the weight of the train to get him through. We were very relieved to see the express approaching Kirkby Stephen. I spoke to the driver and told him that we would follow him to Appleby. When we arrived there, I was pleased to find that there were no injuries to any of the passengers and that the train was undamaged. The passengers had been kept well supplied with refreshments, including milk for the babies on board.'

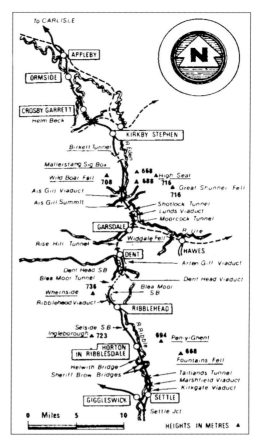

This was merely the prelude to the problems of that winter on the S&C. It was at this stage that traffic was diverted, and every effort was made to clear the line and keep it clear. Slindon records that four days later the only section over which nothing had run since it became blocked was the up line between Mallerstang and Ais Gill. Arriving at Ais Gill from Hellifield with a snowplough, he then inspected it from the down line. The up line was blocked by deep drifts at each end, and many more drifts in between. Nevertheless, he and the plough engines' crews decided to have a go from the Mallerstang end. The plough brake, between the two tenders, was old and wooden-framed. They left it at Kirkby Stephen, lest it collapse when the plough hit the first large and solid drift. Then, having arranged with the Mallerstang signalman for a clear run, they got both engines blowing off and by the time they passed that box were running at full speed. When they hit the first drift everything was blotted out; speed dropped instantly and so much snow got into the motion of the first locomotive (upon which Slindon was riding) that this seized up solid; with its wheels sliding, it was pushed out of the drift at walking pace by the rear engine. But the snow around the motion evidently soon thawed, for the locomotive started off again and the mission was accomplished successfully.

Later in the long-drawn-out process of attempting to clear the S&C, Slindon obtained the use of an '8F' 2-8-0 and marshalled it between two plough engines. This provided the power to clear deep snow that had accumulated in Shale Cutting, north of Dent Head. Parkes, in *Railway Snowfighting Equipment and Methods*, states that this snow was 10ft deep and that snowploughs were driven at 60mph against it. The snow-clearing gangs then loaded the snow into wagons for removal, filling ten trains of 20 wagons every day. Evidently earlier worries about high speed, and inhibitions about tender-first running, had disappeared.

M. Harbottle, writing as District Engineer Inverness in his 1960 article, considered that nothing beat an 0-6-0 engine with a medium or heavy plough to maintain a path for traffic, speedily and in all weathers. The Fowler '4F' 0-6-0 was evidently a favourite locomotive for this purpose. Other instances where snowplough-equipped examples were noted at work were at Miller's Dale in February 1940, and on the Cromford & High Peak on 27 February 1955. On that occasion the '4F' was coupled to an '8F' 2-8-0, with a plough-fitted LNWR 0-8-0 bringing up the rear. Such usage may well have contributed to the longevity of some members of the class. As late in the steam era as 8 June 1965 five snowplough-fitted '4Fs' were noted at Skipton, at least two being fitted with large ploughs extending upwards to chimney-top level.

In Ireland, the LMS-owned Northern Counties Committee was operating Derby-built Class V 0-6-0 No 13 fitted with a medium snowplough in January 1939. No doubt a similar combination was put to use on other rare occasions when sufficient snow lay in the region served. The later Ulster Transport Authority had a snowplough attachment for its 'Jeep' 2-6-4 tank locomotives.

The Southern Railway also used snowplough-fitted 0-6-0s to clear blocked lines. Ex-London & South Western Railway '700' class 0-6-0 No 30368 was in steam at Basingstoke, fitted with a medium snowplough, on 24 November 1962. Two members of this class, which dated from 1897, snowplough-fitted and working back-to-back, attempted to clear the Southern line to Plymouth after the snows of 29 December 1962, but one of them became derailed in a drift and they had to be abandoned for several days. The Southern's 'Q' class 0-6-0s were also fitted with snowploughs, including Nos 30530 and 30543, at Ashford in January 1964.

Locomotives of many other types were also fitted with snowploughs. BR Standard Class 3 2-6-0 No 77003, for instance, was fitted with a buffer-beam plough while working over Stainmore in the early 1960s. At Diggle in January 1963 snow was being cleared by a 'WD' 2-8-0 back-to-back with an '8F' 2-8-0. Other 'WD' 2-8-0s fitted with buffer-beam ploughs were working in northeast England at this period.

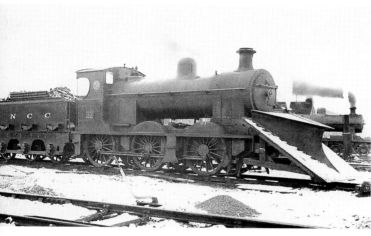

Left:
Snow is rare in Ireland, but LMS Northern Counties Committee 0-6-0 No 13 was operating with a medium-sized snowplough in January 1939.
National Museums and Galleries of Northern Ireland, Ulster Folk & Transport Museum, MS 578

Left:
'K2' class 2-6-0 No 4699 has been fitted with a small snowplough for working over the West Highland line.
National Railway Museum

On the West Highland line, opened in 1894, the snows of early 1895 were tackled by snowploughs from both Fort William and the Glasgow end of the line. I have not, however, been able to establish the type of plough used; the plough from Fort William did become stuck in a 14ft drift near Tulloch. In later years buffer-beam-mounted ploughs were fitted to locomotives of the 'Glen', 'K2' and 'K4' classes. Later still, in British Rail days, a single '4F' for snowplough duties was, I understand, for many years a feature of Fort William shed.

Former Great Western 0-6-0 pannier tank No 3625 was noted at Tyseley motive power depot on 31 January 1966 fitted with a snowplough large enough to conceal the smokebox. Of smaller concerns, the Keighley & Worth Valley Railway was operating ex-Manchester Ship Canal Railway 0-6-0T No 31 fitted with a buffer-beam plough in February 1969. In days gone by, the Isle of Man Railway regularly had problems with drifting snow, particularly in the exposed cuttings on the Ramsey line north of St Johns. Engines being used to haul trains during the winter were fitted with small ploughs, one at the front and another, since the locomotives were not turned, at the back. When drifts blocked the line, the railway's sole 0-6-0T, No 15 *Caledonia*, fitted with a much larger wedge plough, was despatched to clear them, and in this task the locomotive, which saw little regular use otherwise, came into its own.

Clearing snowdrifts on the Isle of Man Railway. In the first photograph (*Above right*), cross-trenches are dug — a standard technique that can be seen in other illustrations. The location here is north of Kirk Michael. In the other view (*Right*), *Caledonia* charges a weakened drift. It is possible that this picture is printed in reverse; a companion picture in the same collection is the other way round, but it seems no longer possible to establish which is correct. *Manx National Heritage*

Above:
In the late 1960s the Festiniog Railway
fitted veteran diesel locomotive *Moelwyn*
with a snowplough, and this, assisted by
diesel *Upnor Castle*, was able to clear the
way to Tanybwlch and beyond.
N. F. Gurley

The Festiniog Railway, brooms or no, had early on equipped some of its locomotives with guards equally to clear snow or obstructions. In 1888, for example, five locomotives were listed as being fitted with small snowploughs, but over many years ploughs seem to have been available for most of the locomotives, to be fitted when needed. Snow tended to accumulate in drifts in the elevated and exposed cuttings towards the inland end of the line; one or more locomotives were run backwards and forwards over it to prevent drifts from forming. This was not always sufficient, and locomotives that got stuck had to be dug out.

Early in the revival era, around New Year 1962, the crew of a works train going up the line had to dig their way through accumulated snow in the cuttings. Later in that decade a substantial buffer-beam-mounted snowplough was made for the 2-4-0 diesel locomotive *Moelwyn*, which dated from 1918; this locomotive and the much more recent diesel *Upnor Castle*, working in tandem, were then able satisfactorily to clear the line following a heavy snowfall in the winter of 1968/9.

In industrial use, small narrow-gauge internal combustion locomotives were fitted with buffer-beam snowploughs on the Leighton Buzzard Light Railway where both the users, sand quarry owners Garsides and Arnolds, had ploughs, and on the British Aluminium Co's Lochaber Narrow Gauge Railway with its exposed route along the mountainsides to the north of Ben Nevis.

Back on British Rail, it was not practicable to fit large snowploughs, of the type traditionally attached to steam locomotives to clear drifts, to the diesel and electric locomotives that came into use in rapidly increasing quantities in the 1960s. Their introduction, therefore, was matched by the construction of quantities of independent ploughs, to be propelled by diesel locomotives, as will be described shortly. But small ploughs could be and were fitted to diesel locomotives. Sulzer Class 26 diesels became the most common motive power over much of the Highlands; when fitted with snowploughs it was found that they could deal with drifts as deep as 4ft. Locomotives of other classes operating in that area were equipped similarly. In the widespread snow of February 1991, the efforts of large independent ploughs were supplemented by locomotives of many classes, which, fitted with small ploughs, were employed to keep lines clear and operated singly or in pairs. They included Class 20s in the East Midlands, a Class 31 between Preston and Hellifield, a Class 37 between Stone and Colwich and a Class 60 between Doncaster, Newcastle and Carlisle. Other locomotives fitted with small ploughs kept lines clear between Northampton and Watford, and Rugby and Stafford. Evidently not all the snow was of the wrong type! By this date too, many modern diesel and electric multiple-units were fitted with small ploughs or deflector shields, defence against both snow and other obstructions.

* * *

Turning now to independent snowploughs, early development of these was very much a feature of the North Eastern Railway. In stating this I am assuming that Sturrock's Great Northern snowploughs of 1854 were, as seems likely, mounted upon locomotives. The North Eastern had some snowploughs by 1886, though of what type is not known. What is clear is that their performance was inadequate in the heavy snowfalls experienced from time to time in the exposed North East of England.

In the snows of March 1886, as mentioned earlier, two plough trains became snowbound on the main line north of Newcastle, one of them near Cramlington, the other near Acklington. In charge of the latter was Wilson Worsdell, who would later be a noted Chief Mechanical Engineer, but who was at that date Assistant Locomotive Superintendent under his brother, Thomas William Worsdell, Locomotive Superintendent. This plough train had five locomotives to propel the plough, and carried 50 men to dig away the snow. W. M. Acworth, in *The Railways of England*, describes what happened to it, quoting, as he put it, 'the lips of the commanding officer':

'We left Gateshead soon after midnight on Sunday, and we began by forcing our way through a drift 1½ miles long and 14ft high. If it had been daylight, we should never have attempted it. But then we came to a cutting, where the snow, falling from the banks above, had solidified the snow beneath into a compact mass; and there we stuck. From Monday morning till Saturday night none of us ever had our clothes off. For thirty-eight hours we were without water, except the melted snow, and without food. At last we got the road clear to Alnwick, and sent an engine down. The man swept the town bare, I believe; anyway, he came back with several hams, and roasts of beef, and shoulders of mutton, two or three clothes-baskets full of bread, and lots of tobacco. That storm cost the Company £100,000.'

It also caused the company to enhance its snow-clearing ability, by constructing two large independent snowploughs. These were built during 1887; each weighed 26 tons, was 30ft 8in long, and ran on six wheels, utilising the frames from a scrapped locomotive. The blade rose at an angle of 30° from the horizontal; the divider, angled forward at the top, took on the form of a prow. They were built of timber, sheathed with metal. Behind the blade was a cabin equipped with cooking stove, lockers and accommodation for the men. As the 'commanding officer' put it to Acworth, concluding his account of the 1886 storm:

'Now we're ready for the next. We've built a good solid house, with a cook's stove, and benches and cushions on which to sleep, and a snow-plough in front, on an old engine frame. But I wish we'd had it in '86.'

It is interesting to see that he reserved the term 'snow-plough' specifically for the snow-clearing apparatus on the front; evidently it was later that the entire vehicle became known as a snowplough.

Why this form of construction was adopted I do not know. The only other definite record of something comparable in Britain at this period that I have been able to trace is the use of the remains of the early Hackworth locomotive *Braddyll* as a snowplough on colliery lines in the region, after withdrawal in 1875. I am inclined to wonder whether there was North American influence. Both Wilson and T. W. Worsdell had worked for the Pennsylvania Railroad at Altoona, and the substantial cabs they provided for North Eastern locomotives are considered to be a consequence. The independent snowplough was evidently known in North America at this period. When a British company built the Mont Cenis Railway over an Alpine pass nearly 7,000ft high in the 1860s, its independent snowplough was based on Canadian experience.

Comparing North Eastern practice with that of the Highland Railway, one may conjecture that it suited the Highland to, in effect, convert some of its locomotives into snowploughs in the autumn; not only was snow likely to arrive, winter by winter, but traffic was seasonal with a lower demand for locomotives in winter than summer. On the North Eastern, by contrast, traffic was more regular round the year, and heavy snow intermittent but sudden, demanding immediate availability of ploughs. In those circumstances independent ploughs would make good sense.

Nonetheless, early in 1888 there were reports in the press that the new North Eastern ploughs had not come up to expectations. Upon enquiring, Acworth was advised by Worsdell:

'We do not use our ploughs for ploughing engines and trains off the line; and therefore, as there were five trains snowed up on the single line between Tebay and Kirkby Stephen, it is quite true that the ploughs were powerless, at the outset. But, as soon as we got the trains and their engines out of the way, we went through in grand style. The next week, on the moors near Consett, with three engines we drove the plough through several hundred yards of snow 9ft deep.'

The danger of ploughing snow towards a snowbound train on the same line was demonstrated with horrifying clarity only a few days after those words were written. On 15 March 1888, as mentioned in Chapter 2, the down 'Flying Scotsman' became snowbound in a blizzard north of Morpeth; the next express reached Morpeth but was sent back to Newcastle, only to become stuck in the snow at Annitsford near Killingworth. The snowplough was working near Consett, but as soon as it returned to Newcastle it was despatched to the rescue of this second express; it left about 10pm, propelled by four locomotives. On board the plough were Wilson Worsdell in charge, two other NER officials, a friend of Worsdell and a reporter from the *Newcastle Chronicle* (according to Acworth, but Teasdale's recent account differs slightly). The plough cleared the down line without much trouble until it came up alongside the snowed-up express. After a discussion, it was decided that the plough should return along the down line to Killingworth, cross over to the up line, then plough towards the express to release it. I cannot help but wonder whether the decision to adopt this course of action was to some extent a reaction to earlier criticisms.

It was of course dark, and it was realised that the lamps of the express would be concealed from the drivers of the approaching plough engines behind showers of flying snow. With the position of the snowed-up train noted, instructions were given that drivers would shut off steam and apply the brakes when they reached a particular bridge some way short of it.

This did not work. Maybe the brakes were obstructed by snow; maybe the rails were coated with ice; maybe there was some other reason. One way or another the plough was still moving, with the momentum of 300 tons of locomotives propelling it at about 3mph, when it struck the locomotive of the express. The blade was driven beneath this locomotive, which rose up on it, demolished the cabin behind, and finished propped up on the smokebox of the leading plough engine.

Those within the plough cabin were feared dead. To gain access into the debris, without bringing the express locomotive down on top of it, was slow and delicate work. But the two officials and the reporter were eventually found shaken but unharmed. Worsdell himself was

discovered buried beneath a heap of heavy jacks, chains and snatch-blocks that had burst from an adjoining locker. It took him several months to recover from his injuries. His friend was less lucky. Jammed beneath the stove, he was very badly burned, and subsequently died.

Nevertheless, it is evident that the effectiveness of the snowploughs was considered to be confirmed. The NER immediately set about building two more, and eventually completed a fleet of 24 independent snowploughs, of which the last were built in 1909. Particulars of them are to be found in K. Hoole and J. Malton's *North Eastern Railway: Diagrams of Snow Ploughs*. There were of course detail changes in design, though common to most was a skirting over the wheels and frames so that the wheels did not become blocked by snow. All but three ran on six wheels; the last four to be built were of all-steel construction, and carried 7 tons of scrap iron as ballast. All had wire brushes behind the blade to sweep the rails. It became the usual (but not invariable) practice to work them in pairs, with a two locomotives back-to-back between them. Like that, not only could they plough in either direction when they were to clear a double-track line but they were also protected from becoming trapped by any accumulation of snow behind them. This could arise either when ploughing during a snowstorm, or from the collapse of snow banks close beside a line that had been ploughed.

Of the three four-wheeled ploughs, one was a curious double-ended vehicle converted from a shunting truck in 1907 for use on the electrified Newcastle suburban lines. Buffers and drawgear were concealed behind hatchways in the blades. The other two four-wheelers were built as early as 1888 and used on the Rosedale mineral branch high on the North Yorkshire moors. Access to this line was by the Ingleby cable-worked incline, three-quarters of a mile with an average gradient of 1 in 5; to work long six-wheeled vehicles over the head and foot of this might well have been difficult. After this line closed in 1929, the LNER thriftily transferred both these four-wheelers to its Great North of Scotland section, as mentioned earlier. At least one of them was still there as late as 1956.

The big six-wheelers were stationed, usually in pairs, at strategic points around the North Eastern system. Gateshead, Darlington, Tweedmouth, Alnmouth and Kirkby Stephen usually seem to have had snowploughs, but they were based at other places too. Occasionally the LNER employed them elsewhere, as in early 1940 when ex-North Eastern snowploughs were used to clear the Cheshire Lines near Manchester. In the snow of early 1941 in the North East, the fleet must have been stretched to its limit with ten pairs of ploughs at work. Early in 1963 a pair based at Middlesbrough was used regularly to clear the Whitby line, powered by two 'Austerity' 2-8-0s back-to-back.

The line that probably needed the attention of the North Eastern snowploughs most often was the Barnard Castle to Kirkby Stephen line over the 1,370ft summit at Stainmore. On this line their activities were recorded by British Transport Films in the documentary *Snowdrift at*

Bleath Gill (1955); this is now available on video from the British Film Institute. The laborious technique of digging cross-trenches in drifted snow is clearly shown, followed by a successful charge by the snowplough. It is evident too that techniques of ploughing up to a snowbound locomotive had long since improved to the point at which it is done with a gentleness that is probably deceptive. The film also shows the need to clear snow and ice from the stranded locomotive before it can be moved, for, as it points out, when a steam locomotive becomes snowbound it is hot, and thaws much of the snow in its immediate vicinity, which subsequently freezes to ice. To clear this, paraffin-soaked cotton waste is set on fire around the motion, and steam lances from an adjoining working locomotive are used.

A second film on a similar theme that was made by British Transport Films was *Snow*. This depicts the railways battling with the effects of the winter of 1962/3. To the best of my recollection from seeing it soon afterwards, it includes some dramatic shots in colour of

snowploughing by steam. It has been available on video but at the time of writing regrettably is not. The British Film Institute holds a viewing copy.

Most strangely, as late as 1949 two double-ended snowploughs were built at Ashford Works for British Railways Southern Region; they were so similar to the double-ended plough built by the NER 42 years before, in 1907, that Hoole and Malton consider that they must have been built to the same designs. But how this came about, and how much use they saw, seem equally uncertain.

The eventual fates of the NER snowploughs have been regrettably difficult to establish with precision. No 900565 (originally NER No 11 of 1891) was withdrawn from Gateshead for breaking up in 1958. Hoole and Malton, however, note 18 ploughs still extant in 1967. But there seems to have been a spate of withdrawals during the early 1970s; three examples that survive in preservation were withdrawn from service at that period. Snowplough No 900574 (originally NER No 20 of 1909) was withdrawn from Darlington motive power depot about 1974 and moved to Beamish North of England Open Air Museum, where it still is. No 900572 (originally NER No 18, also of 1909) was withdrawn from Gateshead in March 1973. One of two snowploughs found in a local scrapyard, it was purchased privately for preservation on the North Yorkshire Moors Railway, where it arrived in 1974. Some restoration work has been done on it, but despite the severe weather conditions from which the NYMR sometimes suffers it has not been necessary to operate it.

This is one of the two ploughs that appears in *Snowdrift at Bleath Gill*; the other, No 900566 (NER No 12 of 1891) reached the National Collection, being kept in store for a while at Preston Park, Brighton, and moved to York in 1977. It has recently been restored at the National Railway Museum, which involved removal and replacement of rotten woodwork, while retaining as many as possible of the original timbers, followed by repainting in the Indian red of the NER for eventual display.

* * *

On some railways, redundant steam locomotive tenders were adapted to become snowploughs. The Midland Railway in the 1920s had two such ploughs stationed at Carlisle and two more at Hellifield, in its attempt to keep the Settle & Carlisle line clear. These ploughs were based on bogie tenders, and were operated with two locomotives and riding vans between them.

Snowploughs based on old tenders were also used by the LNER on the Woodhead route between Manchester and Sheffield. In 1940 a plough train comprising two such ploughs back-to-back with a locomotive sandwiched between them became derailed and then snowbound at Crowden; it had to be dug out. These tenders seem to have received little modification apart from the attachment of a medium-sized plough blade to the front. Such simple conversions were for many years a familiar part of the railway scene. In 1964, for instance, the sole remaining steam locomotive at Ipswich Shed, a 'B1', was attached to such a plough, conversion apparently consisting of fitting a buffer-beam plough to an old tender and painting that end of its tank in contrasting diagonal stripes. The Southern Region in the 1960s converted a batch of tenders, formerly attached to 'Schools' class locomotives, into snowploughs at Eastleigh. Conversion comprised loading the tender body with concrete, adding a cowling over the top, and putting a plough blade in front. At the rear, buffing and drawgear and vacuum brake connection remained intact.

When diesel power replaced steam in the Highlands in the early 1960s, and the traditional large plough enveloping the front of a locomotive could no longer be used, some tender conversions were provided. These were based on LNER 4,200gal six-wheel tenders, with No 2 heavy-duty steel snowploughs adapted for attachment at the front. Concrete ballast was provided, and a roof over the body. These ploughs were apparently intended as no more than a stop-gap, although in January 1984 at least one such plough was in use on the West Highland.

In 1962, however, 'Independent Snowplough No 1' was designed at St Rollox, built, and allocated to Inverness. Once again a redundant tender — an LMS 3,500gal type — formed the basis of it, although little of this seems eventually to have remained but the chassis and two of its three pairs of wheels. The third, leading, pair was replaced by a pair of smaller diameter to accommodate the blade that passed close above them. The shape of the prow looks as though it was derived much more closely from the old No 2 heavy-duty plough than from anything developed by the North Eastern. The upward extension, which formerly shielded the upper part of the smokebox and the chimney, now shielded the cab with which the plough was provided to accommodate crew and tools. The upper corners were cut away so that the driver

Left:
With the withdrawal of steam locomotives in the 1950s and 1960s, redundant tenders were converted into independent snowploughs to be propelled by diesels.
Highland Railway Society

could see where he was going, and the plough cab was narrower than the width of the chassis, presumably for the same reason. Reporting the presence of this new snowplough at Inverness in its issue for January 1963, *The Railway Magazine* stated that it gave an impression of fitness for purpose.

Both this plough and one of the tender conversions were involved in the serious accident at Dava in February 1963, mentioned in the last chapter. It was perhaps fortunate that it was the tender conversion that was in front at the time of the accident, and which was turned over on to its side. No 1 Independent plough seems to have been unharmed, and was taken round to the far end of the blockage to work at it from there.

Evidently it was considered a success, for six more like it, with minor modifications, were built at Cowlairs and stationed at Inverness in time for the following winter. Still more — over 40 — are said then to have been built at Cowlairs, Eastleigh and Swindon using old LNER tender underframes. Springs and axleboxes were sheathed over, unlike those of plough No 1, at least as it was built. More independent ploughs may have been added later. Some at least have been fitted with ice-breaker hoops over their roofs, to clear icicles in tunnels.

In December 1968 — by which date snowploughing by steam was a thing of the past — snowploughs to be propelled by diesel or electric locomotives were allocated thus: Eastern Region, 27; London Midland, 20; Scottish, 12; Southern, 8; Western, 12. Presumably the total

included tender conversions, and the preponderance in the Eastern Region was due to inclusion of the NER ploughs then surviving. In 1979 the Southern still had its allocation of eight independent snowploughs, and in 1981 the Scottish Region still had 12. They were based at Aberdeen, Ayr, Edinburgh, Fort William, Glasgow, Inverness and Motherwell. It appears, therefore, that there were two bases with only one plough.

In the mid-1980s British Rail built another series of independent snow ploughs, smaller than those built before. These were based on redundant bogies from withdrawn Class 40 diesel locomotives. The bogies were well ballasted, and had medium-sized plough blades fitted, of Beilhack design — BR had by this date obtained the Beilhack snow blower to which reference will be made below.

Usually independent snowploughs have been operated — or prepared winter by winter for operation and then not required — in pairs. Locomotives sandwiched between them to provide propulsion, usually but not invariably also in multiple, have been drawn from Classes 20, 25, 26, 30, 31, 47 and doubtless others. Outside Scotland, places at which they have been based include Buxton, Crewe, Bescot, Carlisle, Toton, Peterborough, Bristol and Old Oak Common. The pair of snowploughs based at Buxton seems to have seen as much use as any. Occasions when they have been in action in the Peak District include February 1986, February 1991 and November 1996; by 1996 they had even acquired names, *Snow King* and *Snow Queen*. Other routes that have needed the attentions of independent snowploughs in recent years include the Hope Valley line in January 1979, the Blaenau Ffestiniog-Trawsfynydd line in December 1981, and the Cumbrian Coast line in the vicinity of Whitehaven in February 1996. February 1991 saw independent snowploughs hard at work between Coventry and Stafford, over the Settle & Carlisle line, between the East Midlands and St Pancras, and in south London. There was plenty of criticism of BR's performance that winter, but most of it related to availability of rolling stock; from reading about the period, it is clear that criticisms of lines actually blocked by snow are conspicuously absent. Evidently the snowploughing programme was effective. The trouble is, I suppose, that so long as trains are not actually held up by snow blocks, no one realises how much work is being put into keeping them on the move!

A graphic description of using independent snowploughs — experienced at first hand — was included by Allan C. Baker in his article 'Tales of the West Highland Line', which appeared in *The Railway Magazine* for April 1993. The two following extracts are quoted by permission of the editor. Baker was in charge of Eastfield motive power depot, Glasgow, in January 1984, at the time of the heavy snowfalls mentioned in Chapter 3. What is not made clear is whether the snowploughs to which he refers were the basic locomotive tender conversions, or the rebuilds into independent snowploughs; possibly both, for either could have suffered from the following hazard:

'That Monday [23 January 1984], with two Class 37s and the independent ploughs, we tried to get through to Fort William, still cut off by both road and rail. When charging at the drifts north of Bridge of Orchy, an axlebox on one of the ploughs collapsed. We limped back to Bridge of Orchy with difficulty, then beat an ignominious retreat to Eastfield to get a replacement. It should be remembered that these ploughs were converted from old LNER group standard tenders recovered from steam locomotives, and were still fitted with plain bearing axleboxes. Because of this, we had to stop and clean out any water penetration, then refill them with oil after every few charges at a drift, otherwise there would have been a certain hot box!'

The Oban line had also been blocked, but was clear by the Tuesday night. Baker continues:

'To get through to Fort William was another matter, however! At Eastfield we had an extremely experienced footplate inspector whom I will call Archie, and it turned out to be a good job we did. One day in late autumn, while we were commissioning the ploughs for the oncoming winter as was the normal practice, he came into my office and pointed out that the new "spades" we were fitting were not low enough. These were the adjustable lower extensions which, by means of slotted holes, extended the main blades down towards, and even below, rail level. Archie's point was that, even by using all the adjustment we had allowed in the slots, they would not go low enough. Bowing to his better judgement — at that time I'd only experienced mild Peak District drifts — I had the slots extended to allow the "spades" to go lower. A few days later Archie was back, and in his inimitable Glaswegian tones he told me in no uncertain terms that obviously I had not listened to him well enough. This was Scotland, and the "spades" were still not low enough.

'We went out together to have a look, and it soon became clear to me that, to meet Archie's wishes, the "spade" at maximum adjustment would almost touch the sleepers, and clearly the dangers this would present (if there were obstructions in the four-foot, or the crews were not exactly knowledgeable of where they were) would be too horrendous to anticipate. After a lengthy discussion, we agreed to disagree, but Archie left me saying, "Don't say I didn't tell you" or something like that.

'Now, as I sat at my desk trying to clear the paperwork as the ploughs had another go on the Wednesday, in walked Archie. "Ya know," he said, "they'll never get through if they carry on the way they are. Why don't you and I go up there tomorrow and show 'em?" To cut a long story short we did — because as Archie had predicted, despite the crew charging at the drift all day Wednesday, little progress had been made. The Fort William lads did manage to get through to Rannoch with their independent plough, however, and release the Class 20 — even though it had done so much damage to itself that I seem to remember it being withdrawn subsequently. [It had become not only snowbound, but also derailed.] They did not manage to get any further south, though, and the line remained blocked between Rannoch and Bridge of Orchy.

'Very early on the Thursday Archie and I, together with two Class 37s marshalled between two ploughs, set off from Eastfield. First we watched the lads perform, but after two attempts, which moved but a few feet of snow each time (and there was a quarter of a mile of it!) Archie said, "Right! Now it's my turn!" He had the "spades" removed, and with the burning tackle we carried in the plough, the fitter extended the slots as Archie had originally wanted, so that subsequently we could lower them almost to rail level [*sic*, but sleeper level is perhaps meant]. Of course, he knew exactly where we were, and that there would be no obstructions — points, crossings and so on — in our way. It was also important to ensure that the skids were secure: these are the devices that ride on the rail head as the plough blade digs into the snow, so preventing the springs from depressing and allowing the plough to either derail or hit the rail itself.

'After these operations, we all retreated to the front cab of the rear locomotive and Archie took the controls. He started to set back, further and further, until I wondered if we were off back to Eastfield! Then he gave the two Class 37s everything they'd got, frightening the lives out of everyone except himself! We hit the drift at high speed — I won't tell what it was — and came to a grinding halt, with snow flying everywhere, within a few yards. After recovering our composure, we took stock of the situation and found we had made significant progress — so after clearing the snow from the cab windows we did the same thing again and again, until eventually, yes, eventually, we made it, and by nightfall Rannoch was in sight. It had been murderous on the locomotives, though, and we must have added the equivalent of many miles to them, cringing every time we hit the drift. That night the bauxite got through to Fort William.'

Recent years have seen the quantity of snowploughs reviewed and some have been withdrawn. Those converted from 'Schools' class tenders were attractive to preservation groups for conversion back into tenders, and both the Great Central and Bluebell Railways have had them for this purpose. The Bluebell, however, maintains one in its converted state. It has not yet been needed for snow clearance, but is stationed at Horsted Keynes with a bracket fitted over the top conforming to the curvature of the roof of Sharpthorne Tunnel. Like this, it is propelled into the tunnel by a steam locomotive, with a couple of match wagons intervening, to remove the substantial icicles that form within.

At the time of privatisation, Railtrack inherited 59 of the large independent ploughs and ten of the smaller ones. After a strategic review, the stock of large ploughs was cut back, although all the small ones were kept, but redeployed.

One of the large independent snowploughs, built upon an LNER tender chassis and latterly stationed at Fort William, has been purchased for display at Glenfinnan Station Museum. There it is to be cosmetically restored, an artefact of a type closely associated with the West Highland. I understand that at least three other such ploughs have been purchased for preservation.

Railtrack, according to *On-Track Plant 2000*, has at the latest count 22 of the large independent snowploughs, referred to as drift ploughs. These are based in pairs at depots as far apart as Inverness and Hither Green, Thornaby and Cardiff. The ten smaller ploughs — referred to as patrol ploughs — are considered particularly suited to electrified lines and are based, again in pairs, at Motherwell, Stratford, Crewe, Doncaster and Peterborough.

* * *

By the 1960s, rotary snowploughs were commonplace on railways in North America and on the continent of Europe. Originally they had been driven by steam, and latterly by internal combustion. In operation, rapidly rotating blades cut out the snow, which is then directed through a chute to be blown well away from the track. They were not introduced in the UK, although they had been considered. St Rollox, in 1942, prepared a scheme for mounting a rotary plough attachment on the bunker end of a Sentinel shunting locomotive; the Sentinel's main drive chain would have been disconnected and its engine would instead drive the cutting rotor through gears and shafting. The whole would be propelled into a snow block by another locomotive, in reverse, and fitted with a No 3 plough at the front to ensure that it could withdraw again. This was intended to provide a rotary plough for experimental use at an economical cost; the high cost of a purpose-built rotary snowplough, which would see only intermittent use, was considered to be one of its prime disadvantages.

Above: The Beilhack snow blower from Inverness is seen at work in the Lowlands on 1 March 2001, having been brought down there following widespread heavy snowfall. *Railtrack PLC*

Another disadvantage was that rotary ploughs were considered to need dry powder snow to work effectively, but snow in Britain and particularly in the Highlands is usually wet. It was also thought that they needed still air to disperse the ploughed snow effectively, whereas in Scotland snowfall was all too often accompanied by gales.

However, after the severe problems encountered in the Highlands during the winters of 1978 and 1979, British Rail decided to acquire a rotary snow blower for use in Scotland and to evaluate its use more widely. The contract was awarded to Atkinson's of Clitheroe Ltd for a German Beilhack machine. Beilhack snow blowers had already seen use in many European countries including Germany, Switzerland, Finland and Sweden.

This type of snow blower has twin rotors, side by side, and the blades project forward into the snow to cut it. This is considered to work better in wet and heavy snow than rotary ploughs of earlier types. Pre-cutting propellers, which project above the blades, tackle hard and frozen snow, and the cut snow is thrown out to the side. In the version purchased by British Rail, the rotors have their own 450hp diesel engine; a separate 200hp engine makes the blower self-propelled. BR's Beilhack snow blower was built in 1980 and cost £¼ million; it was based at Inverness. A second Beilhack snow blower was obtained in 1989 for Network SouthEast.

Both snow blowers were inherited by Railtrack at privatisation. Numbered ADB 968500 and ADB 968501, they were in 2000 based respectively at Inverness, with stabling, maintenance and operation contracted to ScotRail, and Stewarts Lane, with stabling, maintenance and operation contracted to Gatwick Express.

The Inverness-based snow blower saw action early in February 2001, when it was clearing the Far North line. At the end of the month it was brought down to Motherwell, hauled by a Class 37, and set to work clearing snowbound lines in that area. It returned north on 9 March.

* * *

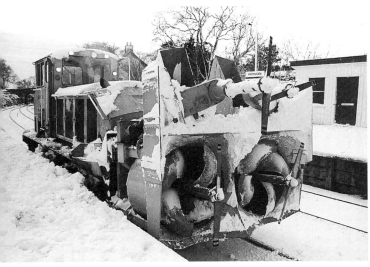

Various other means have been adopted in attempts to mechanise clearance of snow. What was surely one of the most spectacular, yet sadly least effective, was the use of aircraft jet engines mounted upon railway wagons. During the snows of 1947 the LNER, LMS and GWR all attempted to use them. The intention apparently was that the gas turbine exhaust would both melt the snow and blow it away. Typically, the jet engines were used in pairs mounted securely on a flat wagon. Behind this was coupled a tank wagon for fuel, a brake van or similar, and behind that a locomotive to propel this remarkable train into position.

The LNER carried out trials, jointly with the Ministry of Supply, at Louth (on the former Great Northern route to Grimsby), and on the Stainmore route. The Great Western attempted to use two Rolls-Royce Derwent jet engines to clear snow that had stranded trains at Dowlais. The LMS tried out a Rolls-Royce jet engine at Ribblehead and, doubtless the same winter, prepared for, and probably carried out, similar trials near Buxton. There may well have been other trials elsewhere.

Evidently, by the time problems had emerged, preparations made and the clearance train arrived on site, the snow had been lying for some time, and had compacted and frozen. Near

Stainmore it was found that the jet engines made little impression on packed layers of snow and ice. Near Dowlais they are said to have ripped up slabs of ice 6ft long and 3ft wide, and scattered them around. At Ribblehead the hard-packed snow was blown about in lumps and it took several hours to clear 30yd of track. Parkes, in *Railway Snowfighting...*, says that jet engines for this purpose were useless — snow was blown about too violently and often in the wrong direction. George Dow, LNER Press Relations Officer, wrote more temperately that when ice was encountered, the results were not altogether satisfactory, but with certain kinds of snow the turbines were quite effective. And Inspector Slindon, who was at Ribblehead, commented that he would have liked to have seen the engine's effect on fresh snow. One regrets that, evidently, he did not have the opportunity.

On a smaller scale, flame guns and similar implements have been used to thaw snow and ice, particularly in flangeways where there are check rails. High temperature gas torches were used to do this while the West Highland blockage of January 1940 was being cleared. Attempts to use them to clear switch blades were less satisfactory, but nonetheless 800 flame guns were stated to be available for use throughout BR in 1952, and by 1963 their number had increased to more than 1,000.

Steam lances drawing steam from locomotives were used at this date for the same purposes. More remarkably, after the end of steam, at least one diesel was used in the same way. In December 1968, Class 47 diesel No 1698 was being used to free frozen points with a steam lance; presumably the locomotive had a steam-heating boiler to which the lance was connected. Air hoses could be used similarly. In 1963 it was stated that at York, where points were operated electro-pneumatically, connections were provided in the air main to which hoses equipped with nozzles could be connected; these would blow the snow for 10yd and, with an air pressure of 70psi, vaporise it. Seventeen connections covered the entire station trackwork.

* * *

The spread of third-rail electrification in and south of London was initially accompanied by mild winters, and the earliest instance that I have found of hard weather bringing serious problems with conductor rails was in December 1927. On this occasion H. A. Vallance described it in his 1935 paper to the Railway Club as 'snow clogged between the pick-up shoe and the third rail', but it sounds very much like the problem later all too familiar as ice forming an insulating layer upon conductor rails. The Southern Railway's answer to it, at that date, was to continue running trains through the night, after the passenger train service had ceased, to keep the third rail clear.

An intensely cold snap from 28 to 31 January 1940 reduced the Southern to the desperate expedient of coupling steam locomotives to the front of electric multiple-units, either six-car units or two four-car units coupled together. The task of the locomotive was to assist when sufficient power could not be collected from the third rail, and so to prevent the train from stalling. Wherever possible, power was collected from the third rail both for traction and to work lighting, heating and the Westinghouse brakes, and, commented *The Railway Magazine* for March 1940, some remarkably rapid accelerations from stations occurred. In view of this it is alarming to read that since locomotives were equipped with vacuum brakes, they were connected to the trains by the couplings only; although the steam locomotive driver was in charge of the train, he could not operate its brakes, and had to communicate with the motorman by hand signals! Locomotives employed on this task ranged from 0-6-0 goods engines to 4-4-0s, 4-4-2s and 4-6-0s. On the Central Section, however, there were some 0-6-0s and 0-6-2Ts of London, Brighton & South Coast origin, which were still equipped with Westinghouse brakes. These were able to head 12-car electric trains and to operate the train brakes as well as providing power. One is reminded of the much later occasion when an ex-London Transport tube car was being tried out on the Isle of Wight, hauled by a steam locomotive that was able from its Westinghouse compressor to provide compressed air not only to apply the tube car's brakes but also to operate its sliding doors.

Similar expedients were reported in the snows of January 1963 when Southern Region steam locomotives replaced electric locomotives, and diesel locomotives double-headed electric trains. In the hard weather of January 1979, once again diesel locomotives provided supplementary power for electric multiple-units, being coupled at the front, or, on occasion, at the rear to propel them.

By 1940 London Transport was operating sleet locomotives when and where necessary to clear the live rail. They had extra bogies equipped with ice cutters, wire brushes and anti-freeze sprays. Even so, ice up to 2in thick formed on conductor rails that January, and had to be chipped away by hand.

In 1957 the sleet locomotives' traction control equipment was out of date and expensive to modernise, and London Transport introduced sleet tenders in their place. These comprised low four-wheeled bogies to be propelled ahead of a train. They were equipped with three sets of de-icing equipment, to operate on the conductor rail, whichever side it might be, and the central fourth rail. The de-icing equipment comprised crushing rollers and steel brushes, which were lowered when needed by compressed air and raised again by springs, and anti-freeze sprays fed by an axle-driven pump from two 75gal tanks. Brakes were applied by springs and released by air pressure, or manually.

With such equipment, London Transport train services through the hard winters of 1962 and 1963 remained almost normal. Similar techniques were still being used in the 1990s.

The Southern Region too had de-icing trains by 1963, 13 of them operated in the very early morning before commencement of passenger trains to scrape conductor rails and spray them with anti-freeze. By late 1968 their numbers had increased to 15, and an improved anti-freeze fluid was being introduced, which was expected to remain effective for longer than the mixture used previously. Similar trains were operating over the North London line from Broad Street to Richmond, and between Euston and Watford Junction over lines equipped with conductor rails. In 1979 the number of de-icing trains in the Southern Region had been reduced to 14, but it was considered that they could spray most of the system in one night — for which the fluid cost £1,300.

Recent years have seen the construction of trains able to spray de-icing fluid on to conductor rails or clear leaf mulch from running rails, according to the season. From that has developed the concept of multi-purpose vehicles (MPVs), to which reference is made towards the end of Chapter 11.

Chapter 5

Snow and Ice: Precautions

Prevention, as they say, is better than cure, and there are many measures that railways have taken, and do take, to alleviate the probable effects of snow and ice before they occur.

From early on, railways made extensive use of the electric telegraph both to give warning of deteriorating conditions and, after a heavy snowfall, to establish the situation so that remedies could be applied. On the Highland Railway, stationmasters had instructions to telegraph reports of weather conditions to the Traffic Office and to the Engineer's Department at Inverness. They had to provide information and advice on whether snow was likely or falling, whether the wind was light or strong, whether snow was drifting, whether trains should be hauled by snowplough-fitted locomotives, and whether snowploughs were needed to clear the line ahead of trains.

By the 1950s in the same district there were Meteorological Office weather reports to provide an overall picture, but they were supplemented by reports from stations to Control, from permanent way inspectors to the District Engineer, and by advice from train crews of difficulties in running. With foreknowledge, steam could be raised in snowplough locomotives, and the loadings of freight trains reduced. The LMS had required that when snow was thought to be imminent, all trains heading north of Blair Atholl must be hauled by locomotives fitted with snowploughs, and if they included loose-coupled wagons these were to be double-coupled to prevent them from becoming detached from one another.

London Transport, in association with the Meteorological Office, set up in the 1950s a series of unmanned weather recording installations adjacent to its surface routes. The incentive was to obtain data on the risk of iced-up conductor rails; weather forecasts, LT had learned, referred to air temperatures at a height of 4ft above the ground, and there was little data on how this related to rail temperatures.

The first installation was made at Barons Court in 1950, recording, simultaneously, air temperature and humidity at 4ft, air temperature and humidity at rail level, rail temperature, and ballast temperature. To measure rail temperature, a short length of rail was laid alongside the track, with a hole bored in it into which the thermometer bulb was inserted. Two more installations were made on the Stanmore line, one in a deep cutting near Kingsbury and the other on a high embankment near Queensbury.

From the data obtained it was found, among much else, that the daily range of temperature was greatest in the conductor rail, and least in the air at the 4ft level. Nevertheless, the Meteorological Office was able to establish a means to estimate rail temperatures from the usual forecast for air temperature at 4ft. This led to more economical and, presumably, more accurate use of de-icing equipment. The Barons Court installation was then closed down, and that at Kingsbury transferred for a time to High Barnet, notorious for its coldness. In 1958 two further installations were made, one at Theydon Bois on the Central Line, where winter weather was as severe as any on London Transport, and the other at Chorley Wood on the Metropolitan Line, which at that time was still worked by steam; the weather recording station gathered data in advance of the planned electrification.

In the 1990s the London Weather Centre was sending a daily 24-hour weather forecast to London Underground's network control centre, which was then sent out to all lines.

British Railways had, by 1963, arranged with the Meteorological Office for railway control centres to be warned when snow was expected. Fourteen meteorological stations were involved, and 51 control centres were supplied with information. In the year 2000, by which date it had been found that excessive ice or frost on overhead cables reduced power transfer to trains, a series of five computerised monitoring stations was set up beside the East Coast main line. Information gathered was passed automatically to the control centre at York, and relayed to train operating companies.

Railtrack established a weather team in Glasgow in 2000, to study the effects of weather on the rail network and to find ways to mitigate its impacts. The team is concerned with the effects of snow and excessive cold, and its activities have included relocation of snowploughs and considering the implications of global warming — that is to say, less frost and snow with quicker thaws — on specifications for drainage, and for overhead line equipment. But its concerns go far wider, to the effects of rain, wind, heat and autumn leaves, and its activities have included remote monitoring of anemometers, clearance of vegetation, and identifying locations at risk from flooding. Factors affecting the latter include changed ploughing patterns, and increased run-off from new building developments.

* * *

To return to problems of snow and ice, reliance upon telegraph and telephones for communication had the disadvantage that overhead lines were themselves likely to be knocked out by blizzards and accompanying hard frosts. The Highland Railway located its telegraph poles in the most sheltered positions possible, but there was little else it could do. H. A. Vallance, in his 1935 paper, noted that in extreme cases telegraph wires were collected into an insulated cable, well supported.

Eventually a partial solution emerged in the late 1970s. After the incident in January 1978 when a passenger train became snowed up near Altnabreac with its whereabouts unknown for several hours, temporary radio equipment was installed on all trains between Inverness and Wick. In 1980 ScotRail replaced poles and wires by radio links over 103 miles of the Far North line between Tain and Georgemas Junction. These also provided speech communication between Inverness Control and signalboxes and locomotives. Drivers were then able to report weather conditions directly, and delays in sending assistance to immobilised trains were much reduced.

Then in July 1984 traditional signalling and signalboxes, as well as wires and poles, were replaced by the Radio Electronic Token Block (RETB) system between Dingwall and Kyle of Lochalsh. The lines north of Dingwall were equipped with it in December 1985, and between Dingwall and Inverness in August 1988. Meanwhile the West Highland lines, including the remaining section of the Callander & Oban west of Crianlarich, had been equipped with RETB, which came into operation in May 1988. In recent years development of mobile telephones has enhanced still further the possibilities of communicating with trains during the course of their journeys.

The Highland Railway, however, could and did protect point rodding from snow by boxing it in, and this practice was perpetuated by the LMS and by BR. Also, in many places the Highland carried signal wires on poles, elevated above the level to which they were likely to be affected by snowdrifts. To keep water columns from freezing, the usual external brazier was inadequate; on the HR water columns comprised a cast-iron column of large diameter, within which heated air surrounded a smaller-diameter water pipe.

The susceptibility of the cuttings on the Highland Railway's main line to become blocked by snow became all too apparent during its first hard winters in the 1860s. Construction commenced of snow fences at the worst-affected places, to keep the snow out. Built of old sleepers set on end and an inch or two apart, they were placed some yards out from the cuttings found to be at risk, and became a familiar part of the Highland Railway scene. In some places two or three lines of fencing were needed, and sometimes snow fences were positioned on both sides of the line.

Snow fences were still part of the civil engineer's armoury against Highland snow in the 1950s. It had been stated that snow accumulated against them on their windward side, but Harbottle, in his 1960 article, pointed out that their function was often improperly understood; a snow fence was not a barrier, but a windbreak to produce still air in its lee, where the snow was deposited. Therefore it needed to be positioned 60 to 90ft back from the top of the cutting. This meant that snow fences were outside the railway boundary, but landowners gave permission without charge. The design of snow fences was based upon experience; old sleepers were, perhaps surprisingly, becoming expensive, and sawmill offcuts were being used instead; successful trials were also carried out with chestnut paling.

Elsewhere, snow fences were used extensively on the West Highland line, their timbers being supported, recently at least, upon frameworks of old rails. They were also constructed beside the Great North of Scotland's Deeside line near Ballater, and at Dent on the Settle & Carlisle, where three tiers were installed up the hillside in an attempt to prevent snow from drifting on to the track.

Despite the extensive use made of snow fences, I remain not entirely convinced of their effectiveness. Perhaps some were positioned too close to the track to be of value; certainly, during recent winter journeys over the Highland main line and over the West Highland, it appeared that the snow fences were now mostly derelict, without many adverse consequences. Maybe their effectiveness varied with the conditions experienced in any particular snowstorm.

The most remarkable structures of this sort, however, were the Highland Railway's 'automatic snow fences', alternatively called 'snow blowers'. These were the patent not of anyone intimately connected with the company, but of a Lancashire gentleman, Mr W. L. Howie. Mr Howie reasoned that snow fell in cuttings because wind passed over the top, and allowed the snow to fall through still air to the ground below. Wind blowing along the surface of level ground drove the snow before it and prevented it from settling. He therefore proposed that over the sloping side of a cutting should be built a sloping roof — perhaps better visualised as a ceiling since its underside is what matters — with its lower part reaching close to the ground by the track, but with the upper part extending to several feet above ground level at the top of the cutting. The effect, he reasoned correctly, would be to catch a cross-wind, and with it the falling snow, and deflect it downwards and at speed across the track for the snow to be scattered beyond. Building a second similar structure on the opposite bank of the cutting produced, as Harbottle points out, a blower that acts on the principle of a Venturi, to even greater effect.

The Highland was sufficiently impressed to construct a trial snow blower near Halkirk in the 1880s. As always seems to happen in such circumstances, the winters then turned mild and for several years there was insufficient snow to put it to the test. But the Highland had another similar problem, on its Hopeman branch at Burghead, where the line ran along the foot of sand dunes from which sand drifted over the track in westerly gales. Between track and dunes therefore the company built a blower — a big one, for grains of sand, being denser than snowflakes, needed a sharp draught to blow them away. Acworth, in *The Railways of Scotland*, quotes a report by the company's Assistant Engineer:

'No sand opposite fence ... the agent [stationmaster] and leading surfaceman gave me their opinion that 40 men could not have kept the line clear on Friday night, and that, if the fence had not been there, there would have been at least four feet depth of sand over the rails.'

Eventually there was enough snow to confirm that blowers worked with snow as well. In addition to the snow blower at Halkirk, which lined 47yd of track, two more were then built at trouble-spots between Kinbrace and Forsinard, one blower being 48yd long and the other 71yd. Another two were built as recently as the mid-1950s to protect points leading to the loops at Scotscalder and Georgemas Junction.

Snow blowers did not come into more general use. They were expensive to build and maintain, liable to catch fire, and hampered re-laying operations. Indeed, in the ordinary course of events, maintenance gangs evidently regarded them as a menace on account of the tremendous draughts they set up on those days, all too common in the North of Scotland, when it was blowing hard but not actually snowing.

The expedient of protecting a railway against snow by covering it over completely with snow sheds has been resorted to frequently in other countries, such as Norway and the United States, but only once in Britain. This location is Cruach Cutting, north of Rannoch on the West Highland line, which proved in the early days to be very susceptible to blockage by accumulations of snow. So over a length of 205yd the sides of the cutting were extended upwards by low concrete walls, and old rails, curved, were placed between them across the cutting to support the roof, which was made of corrugated iron sheets. Above the centre-line of the track, the roof was made so that it could be removed in summer to allow for escape of smoke and steam. This snow shed remains *in situ*, apparently ready to fulfil its purpose when needed.

Another unusual precaution against the cold was the heating of the water supply for Garsdale water troughs on the Settle & Carlisle line. These were installed in 1907 at an altitude of more than 1,000ft, and were said to have been the highest water troughs in the world. They were located on one of the few sections of the line that was level, and where no doubt locomotives needed their water supplies replenished after the long drag up the 1-in-100 gradients on either side. The water supply was steam-heated to maintain its flow. Nonetheless the troughs frequently froze up and maintenance men had to hack the ice out with picks and remove it with shovels. The troughs were eventually removed in the 1950s.

* * *

The traditional means to prevent the switchblades of points from freezing up was for men to clear them of snow and keep them clear. This was inefficient — and at times of heavy snowfall ineffective — expensive and wasteful of labour. In Britain it was London Transport that led the way with installation of point heaters. In 1943 a patent was granted to Mr J. H. Condy and his employer, the London Passenger Transport Board, for a point heater incorporating a hot oil circulating system. Heaters of this type were then installed on London Transport surface railways.

In operation, oil in a reservoir was heated by an electric immersion heater deriving power from the traction supply and controlled by thermostats. Heated oil was circulated through pipes forming a closed system. The pipes passed through longitudinal holes bored through the

Right:
London Transport's prototype point heater, using a recirculating hot oil system, was installed at Greenford and is seen here in November 1948. Hot oil was circulated through the pipe, which passes through the slide chairs. *London Transport Museum*

Lower right:
London Transport as well as BR used Mills Arma propane-fuelled infra-red point heaters. Two burners with their supply pipe can be seen adjacent to the stock rail in this installation at Acton Town in 1963. *London Transport Museum*

slide chairs, outside the rails, and were welded to the foundation plates of the point operating mechanisms, electro-pneumatic or whatever they might be.

Such heaters were found to keep points working freely even in the most severe weather, and by 1961 there were more than 600 installations in use. On British Railways it was another matter. During the 1950s the lack of point heaters, when such equipment was already common on London Transport and on the railways of other countries subject to snowfall, became a matter of controversy. Up to about 1959 there appear to have been only three installations. Two of these, using electric heaters, were at Buxton and Dunford Bridge, at the east end of Woodhead Tunnel. There was also a single point heater at York, of French manufacture and using propane.

In 1959, however, BR decided to install at York six more sets of point heaters, using the hot oil circulation system similar to those of London Transport. Such heaters can work only where there is a suitable electricity supply, which may be why BR then decided to try out another system, the Arma infra-red switch heater, fuelled by propane. It had originated in the Netherlands, where it was already much used. In operation heat was radiated to the stock rails by a set of burners mounted on pipes supplying the gas. Inside the iron casing of each burner was a ceramic block, within which combustion took place; there was no naked flame to blow out.

BR initially installed some sets as an experiment, for instance a single set at Penistone. But experiments must quickly have been satisfactory, for late in 1961 it was announced that the North Eastern Region was installing no fewer than 568 sets at important junctions on the East Coast main line. At York alone there were to be some 100 sets, and it was considered that, whereas 200 to 240 men had previously had to be taken from other work and set to clearing points when snowfall demanded, now only 24 would be needed. Installation of each heater meant fitting two brackets held by coach screws, and attaching the assemblies and gas pipe; it could be done in 15 minutes.

Having started late, BR then worked hard to catch up. By early in 1963 it was reported that 719 point heaters were in operation — 710 gas and the remainder electric. And that number was almost to be doubled, with 148 more heaters in the North Eastern Region, 350 in the Southern and 200 in the Western. These were evidently to be propane fuelled, except on the Southern where 135 of them were to use town gas. Yet more heaters were to be installed by the Eastern, London Midland, and Scottish Regions, but at £200 per unit they could be justified only at important junctions. BR then had some 100,000 sets of points.

Spurred on no doubt by the Arctic conditions of early 1963, BR had 2,180 sets of point heaters installed by the end of that year, and 4,115 a year later. By the end of 1968 there were 7,131 installations, 6,721 using either propane or town gas, and 410 electric, on electric lines where power was easily available.

After that, installation of point heaters no longer seems to have been newsworthy, although it certainly continued. At the present time, the quantity of points on Railtrack's system is down to 23,000, but of these 18,000 are equipped with heaters. Only 5% of these are gas, the remainder being electric of various types. All are automatically controlled, with manual override. Sensors detect temperature and precipitation, and activate the heaters at pre-set temperatures.

Various other expedients have been adopted to mitigate the effects of severe weather. In 1989 it was reported that Ipswich Tunnel, 365yd long, suffered constant ingress of water that formed ice above and upon the overhead wiring. There was risk of damage by passing trains both to the wiring and to the trains' own power equipment. BR had tried blowing hot air into the tunnel from powerful gas heaters at each end, but this was unsuccessful. It then installed, successfully, 30 4.5kW electric heaters suspended from the tunnel roof and aimed at the overhead line equipment. These were activated by thermostats; treadles activated by approaching trains turned them down temporarily lest their glare affect drivers.

Since the early 1990s DMUs of certain classes running in Scotland, such as Class 156, have been provided with protective covers for their automatic couplings, when not in use, to protect delicate electrical connections from snow. They are placed in position or removed by drivers and maintenance staff. These covers are known officially as 'coupler snowbags'; more often, I suspect, they are known by their unofficial nickname of 'willy warmers'!

Following the overnight 'disappearance' of the snowbound passenger train at Altnabreac in January 1979, British Rail decided that survival hampers should be carried in winter on all passenger trains running north of Inverness, and over the West Highland lines. These were carried in the guards' compartments and contained emergency rations for 50 people for 24 hours, with heating, lighting and cooking equipment and a supply of blankets. It seems, however, that with milder winters they were never used in earnest, at least to any great extent, although disposal of their unconsumed contents, before they finally went out of date, may have been a valued perk for staff! The hampers did not outlast conversion of train services over these lines from locomotive-hauled coaches to DMUs, if only because of space restrictions on the latter. Today, most trains on the lines concerned are in any case served by refreshment trolleys.

Chapter 6

Snow:
The Positive Side

There are a few — but not very many — positive effects of snow, circumstances in which the attractiveness of rail travel is increased, to the mutual benefit of user and operator. The initial development of Scottish ski resorts, for instance, occurred just in time for the hard winters of the early 1960s. Throughout the skiing season of 1962/3 British Railways was offering excursion fares, at three-quarters of the full rates, to resorts near the skiing areas. The attractions of rail travel compared to road in such conditions are clear.

They were demonstrated much more dramatically in the aftermath of the heavy snowfall in the West Country that New Year. First, many residents of the London area who had driven down to the West Country for the festive season left their cars behind in the snow and returned by train. Subsequently British Railways Western Region did a brisk business conveying the deserted cars back to London, where their owners collected them from Kensington Olympia station.

At this period British Railways was also busy carrying passengers whose intended airline services had been cancelled, and special trains were provided. BR ran special freight trains to carry supplies of food and fuel to places where shortages were occurring. Salt was brought by the trainload from Cheshire to the South of England, for use in clearing roads. This latter traffic may perhaps have been of greater short-term benefit than long-term.

The superiority of rail over road in snow was well demonstrated again in November 1965. Roads over Shap were blocked by snow, but British Rail's first liner trains, carrying freight containers between London and Glasgow, were not merely running but running ahead of schedule.

Yet the apparent greater reliability of rail over road transport in conditions of heavy snow is in truth really one of lower unreliability. In these conditions, then and now, many trains are late and cold, or cancelled. Travellers and forwarders of freight, who in such circumstances turn to rail of necessity rather than free will, are likely to return to their accustomed modes as soon as conditions are back to normal. Exceptionally, it was reported early in 1982 that bulk milk traffic was returning to rail, after its successful carriage by special trains over two hard winters.

The snows of 1962/3 came at a time of great change, when no branch line seemed safe from closure. Then, from one end of England to the other, train services that, it had seemed, could be dispensed with were suddenly found to be indispensable. On the Isle of Wight the railway provided for hundreds the only sure means of getting to work. On the Alston branch, a snowplough cleared the line while nearby roads were blocked, and the villages served received essential food by rail. The main road from Taunton to Minehead was blocked by snow for a week, but the Minehead branch line continued to operate. Regrettably, almost as soon as the snow had thawed it seems that the lessons learned were ignored and many such lines were later closed.

However, on a few occasions railways and stations closed to passengers have been reopened temporarily when roads have been blocked by snow. The branch from Malton to Driffield in Yorkshire appears to have been thus temporarily reopened on two occasions, in December 1950 and in February 1953. On the latter occasion, the temporary train service was

Somewhere in the left background of this picture is the A9 main road, but no traffic appears because it is closed, blocked by snow. The railway triumphs as two 'Black Fives' breast Druimuachdar summit, in the Alpine conditions of 3 January 1953, with 12 or more coaches forming the 11.55 Perth-Inverness. *W. J. V. Anderson*

announced on BBC radio the evening before it commenced, and 39 passengers travelled on the first train, the 8am from Malton on 12 February. Two trains ran each way daily, and milk was carried as well as passengers. The service lasted until 16 February.

British Railways dispatched a special train down the closed branch from Buxton to Ashbourne — the route included part of the Cromford & High Peak Railway — on 21 January 1963 when roads nearby were blocked by 20ft drifts. The train carried passengers, and bread, milk and other necessities of life; it was double-headed and preceded by a snowplough.

While the Settle & Carlisle line was blocked by snow in 1947, Inspector Slindon records being approached by a farmer who was completely out of feed for his livestock, despite having three wagons of hay consigned to him. Slindon was able to locate the wagons held up at Skipton, and arranged for them to be moved forward by light engines booked to depart for snow clearance at 5.30 the next morning. At the appropriate point the farmer was waiting; railwaymen unsheeted the wagons and pushed the hay bales down the embankment, whence the farmer took them away by sledge.

In February 1979 bus services in the vicinity of Dronfield, between Chesterfield and Sheffield, were halted by snow and severe weather. Dronfield station had been closed since 1969, but in these circumstances BR reopened it temporarily between 15 and 19 February. This gave a fillip to a campaign for permanent reopening, and that was indeed achieved in 1981.

When the Dingwall-Kyle of Lochalsh line was under serious threat of closure in February 1971, campaigners for its retention arranged a bus trip from one terminal to the other, to demonstrate the inadequacy of the proposed replacement. The bus had to contend with steep icy hills, snowy single-track roads, sharp bends, wandering livestock and, at one point, had to await removal of a car that, having skidded and put one of its front wheels into the ditch, was obstructing the road. The railway is still open.

The Cambrian Coast line also narrowly escaped closure in the early 1970s, and although trains became snowed up north of Tywyn during the exceptional snow of 8/9 January 1982, as described in Chapter 2, the section between Machynlleth and Tywyn was to demonstrate its

Above:
Trains kept running in the snows of
1962/3. An 'A3' passes Hadley Wood with
the 2.5pm King's Cross-York on
29 December 1962. *Brian Stephenson*

value while roads in the district remained impassable. On 10 January, despite deep snowdrifts, half a dozen delayed passengers finally reached Tywyn from Machynlleth in the rear cab of a Class 25 diesel running light, and on the evening of 12 January a DMU with a locomotive coupled in front brought milk and bread to Tywyn, where supplies were running short.

Heritage railways based on former BR branches have also made a worthwhile contribution. By February 1978, when a severe blizzard struck the West Country, the Minehead-Taunton branch had been closed and reopened, from Minehead to Bishops Lydeard, as the West Somerset Railway. Volunteers who were young in spirit lit up Bagnall 0-6-0 saddle tank *Vulcan* to see how far they could get through the snow. After several days of charging the drifts — drifts so deep that one of them knocked the lamp off the iron at the base of the chimney — they eventually got through to Bishops Lydeard. The road over the short distance from Taunton to Bishops Lydeard was just passable, but the road onward to Minehead was not. So for four days the railway, with a bus link from Taunton to Bishops Lydeard, became the means by which passengers, mails, newspapers and foodstuffs reached Minehead. *Vulcan*, coupled to a Mk 1 coach and a driving trailer from a DMU, provided the train. For several winters thereafter, I understand, volunteers at Minehead were waiting eagerly to be snowed in again!

On 8 February 1991, despite hard frost and deep snow, volunteers of the Keighley & Worth Valley Railway maintained its Saturday shoppers' railbus service (all except the first, because it took too long to clear the points of snow). Their efforts were rewarded by the frequent sight of local residents on their return journeys, laden down with supermarket carrier bags.

Heavy snow fell in the vicinity of the East Lancashire Railway on the afternoon of 27 January 1995. Roads became blocked as lorries jack-knifed, and commuters returning from Manchester were stranded. ELR staff and volunteers quickly assembled a passenger train with a diesel locomotive at each end and this, working between Bury and Rawtenstall as frequently as possible between 16.00 and 20.00, carried more than 500 passengers free of charge.

Chapter 7

Flooding: Flash Floods and Washouts

The autumn of the year 2000 was the wettest on record in England and Wales, and much wetter than usual in Scotland and Northern Ireland. The extensive floods that resulted will go down in history, yet for railways such problems are far from new.

Flooding may be divided into three types. They are of course interlinked, and linked too with other weather phenomena, yet they may be defined thus. First there are flash floods, which are associated with heavy rainfall and a sudden thaw of snow. Then there are inundations, associated with swollen rivers, in which railways disappear under water along with, probably, much of the land on either side — or perhaps remain above it, leading to subtler problems with waterlogged embankments. Third, there are tidal incursions by the sea.

Let us first consider flash floods. Such floods cause washouts of bridges and erosion of earthworks, ballast and track. They also wash debris from high ground down on to track. The flows in watercourses have certainly increased in recent years, as marshy ground has been drained so that it no longer absorbs rainfall, while more and more land has been developed — used for buildings and roads from which water runs off more quickly than before. Nevertheless, the problems have been around for a long time. Extensive flood damage to railways in the West Country in 1960 was attributed at least in part to drainage operations on the high ground of Dartmoor, preparatory to afforestation.

What appears to have been the first occasion on which an accident to a train resulted from a washed-out bridge occurred in 1846. On the night of 19/20 January there was heavy rain over Kent, and the River Medway rose in flood, weakening the timber bridge by which the South Eastern Railway crossed it at Penshurst. Of this the crew of the regular night up goods train were sadly unaware. When the locomotive, long-boiler 0-6-0 No 120, ran on to the bridge, it collapsed with a loud crash; the locomotive went down into the river, and its tender and several wagons followed. The driver was killed while attempting to jump clear; the fireman, who was his brother, survived.

The North British Railway was opened from Berwick to Edinburgh later in 1846, but it had been open less than three months when a severe storm brought the burns, or streams, that crossed its path into spate and turned rivers into torrents. Over the 19 miles between Cockburnspath and East Linton, bridges, culverts and embankments were devastated; many of the bridges were washed away, and where the railway followed the valley of the Eye Water up to Grantshouse, six of the seven bridges over this watercourse were affected.

Finding horse-drawn road vehicles to fill in the gap pending repairs produced its own problems, for all the stage coaches had been withdrawn when the railway opened. At one point in the repair programme, sufficient work had been done for passengers to be carried by train over a section, temporarily isolated, in the middle of the 19 miles, while road transport still covered the gaps at either end. This sounds as though some locomotives and rolling stock had been marooned on the centre section by the floods.

Full repairs took a couple of months, and the line was reopened throughout at the end of November. The storm that caused the floods was described as the worst since the 1770s; this is suggestive of problems occurring in the same locality at long intervals, and they were indeed to do so again — but for the moment all seemed well.

Elsewhere, records show that similar problems recurred from time to time. In August 1857, for instance, heavy rain flooded the Great Northern Railway's main line near Carlton. Both up and down lines were washed away, and an up fish train and a down passenger train were alike derailed. There were injuries to passengers, who eventually took the company to court and (perhaps surprisingly) obtained substantial compensation.

A much more serious accident — although not, fortunately, directly involving a passenger train — took place on 16 November 1866 at Apperley, a few miles from Leeds on the Midland Railway's line to Lancaster. Here the line crossed the River Aire on a viaduct; heavy rain upstream had already caused the river to overflow its banks to a width of half a mile. The increased flow also weakened the viaduct. This was discovered that night by a platelayer returning home, who was walking over the viaduct when suddenly he all but fell into a rent that had appeared in the masonry of one of the arches. He had to jump across, then hurried on to Apperley station, where the stationmaster arranged to stop down trains; then both men and a porter rushed back along the line to halt an up goods train that was due. Even before they reached the viaduct they saw it approaching on the far side. They waved red lights, and the driver spotted them and shut off steam; the fireman applied the brakes, and both driver and fireman then prudently jumped off. Propelled by its heavy train the engine ran out on to the broken arch of the viaduct, which, as F. S. Williams puts it in *The Midland Railway*, went down like a pack of cards. It carried with it engine, tender, guard's brake, and a trainload of meat intended for the London market.

To recover the locomotive, a gang of 30 men was sent from Derby. They laid rails down into the river under the wheels, then winched the locomotive up inch by inch on to the riverside meadow, then up an incline on to the line. To reconstruct the viaduct the piers were rebuilt, and 60 iron girders were manufactured, delivered and fixed in position — and the whole operation, which had been estimated to take six months, was completed in five weeks. A cynic might wonder whether we have since made any progress at all.

When the main line of the Highland Railway (as it became) was being built in the early 1860s, it was lined by almost a mile of breastwall, south of Dalwhinnie, as a precaution against flooding by the River Garry. The wisdom of such precautions was demonstrated in January 1868 when a sudden thaw brought floods that damaged the railway in several locations but not, presumably, that one.

By that date railways had penetrated another region where rivers are apt to run riot when heavy rain falls over the mountains — Central and Mid-Wales. Of these rivers, probably the Severn and its tributaries have brought railways as much trouble as any. It rose in flood in February 1868 so quickly that the driver of an early morning up goods train found, when descending the long gradient from Talerddig to beyond Carno, that floodwater was almost up to the footplate, and well on the way to putting out the fire. But it did not, and the wooden bridge over the Severn at Caersws was found to be holding, so the train reached its destination at Newtown safely. On the return journey, however, when the train was gingerly approaching the bridge along its approach embankment, the engine suddenly toppled right over. Although the bridge remained sound, floodwater had scoured away the embankment. Driver and fireman were killed.

But that was not the end of the affair. The first up passenger train, bringing a director and the traffic manager to the scene, was approaching when it was discovered that pressure of floodwater had rendered unsafe another bridge, near Pontdolgoch. The train was halted only just in time.

Floodwater showed what it could do on the Settle & Carlisle line even while it was still under construction in the 1870s. While the cutting at the north end of Blea Moor Tunnel was being excavated, there was a cloudburst over the hills. With little or no warning, a sheet of water came down the hill like a wave, said to have been 5ft high. It poured into the cutting, engulfing the seven men at work there before they could escape, and drowning two of them. A horse that was drawing a wagon loaded with spoil towards the tip was also overtaken, and both horse and wagon were buried beneath hundreds of tons of debris swept down the mountain. In nearby Dent Dale, where 2½in of rain was recorded in three-quarters of an hour, seven road bridges were washed away.

Above:
A bridge at Selham, on the Midhurst branch of the London, Brighton & South Coast Railway, was washed out in December 1886. Remarkably, a telegraph pole seems to have descended vertically into the gap. *National Railway Museum*

A culvert near Ladmanlow, on the Cromford & High Peak Railway, became blocked by melting snow in March 1881. With heavy rain falling, water ponded up until it eventually carried away the embankment.

On the Callander & Oban Railway, which had been completed through to Oban only in 1880, the bridge over the Nant burn, just east of Taynuilt station, was washed away in a storm in November 1882. It was replaced by a timber bridge as a temporary measure, and this lasted for several years until replaced by a substantial two-span bridge, of wrought iron girders between masonry abutments, and with a central pier of cast-iron cylinders, which was completed in 1887. The Midland — its expeditious action in replacing Apperley Viaduct has already been noted — was a byword for prosperity. The C&O was not.

A bridge washout in December 1886 at Selham, on the London, Brighton & South Coast Railway's branch to Midhurst, left the single track suspended over a substantial gap.

The exceptionally deep snow that was experienced in the Highlands in January 1892, and its immediate effects, were described in Chapter 3. This snow was followed, however, by an exceptionally rapid thaw. As the snow melted, the rivers rose — at the rate of 1ft per hour in places. Strathspey, traversed by the Highland Railway between Newtonmore and Grantown, was particularly badly affected. With the thaw came what seemed at first no more than an ordinary spate, but 24 hours later valley, farms, roads and railway were largely under water.

The worst damage was to the Highland Railway between Kingussie and Kincraig. Here the line runs almost straight for several miles, much of this on an embankment up to 10ft high; meadows lie between the railway and the River Spey. The river was lined by floodbanks. On

this occasion the rising water first overflowed the floodbank, then rapidly eroded two large breaches in it. In a very short space of time the meadow was inundated to a depth of several feet, and the gale that was blowing sent breaking waves over the railway embankment. Then the rails too disappeared beneath the swelling flood. The 7.35pm from Inverness was the last train to get through, and narrowly escaped having its fire extinguished. The embankment was then breached, and rapidly washed away. The midnight train from Perth actually left Kingussie, but surfacemen — that is to say platelayers — were on watch and by good fortune were able to signal it to stop; it set back to Kingussie station. By daylight it became clear that some 70yd of embankment had been washed away, and the breach was as much as 10ft deep. The adjoining highway, too, was under water to a depth of 7 to 10ft.

By good fortune the railway's Assistant Engineer was in the district, and its Traffic Superintendent was on board the train from Perth. Preparations began immediately for repairs, and a force of 250 men was eventually assembled. Highland Railway employees came from stations as far afield as Buckie and Dunkeld, and contractors' men from the direct Aviemore-Inverness link line, then under construction, were called in too. Frequent special trains delivered fill and ballast to be tipped into the breach.

The rails had not been broken; they remained suspended above a gap into which hundreds of tons of spoil were being tipped with limited effect, while urgent mails and parcels were held up in increasing quantities at the railheads on either side. The desperate — and to modern eyes startling — expedient was adopted of transferring the mails, and the Post Office sorters in charge of them, across the gap on surfacemen's trolleys. This meant a sort of switchback ride: the trolley with its load was given a shove by a gang of men from one side. It then ran down into the dip, where its weight submerged the rails below the surface of the flood, but, if the force of the shove had been correct (and with increasing experience it usually was) continued up the slope on the other side to be met by a second gang who helped it to its destination.

This was dangerous work, and on one occasion sorter and mailbags overbalanced into the flood. They were rescued, apparently little the worse for their wetting. The PO sorter was not the only person to have a narrow escape. An inspector examining the work at the head of one of the embankments fell into the fast-flowing water, but was quickly rescued although bruised. A workman who fell in disappeared beneath the water, but, while being swept away, came to the surface where he was able to grab a shovel that one of his colleagues held out to him.

Although work continued day and night, it took four or five days to complete. The same floods inundated the Great North of Scotland line between Nethy Bridge and Grantown to a depth of 6ft, but fortunately breached no embankments. Part of the Dingwall & Skye line was washed away too.

Clearly, flash floods and inundations are so closely associated that it is not always easy to categorise any particular instance of flooding as one or the other. I have described this flooding here because the washout near Kingussie appeared as its most important feature.

When heavy rain fell over East Anglia in August 1912 the resulting flooding washed out seven bridges, and four more were damaged. Probably the most serious loss in terms of effect, for the holiday traffic was at its height, was the three-span brick viaduct that had carried the main line south of Norwich over the River Tas between Forncett and Flordon. This was completely washed away by the river, which rose by 9ft. For speed of reconstruction, the replacement comprised brick piers with three timber spans fabricated at Stratford. There were other serious washouts at Homersfield, on the Waveney Valley line, at Trowse, where a bridge carrying a road over the railway and two rivers collapsed, and near Fakenham. In the latter case the bridge over the River Stiffkey collapsed while a freight train was crossing. The locomotive, with its crew, reached the safety of the far embankment, but the wagons finished up in a graceful downward arc, with only the sagging rails to prevent them from descending into the torrent below.

Despite all this, inundations seem to be the most marked aspect of those particular floods, so I will return to them in the next chapter.

* * *

That brings us back to the Highland Railway for the next incident, which was indeed caused by a flash flood of quite astonishing suddenness and ferocity — the Baddengorm Burn washout of 1914.

Despite the extreme conditions under which the Highland Railway operated, it had never suffered a fatal accident to a passenger, but this record was sadly to be broken. The middle of June that year was exceptionally sunny and hot in the Highlands; Balmoral, on 17 June, reached 88°F, the hottest temperature recorded anywhere in Britain on that day. In such conditions the surface of the ground, usually so spongy and absorbent, becomes baked hard and impervious; rain does not sink in, it runs off. And the exceptionally hot weather gave way, as might be expected, to thunderstorms. These were exceptionally severe, although localised.

At Carrbridge, between Aviemore and Inverness, the morning of 18 June was pleasant but thundery. In the afternoon, the thunderstorm broke. Eye-witnesses later said that the rain came down in sheets, the hailstones were jagged lumps of ice, there was a roaring in the hills. Some 3 or 4 miles to the north west, on the high slopes of the ridge that culminates in the hill called Carn Glas-Choire, there were no witnesses to the storm, for no one lived there. But there it was that the storm became a cloudburst, with unprecedentedly heavy rainfall over a short space of time. Visiting the area shortly afterwards, Alexander Newlands, Chief Engineer to the Highland Railway, traced the burn called Allt a Bhaine almost to its source, where he found it mostly dry. But the sight, he wrote, beggared description. The burn had gouged out for itself a new bed some 15ft deeper than the old; in the gorge so formed, 30ft wide, boulders weighing 3 or 4 tons were tumbled together. The burn joined a larger one, the Allt Ruighe Magaig, running south. Boulders had been dislodged from their banks, and new deposits of deep soft sand laid down elsewhere; where the burn approached the main road from Carrbridge to Inverness, the banks had been torn away to a height of 20ft, and trees uprooted and carried with the flood. Clearly this had been no gradually swelling flood, but a wall of water 20ft high — a tidal wave.

The main road crossed the burn by a bridge that had stood for 120 years or more. The flood blocked its arch with debris, formed a lake upstream, overflowed on to the road and swept the bridge away. Below this point, a third burn came in from the west, the Bogbain Burn; in flood but not exceptionally so, it added its contribution. From the confluence, the combined burn was known as the Baddengorm Burn. The wall of water hurtled down its gorge towards the point, 1,100yd on, where the railway crossed it by a brick-arched bridge of 15ft span between abutments of granite. Once again, it started to block the arch with tree trunks and debris. The course of the burn veered to the west as it entered the bridge, and the torrent started to eat away the embankment behind its south abutment.

Meanwhile the 11.50am from Perth to Inverness was travelling northwards. It comprised a 4-4-0 locomotive with its tender, a horse-box, a Caledonian Railway through coach from Glasgow, a Highland through coach from Edinburgh, and three more HR coaches from Perth. It left Carrbridge at 3.25pm in the half-darkness and pouring rain of the storm, but despite this the fireman observed that the River Dulnain, which the line crosses on leaving the station, was no higher than usual. Half a mile further on they came to the bridge over the Baddengorm Burn. Beyond it the fireman could see water by the rails; knowing that the Baddengorm flowed into the Dulnain, he wondered what could be wrong. The driver observed a lot of water and debris below the bridge, with the water rushing through. Then, as they crossed the bridge, the engine swayed and, despite the driver's attempt to accelerate, the train came to a stand. The tender, the horse-box and the Caledonian coach had crossed the bridge but had been derailed. The driver got down and walked back beside the train, over the bridge, to advise the guard of the derailment.

Just after he crossed it, the bridge, already weakened, was swept away. Down into the torrent — later found to be running 20ft higher than normal — went the second, third and fourth coaches. The last coach, the guard's brake, remained safe on the Carrbridge side of the gap. It was eventually found that the rushing water, as well as washing away the bridge, had eroded a gap in a 26ft-high embankment that was 120ft wide at the top, and 50ft wide at the bottom.

The second coach finished on its side. The fourth was up-ended on the sloping side of this gap. Their passengers, with difficulty, clambered to safety. The third coach finished in the bed of the burn; it was almost entirely destroyed and its passengers were swept away. One had an extraordinarily lucky escape — he was swept into the branches of a tree that was half-submerged in midstream. From this perilous perch he was rescued several hours later. Five others were drowned. So strong was the rush of water that two of the bodies were found almost 5 miles downstream.

The Baddengorm Burn quickly reverted to its normal level. When Mr Newlands inspected it 9 hours after the tragedy, it was no more than 2ft deep; a plank had been thrown over it for people to cross without difficulty. This, at least, aided the tasks of recovery and repair. A new bridge, of steel girders on concrete abutments and with a span 10ft greater than the old, was built with such remarkable speed that the line was reopened 25 days later.

Lightning, it is said, does not strike twice in the same place. But the Baddengorm Burn knew nothing of such a rule, and on 8 July 1923 the new bridge was put to the test. This was, fortunately, a Sunday; since the Post Office had ceased making Sunday deliveries, the Highland Railway had ceased running Sunday trains, and the LMS, which had just absorbed the Highland, continued the policy. No trains were therefore involved. But otherwise the damage was estimated at five to ten times greater.

Once again a thunderstorm, even heavier than before, was the culprit, with a cloudburst a little to the west of the earlier one. This meant that the bulk of the water and debris came

On 18 June 1914 the bridge by which the Highland Railway's Aviemore-Inverness line crossed the Baddengorm Burn was washed away — the water had risen 20ft above normal — with a derailed train stationary upon it. This is the scene afterwards, with the water level returning to normal. The five passengers who were killed were swept away from the coach at the foot of the picture. *Iain Morrison, Scottish Railway Preservation Society collection*

down the Bogbain Burn — and the railway followed the course of this normally tiny watercourse, crossing over it several times. Three bridges were washed away, and the flood overflowed on to the main road. Running down this, it encountered the bridge by which the railway crossed the road, and washed this away too. Some 700yd of embankments were also destroyed. But the new bridge over the Baddengorm Burn stood sound, although the water level rose 30ft to the level of the rails, and the embankments on either side were washed away.

Repairs naturally took longer than before, although not very long, the line being reopened on 31 August. Today, as one's Class 158 DMU sweeps downward from Slochd towards Aviemore, it is remarkably difficult to distinguish the locations of these amazing happenings at all.

* * *

The Great Northern Railway of Ireland line from Omagh to Londonderry ran close beside the River Mourne at Newtownstewart, Co Tyrone. On 6 October 1929 the river rose in disastrous flood; at the station it washed out ballast and trackbed from beneath both tracks, and washed away much of the down platform too. The occasion was by no means unique — a flood in the 1950s again saw the river running between the platforms and over the level of the rails.

A washout from a most unusual cause occurred near Sun Bank Halt, on the GWR between Trefor and Llangollen, in September 1945. Running along the hillside, 37ft above the railway, was the Llangollen Canal; owned by the LMS, it had been statutorily abandoned as a navigation the previous year. It has subsequently become the most popular cruising canal in Britain, but in 1945 it was being maintained only as a water channel.

On 7 September, in the early hours of the morning, the bank of the canal gave way and the resulting torrent poured down upon the railway below. There it washed out the embankment and left rails suspended over the gap. Unfortunately, however, the block telegraph wires were unharmed, nor did anyone see the washout; without any warning of obstruction, the engine of the first train went into the gap at about 35mph. The mail and parcels vans of which it was comprised piled up on top of it and caught fire. The driver lost his life, the fireman was injured and the guard severely shocked.

The canal along this length has a long history of bank trouble, both before and after this accident. The breach on this occasion was considered to be the consequence not of an undetected and increasing leak through the canal's own clay puddle lining, but of erosion of the boulder clay beneath by natural water channels.

The heavy snows of 1947 were followed by a rapid thaw accompanied by heavy rains. That March the swollen River Wye carried away part of the viaduct by which the Hereford-Ross branch crossed over it at Strangford, and there were many other cases of damage to bridges and track. The greater effect, however, lay in inundation of low-lying ground, to which reference will be made in the next chapter.

* * *

August 1948 brought what was probably the worst series of washouts and associated disasters ever to strike the railways of any particular part of Britain. This was the flood damage experienced in the Scottish Borders on 12/13 August. It was only by the greatest good fortune that no one was injured, although many were inconvenienced.

George Dow, then Public Relations Officer of BR's Eastern Region, compiled the text for a booklet about the damage, its effects and the repairs, but the proposed booklet was replaced by a film and remained unpublished. The text eventually appeared 20 years later as a three-part article in *Railway World* (September, October and November 1968). O. S. Nock, in his *Scottish Railways* (1950), also went into the subject at the time in some detail.

Unlike Carrbridge, the cause was not a single storm or cloudburst, but the culmination of six days of heavy rain that commenced on both sides of the border on 6 August. On 12 August it escalated into a deluge, which continued for a further 24 hours without respite.

The first hint of trouble came at 1.50pm on the 12th, when the driver of a Newcastle-Edinburgh express stopped his train out of course at the wayside station of Chathill to report to the stationmaster that ballast was being washed away. He was able to continue his journey, but before long the station was flooded and level crossing timbers were starting to lift. The station was closed, then reopened again, at least on the up line, to allow two expresses to pass that had been held up. They could not return northwards, for the line between Scremerston and Goswick had been out of action, flooded, since 3pm.

Further north on the East Coast main line increasingly serious problems were emerging. The relief stationmaster at Grantshouse received a report of a landslide on the down line, and set off on the footplate of the 2.30pm from Edinburgh to inspect. He found the line covered with earth and water to rail level. When he arrived at Reston, the next station, he heard by telephone from his signalman at Grantshouse that the Eye Water had burst its banks and was flooding the station. This was the same Eye Water that had done so much damage long before, when the railway was new. It had since seemed quiescent, but now it was going on the rampage again. The relief stationmaster attempted to return to Grantshouse by road, but was foiled by flooding a mile short of his destination. Ahead lay one of the bridges that carried the main line over the Eye and, even as he watched, the floods brought it down. 'It seemed to come down slowly at first,' Dow quoted him as saying later, 'then with a rush all the masonry fell into the seething water below.'

By then, arrangements were being made to divert trains. The 'Flying Scotsman' had that summer reverted to running non-stop from London to Edinburgh, a symbol of post-war recovery. On 12 August the down train got as far as Alnmouth, then it was stopped, taken back to Newcastle, and diverted to the Waverley Route. It got as far as Hawick, where it was stopped again, for another diverted express had been halted ahead of it at Tynehead, where a landslide blocked both lines at about 9pm. The deluge was continuing to wreak its havoc. The 'Flying Scotsman' was taken back from Hawick to Carlisle. It set out again, via Carstairs. Third time lucky, it reached Edinburgh successfully, but 10 hours late.

At least it made it. Passengers on the express at Tynehead were eventually rescued by a convoy of buses, preceded by a police car to check the state of the roads. And the few passengers on the 4pm from St Boswells to Reston had to spend the night at Chirnside station, cut off both by rail and by road. Three freight trains were stranded, all of them on the main line, at Reston, Ayton and Cockburnspath.

Between 3.40pm on 12 August and 5.25am the next morning, more than 80 reports of mishaps reached Edinburgh District Control Office. There were floods, landslides, floating sleepers, fallen trees and telegraph poles, signalling equipment damaged and, as we know, bridges washed away. Between Dunbar and Berwick alone, 11 bridges and culverts were destroyed, three more were damaged, and there were 14 other places where there were landslides, washouts and slips. The floodwater had rushed through Penmanshiel Tunnel, and at Ayton, where a culvert through a 52ft-high embankment had collapsed and become blocked, the embankment was acting as a dam and the lake thus formed stretched away out of sight to the west. Where track had been flooded, it was covered by a trail of debris, rubbish, and uprooted trees and bushes.

The list of lines blocked in the Scottish Region was eventually this:

East Coast main line, between Dunbar and Berwick;
Waverley Route, between Hardengreen and Galashiels;
St Boswells-Kelso-Tweedmouth branch, between Sprouston and Carham;
St Boswells-Duns-Reston branch, between Greenlaw and Reston;
Branches to Jedburgh, Dalkeith, Peebles, Polton, Penicuik, Lauder, Eyemouth, Haddington and Gifford.

South of the border, on the North Eastern Region, the East Coast main line was blocked south of Tweedmouth, and the Alnwick-Coldstream branch was broken by a washed-out bridge between Ilderton and Wooler.

As can be seen from the list of lines blocked, the extensive closures of later years had not then struck the railway network of the Borders, and there were far more options for diversions than there would be today. In one important location, though, railwaymen were worse off then than now, for there was no direct link to enable trains from the former LNER station of Edinburgh Waverley to run direct on to the former LMS line from Princes Street to Carstairs and Carlisle. Each train taking this route had to come to a stand at Haymarket West, where a pilot engine came on to the rear to draw it back to Dalry Road Junction. There it could resume its forward direction of travel. This zig-zag manœuvre, which was of course carried out the opposite way round for arriving trains, cost each train making it about 20 minutes.

Nonetheless, all passenger trains, and freight trains carrying perishable goods such as fish, had initially to be diverted via Carstairs and Carlisle. For other freight trains — and at that date freight traffic between Edinburgh and Berwick was running at the rate of 1,000 wagons a day in each direction — there was insufficient capacity and they were, for the time being, cancelled.

Some of the blockages were far less serious than others. The East Coast main line south of Tweedmouth was reopened on the afternoon of 13 August, and some of the branch lines where damage was light were reopened the same day, or a few days later. The damage between Dunbar and Berwick, however, was so severe that resources were concentrated first on clearing the Waverley Route, relatively little damaged, and the branch from St Boswells, which linked it to the East Coast main line at Tweedmouth. By great effort both were reopened

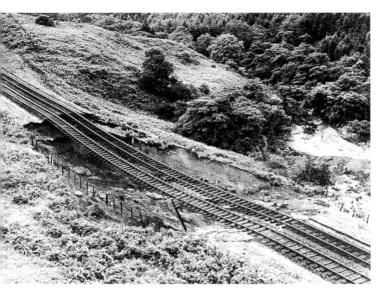

Left and below left: Just two of the many washouts that occurred on 12/13 August 1948 along the East Coast main line between Berwick and Dunbar. *(both) National Railway Museum*

throughout by 16 August, and so became available as a diversionary route despite the 11½ miles of single track on the branch. Curiously, Dow makes no mention of the Riccarton Junction-Hexham line, neither of damage to it nor of its potential as a diversionary route, for it would have provided a shorter route between Edinburgh and Newcastle than that actually used. I surmise that it may have been subject to weight restrictions that would have prevented its use by the largest locomotives.

These were certainly able to use the St Boswells-Tweedmouth route, although additional stops were allowed for locomotives of express trains to take water, at Galashiels for up trains and St Boswells for down. This in turn seems to have put locomotive crews rostered for the 'Flying Scotsman' on their mettle. Although the diversionary route meant a total journey of 408½ miles between London and Edinburgh compared with 392¾ by the main line, on no fewer

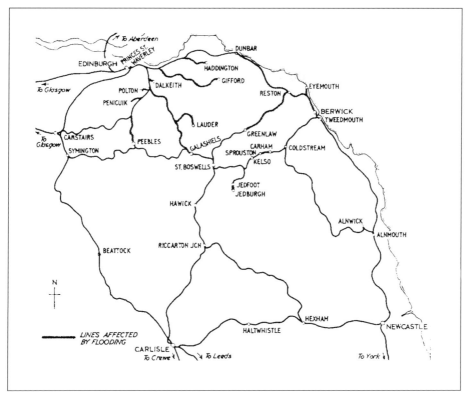

Map labels:
To Aberdeen
EDINBURGH PRINCES ST. WAVERLEY
DUNBAR
HADDINGTON
To Glasgow
DALKEITH
GIFFORD
POLTON
RESTON
EYEMOUTH
PENICUIK
BERWICK
TWEEDMOUTH
LAUDER
To Glasgow
CARSTAIRS
PEEBLES
GALASHIELS
GREENLAW
SYMINGTON
CARHAM
SPROUSTON
COLDSTREAM
KELSO
ST. BOSWELLS
JEDFOOT
JEDBURGH
HAWICK
ALNWICK
ALNMOUTH
N
RICCARTON JCN
BEATTOCK
HEXHAM
NEWCASTLE
HALTWHISTLE
LINES AFFECTED BY FLOODING
CARLISLE
To Crewe
To Leeds
To York

than 23 occasions they conserved their water supplies so well that the 'Flying Scotsman', up or down, made the journey without stopping. Dow stated that these were the longest runs ever made by trains in Great Britain without any intermediate stops, and I see no reason to suppose that they have since been exceeded.

With the opening up of this diversionary route, freight trains recommenced as well. But it had only limited capacity for them; many went south from Edinburgh via Carlisle, reaching that point either by the Waverley Route, by Carstairs, or even by Kilmarnock.

The main line between Dunbar and Berwick had still to be reinstated. A few years earlier, during World War 2, the liberation of Europe had involved quick reinstatement, on a temporary basis, of innumerable railway bridges that had been bombed or blown up. Evidently there was still in 1948 a reservoir of expertise in this work, and indeed of the equipment required. The help and advice of the War Office were sought and given. In order that the line could be reopened as quickly as possible, it was decided to install temporary bridges of standard military type with the spans carried on steel trestles protected by steel sheet piling, and materials were provided by the Royal Engineers' railway bridging depot at Longmoor. Even with this aid, however, it was a big task, involving innumerable railway staff from far and wide, and contractors too.

A most urgent need was to release the water impounded behind the embankment with the blocked culvert, before the embankment itself collapsed and sent a tidal wave down on Eyemouth village. A trench was cut through the embankment to release the water through a control sluice, but with further rainfall this proved inadequate. Emergency pumping equipment with a capacity of 5 million gallons per day was therefore borrowed from the Metropolitan Water Board, and with this aid the danger was alleviated. Elsewhere, debris — 6,500 tons of it — had to be removed, and landslips made good with 50,000cu yd of fill.

115

By these means, the line was reopened for freight traffic on 25 October, only 11 weeks or so since the damage was done. A week later, after freight trains had bedded down relaid track, passenger trains returned too, on 1 November.

The temporary bridges had been designed so that they did not obtrude into the space required to build concrete abutments and wing walls for their permanent replacements. This was done over the next 18 months; embankments were reinstated behind them, and steel spans were installed. Through the embankment that had acted as a dam, a new 200ft culvert was bored and lined with reinforced concrete segments. Permanent reinstatement of all the works on the main line was completed on 21 May 1950.

Reinstatement of seriously damaged works on the branch lines was treated with less urgency. The 3-mile branch from Burnmouth to Eyemouth crossed the Eye Water near its terminus by a 60ft-high viaduct of six wrought-iron lattice girder spans. Substantial repairs were needed, including reconstruction of the centre pier which, undermined by the flood's scouring action, had collapsed. The work was done, however, and the branch was reopened after an interval of more than ten months, on 29 June 1949.

Other branches were less fortunate. That to Gifford, built as a light railway and by 1948 open only for freight, had been breached by a bridge washout beyond Humbie, which was the penultimate station. The bridge was never repaired, and the rails beyond were lifted in the mid-1950s; nonetheless, this section was not closed formally until 1 January 1959! The branch from St Boswells via Duns to Reston was reinstated, but for passenger trains between Duns and Reston only; the remainder became restricted to freight trains. The Alnwick-Coldstream branch had been freight-only for many years; the washed-out bridge at Ilderton was not repaired, and subsequently the line was worked as two separate branches, from Coldstream to Wooler and from Alnwick to Ilderton. In truth, however, on these last three branches the floods had only accelerated a process that was happening anyway. All these branches are now long since closed, and indeed in this region only the main line survives.

* * *

The same process was happening elsewhere. In Mid-Wales the narrow-gauge Corris Railway ran from an interchange station with the standard gauge at Machynlleth, northwards to serve slate quarries near Corris and Aberllefenni. Half a mile from Machynlleth it crossed over the River Dovey on a bridge of steel girders on masonry piers. The Dovey was notorious for fluctuations in its flow, for sudden spates and extensive flooding. By the mid-1940s it was altering its course, as it approached the bridge, to curve round ever closer to the railway embankment.

The Corris Railway had been taken over by the Great Western in 1930, losing its independence and, shortly afterwards, its passenger trains. By the mid-1940s slate traffic was in decline too, freight trains were down to three per week and the future of the line was under constant review. At the start of 1948 it became part of British Railways. By August the river was threatening to erode its way through the embankment and reached the track. The line's two locomotives were brought down to Machynlleth lest they be marooned in their shed near Corris. What turned out to be the last train ran on 20 August, after which further flooding made the track unsafe. It was not repaired — the line, instead, was closed. The two locomotives remained at Machynlleth, sheeted over, until purchased by the infant Talyllyn Railway Preservation Society for £50 the pair in 1951.

A few miles upstream, the Dovey was equally responsible for precipitating closure of the branch from Cemmes Road to Dinas Mawddwy. This branch followed the upper part of the valley of the Dovey, which several times had caused train services to be suspended temporarily. Like the Corris, the branch had long since lost its passenger trains, and after World War 2 its freight trains were down to two a week. Once again, what later transpired to be the last train ran on 5 September 1950. Heavy rain followed, and the Dovey in spate displaced the bridge by which the railway crossed it near Cemmaes station, and the railway was closed. Later the bridge was shored up sufficiently for 'Dean Goods' No 2323 to pass over it while working the demolition train.

On the Midhurst-Chichester goods line of the Southern Region, a culvert was undermined by flooding in 1951. In consequence, on 19 November, 'C2x' class 0-6-0 No 32522 finished in the bed of the steam. Damage to the embankment prevented use of a crane to recover it, and it was eventually raised the following February by lowering the track down to the locomotive to form a ramp, up which it was drawn by means of steel cables attached to another locomotive.

In October 1954 unusually wet weather brought flooding to northwest England, with two culverts partially collapsed on the Coniston branch. At a bridge between Cockermouth and Workington the swollen River Derwent demolished a wing wall and scoured out the embankment behind the abutment. Large blocks of stone that were tipped into the breach were swept away, until the water level started to subside again and the flow was reduced.

This was followed by torrential rain in Ireland on 8 December. Half a mile out of its Dublin terminus the Great Northern main line to Belfast crossed the River Tolka by a two-span bridge. The river, usually 3 or 4ft deep, came up to 20ft and washed away the central pier. Clontarf station, 1½ miles from Dublin, became a temporary passenger terminus, linked to Dublin by Great Northern buses. Goods traffic was diverted via Navan. A month later a temporary bridge had been installed over the Tolka, pending construction of a permanent structure.

The year 1956 produced another wet summer in Scotland. At the end of July heavy rain led to washouts on both the original and the direct lines between Aviemore and Inverness. Between Culloden Moor and Inverness, floodwater coursing down a cutting eroded the ballast and the formation from beneath the down line, so that the track subsided several feet into the space that was left; the up line, remarkably, continued to be usable.

A month later, on 28 August, heavy rain over 24 hours produced flooding in the Borders, in the districts most affected in 1948. The effects were less serious than before, but still serious enough. Floodwater again poured through Penmanshiel Tunnel, leaving debris on the track and washing away ballast, and the Eye Water again flooded Grantshouse station after bursting through a retaining wall. The up 'Elizabethan' morning express to King's Cross, which had left Edinburgh, was brought back and set off to go via St Boswells and Tweedmouth as in 1948. But that branch became flooded too, and the train was further diverted to follow the rest of the Waverley Route to Carlisle. The up 'Flying Scotsman' was sent by the Waverley Route too, but when the line had to be closed because of flooding near Melrose, it had to be brought back to Edinburgh and sent via Carstairs. Comparable diversions and dislocations followed, but it proved possible to make good the flood damage by 30 April.

A violent thunderstorm affected southeast England in the early evening of 5 September 1958. Floodwater flowing through Sevenoaks Tunnel washed away ballast and earth, and on the London, Tilbury & Southend line ballast was washed out between Upminster and Laindon, between Stanford-le-Hope and Pitsea on the alternative route, and between Upminster and Ockendon on the branch linking the two. But the greatest effects of this storm lay in landslips and inundations, and it will feature again.

* * *

Railways in the West Country were much damaged by extensive flooding over several days in September/October 1960. On 30 September floodwater first reached track level of a bridge on the Southern line between Exeter and Crediton, then washed it away. With further flooding interrupting the work of repairs, it was 12 October before the line could be reopened.

On the afternoon of 1 October the Great Western main line was blocked for several hours at Hele & Bradninch when the River Culm overflowed on to the track. Earlier the same day, on the Culm Valley branch, track near Culmstock had started to subside under the 7.15am from Hemyock. Inspection, when firm ground had been attained, revealed that the locomotive was as a result riding on top of the buffers of the first coach. Subsequently the line was washed out. On the Moretonhampstead branch water that overflowed from the abandoned Stover Canal swept away the track, and on 6 October on the Southern line there was a further washout between Yeoford and Coleford Junction. Once again, these floods were accompanied by serious landslips, which are described later.

After only a brief respite, heavy rain returned to the West Country over the night of 26/27 October. The GWR main line was under water again at Hele & Bradninch, and the Barnstaple, Exe Valley and Minehead branches were breached. No sooner had the main line at Hele & Bradninch been partially restored than the rising River Exe reached and exceeded track level at the bridge that carried the Southern line over it at Cowley Bridge Junction. It then ran away down the combined main line towards Exeter, flowing though a permanent way store en route and carrying with it barrels, fence posts and sleepers. At first, trains hauled by steam locomotives were allowed through at slow speed; diesels, newly introduced, were not, lest the water damage their motors. But before long all trains were halted. Meanwhile, Exeter St Davids was not only becoming extremely congested with trains continuing to arrive both from the west and, via the Southern route, the east, but was also rapidly disappearing under water itself. Flooding eventually reached axlebox level. The following day the waters started to subside and things gradually got back to normal.

* * *

Mid-Wales was hit by severe flooding in the middle of December 1964 when rivers rose following heavy rainfall. Between Welshpool and Aberystwyth on the Cambrian main line there were five separate breaches, which were in due course repaired. More far-reaching was the effect of the flooding on the Ruabon-Dolgellau line. A series of breaches on 13 December meant that trains were replaced by buses the following day; however, between Ruabon and Llangollen, and between Bala, Bala Junction and Dolgellau, trains were running again on 17 December. On the intervening section, the breach at Llandderfel was serious. Closure of the entire line had already been announced for 18 January 1965, and the central part of the line was not brought back into use; temporary replacement buses ran until the official closure date. This was, probably, the most important route upon which flood damage prompted closure that was permanent. Or supposedly so — sections of the route have been revived as the Llangollen Railway and the Bala Lake Railway.

Back in December 1964, flood damage also greatly hampered the reopening of another line in the same district. The Welshpool & Llanfair Light Railway Preservation Co Ltd had reopened the 2ft 6in-gauge W&L between Llanfair Caereinion and Castle Caereinion in 1963. On this section the line crossed over the River Banwy on a bridge of three girder spans upon masonry piers. By the late evening of 12 December, after a week of heavy rain had turned into a downpour, water foamed against the piers as though against the bow of a ship; the river had already risen sufficiently to put the line under 2ft of water near Llanfair, and at the bridge it eventually rose some 15ft above its usual summer level. By morning it could be seen that one of the two piers had been undermined — it had been shifted by the current and the spans sagged down on top of it.

This, for a preservation group with limited funds and no capital reserves, was a disaster that might have been terminal. Without the bridge, trains could operate only over the 1¼ miles between Llanfair and Heniarth, which would drastically reduce the takings.

In fact, trains had only to do so for the first part of the following summer season. Members and friends rallied round, raising most of the £2,750 required (this was 1966!). The 16th Railway Regiment Royal Engineers, as an exercise, contributed expertise and equipment to a job that they did, jointly, with the railway's own volunteers. The sagging spans were jacked up and supported temporarily on steel trestling and the damaged pier was demolished. Within a coffer dam, a concrete base was made for the new pier, fabricated from steel. Once this was complete, the spans were lowered on to it. The line over the bridge was reopened to traffic on 14 August 1966. Thirty-one years later, in 1997, this pier itself was found to be badly corroded. Strengthening works were completed over the next two years, and a stone facing was provided.

* * *

Dramatically, the washout of a railway bridge near Godalming in September 1968 was observed by two policemen; they dashed to the station, alerted the booking clerk, then ran on to the platform to alert the driver of a Portsmouth-London train that was about to leave. It did not. Meanwhile the booking clerk was passing a message to the signalbox to stop other trains.

This was a period of severe storms and much other damage was done. In East Anglia two bridges were washed out, one of them almost completely swept away; this bridge was on the Norwich-Ipswich line between Diss and Burston. The other was between Kennett and Higham on the Bury St Edmunds-Newmarket line, where one of two brick arches was destroyed and the centre pier and remaining abutment undermined. At both locations temporary girder spans of military type were installed pending permanent reconstruction.

When an embankment between Wath and Penistone was damaged by flooding on 23 December 1968, trains were diverted via Barnsley for several days. The diversionary route was not electrified so one, and on occasion two, diesel locomotives hauled trains over it complete with their electric locomotives. Up a 1-in-41 gradient, a banker was also provided at the rear.

A severe washout in 1971 brought about the end of the Lochaber Narrow Gauge Railway. This line's Upper Works Railway was of 3ft gauge, lightly laid and operated by internal combustion; it has already been mentioned in connection with its snowploughs. Most of it had been built in the 1920s as an aid to construction of hydro-electric installations for manufacture of aluminium; these included a 15-mile-long tunnel for water supply. The railway had subsequently been kept up as an aid to their maintenance.

In the 1960s it was busy, but the frequent mountain torrents that it crossed by culverts and bridges gave problems — as is, perhaps, only to be expected in a district chosen for its suitability for generating electricity by water power. In February 1962, for instance, 16 culverts were washed out, and on 10 August 1969 a cloudburst washed out six culverts and two bridges. The damage was repaired, but in 1970 a forestry road was constructed that also reached one of the water intakes formerly served only by rail. Then, on 21 October of that year, there was a severe storm. At a point some 400yd above one of the bridges a landslip blocked the burn and caused a build-up of water, which, when released, carried away the bridge and eroded a gap in the railway 70yd across, with track slewed down into it on both sides.

By then, most of the land through which the railway passed was occupied by the Forestry Commission. Rather than restore the railway, the British Aluminium Co Ltd, which owned it, set about a programme of road construction jointly with the Forestry Commission, roads that would both meet forestry needs and provide access to the intakes. That took time, and for some years isolated sections of the railway were still used to provide access to intakes from the nearest road, the last such section passing out of use in 1977. Recommendations that part of the railway should be reinstated to provide passenger access to the Nevis Range ski area have regrettably been ineffectual so far.

In the same area, heavy rain caused the washout of the abutment of a bridge east of Glenfinnan on the Fort William-Mallaig line on 31 August 1973. A temporary bus service was introduced between Fort William and Glenfinnan, but trains continued over the section beyond. Train services resumed throughout on 31 October, after construction of a new bridge of two spans.

* * *

The weather during October 1987 was appalling and became notorious for the hurricane that swept across the South of England; its effects are described in Chapter 11. It was not this, however, but the heavy and prolonged rain that fell over southwest Wales during the next few days that led to a particularly serious accident. This accident remains one of the most severe, in terms of persons killed in an accident resulting from natural causes, in the recent history of British railways. It was the collapse of the bridge over the River Towy at Glanrhyd on the Central Wales line on Monday 19 October 1987, in consequence of which four people lost their lives.

Throughout southwest Wales from 2 to 8in of rain fell over some 27 hours between the evenings of 17 and 18 October. By the night of 18 October, ballast was being washed out near Fishguard, and there was flooding at Carmarthen. At 19.20 the Welsh Water Authority issued a Red 2 flood warning for the upper River Towy, the valley of which the Central Wales line follows from Llandeilo to Llandovery. This was the most serious warning possible for that district, and the first time it had been issued since the system had been introduced in 1980. But although warnings were public and issued to the Police, they were not issued to British Railways, nor had BR been included in the distribution of an instruction booklet about the warning system.

But on that Sunday evening a light engine was travelling back down the line after a day spent on engineering works. South of Llandovery, the driver noticed that the track was flooded, but not above rail level. About 21.15 he stopped his locomotive briefly on Glanrhyd bridge; he could see the surface of the water reflected, and estimated it about 3ft below the level of the bridge. Continuing, he came to a place where floodwater was washing out the ballast, and another where it was running above rail level. At Llandeilo he stopped and telephoned the signalman at Pantyffynon, who was responsible for the whole line, to report these three instances of flooding.

Consequently when the first train on Monday morning, the 05.27 Swansea to Shrewsbury, reached Llandeilo shortly after 07.00 it was carrying an operating manager who had been on call and who had come to assess the situation. The train was a two-car diesel multiple-unit dating from 1960 and fitted with headlights. Waiting for it at the first flood was the Permanent

Above:
Glanrhyd bridge on the Central Wales line was washed out on the night of 18/19 October 1987, and the 05.27 Swansea-Shrewsbury went into the swollen River Towy. The rear car rests on one of the collapsed spans, while the front car has been swept away by the flood. It finished at right angles to the bridge. One rear corner only emerges from the water, the remainder is submerged. *PA Photos*

Way Section Supervisor, who had managed to get there by road from his base at Llandrindod Wells, hitching a lift on a lorry through floods too deep for cars. Having inspected the flooding, he was able to signal the train through it by hand lamp at 5mph. He then joined the operating manager and the driver in the cab. At the second flood he instructed the driver to slow down to between 3 and 5mph.

To inspect a line for such problems in this way, using a passenger train, was permissible; to use a separate locomotive on a line with long single-track sections, from which the locomotive would have to emerge before a train could follow, would have led to delays during which, for instance, floods could become much more severe before the train arrived.

What the railway staff in the cab were looking for, in the half-light of the grudging dawn of a wet morning in late October, was flooded or damaged track. This, on previous experience, was not unlikely. They were not anticipating the sudden collapse of a structure, believed sound, without previous warning. Despite all that I have written earlier in this chapter, this remains a very rare event — and for a train to be directly involved is rarer still.

The train ran slowly up the gradient that led to Glanrhyd Bridge. End-on, the view of the first span showed nothing amiss. It was only when the train was almost upon it that the driver could see that it and subsequent spans had collapsed into the swollen river. He made an emergency application of the brakes. It was too late.

The front car containing the three railwaymen and six passengers went into the raging waters and started to settle. The rear car remained up-ended on the brink; its rear was dry, but the guard's compartment at its forward end was partly under water, which was pouring in through a broken window. Water was also coming in between the cars and through the windows of the front car. The front car started to fill up. The lights had gone out. As ill-luck would have it, all six passengers had chosen to sit in the front car.

When the train first stopped, the manager was able to look back through a cab side window, and saw that the back of the rear car was out of the water. He waded back through the front car, was able to get to the rear car, and established that it was possible to get out of a door at the back and on to the bridge. He got back into the train and started calling to passengers, 'This way out'. The guard, from his place of relative safety, went through to the front car to tell those in it to come back to the rear. One at least of them was initially reluctant to go in the direction from which the water appeared to be coming. But, half-walking, half-swimming, hanging on to the luggage racks, and struggling through the flexible gangway, passengers were starting to make their way to safety. The guard, by now in the gangway connection attached to the rear car, helped them up through it. But three passengers, and the driver, who is believed to have been bringing up the rear, were still in the front car when it became able no longer to resist the current, broad side on. With a loud crack it was swept away, finishing at right angles to the bridge, on its side and almost entirely submerged. Those still within were drowned.

There is no doubt that the bridge had collapsed before the train arrived, for a nearby farmer saw it so, through the dawn gloom. Even before he had time to telephone a warning, the train appeared on the scene.

The bridge had consisted of five spans. The piers and abutments, of masonry, dated from construction of the line in the 1850s. The superstructure had been renewed in 1958. The bridge had been regularly maintained, including underwater repairs to pier 2, which was located in the deepest part of the river, in 1982.

A detailed survey of the remains of the bridge and of its surroundings eventually established the likely cause of its collapse and the sequence of events. They were remarkable. The initial cause was to be found not at pier 2, but at adjoining pier 3, and furthermore at its downstream end, which had been undermined by erosion. Pier 3 lay out of the main flow of the river, which was to the far side of pier 2. Downstream of the bridge, however, was a marked eddy or swirl that had produced an upstream current on pier 3 sufficient eventually to undermine it. This pier broke its back, and as it collapsed one of its spans slewed sufficiently to force pier 2 to collapse also, and upstream.

In his eventual report, the Department of Transport's Inspecting Officer was critical of a lack of understanding among railway engineers of the complex hydraulic behaviour of watercourses. Measures were taken to improve this, and to ensure that water authority flood warnings were received by British Rail.

At the inquest, the jury returned a verdict of 'Unlawful Killing'. The case was referred to the Director of Public Prosecutions, and British Railways faced the possibility of criminal charges. It was September 1989 — almost two years later — before he announced that no prosecutions would be brought. This had the unfortunate consequence that, in the meantime, not only was publication of the Inspecting Officer's report deferred, but that it was inappropriate for him even to discuss proposed action with railway officers, lest agreement over recommended changes be taken as evidence of previous fault.

In other words, improvement of passenger safety was taking second place to finding someone to blame. Those who are quick to demand prosecutions in the wake of railway accidents would do well to take this aspect into consideration.

* * *

On 7 February 1989 came a washout on an even larger scale than Glanrhyd — the River Ness in flood swept away the Ness bridge at Inverness, a masonry viaduct that carried the line from Inverness to the North. No trains were directly involved, for the danger had been foreseen and the line had been closed to traffic.

The collapse of the bridge had the effect of isolating the lines to Kyle of Lochalsh, Wick and Thurso from the rest of the railway system. Not many years before, such a disaster would probably have prompted their closure. By 1989, however, ScotRail considered it had a commitment to maintain them — indeed, it was committed to introducing 'Sprinter' DMUs in place of locomotive-hauled trains, with corresponding accelerations, that spring. It was immediately announced that the bridge would be rebuilt.

Yet there seemed to be no sense of urgency. Not many years before, in such circumstances a temporary bridge would quickly have been provided, to serve until the permanent bridge was complete. If this was considered, it was not publicised. Rather, ScotRail took advantage of the recently completed Kessock road bridge, over the Beauly Firth, to institute a temporary bus service from Inverness to Dingwall, which became the terminus for trains to and from the north and the west. To a cynic like the author, this seemed a good way of demonstrating to rail passengers just how much shorter and quicker the road route had become!

However, six Class 37 locomotives and 16 carriages had been isolated north of the viaduct, sufficient to work train services, and a temporary maintenance depot was established at Muir of Ord. In due course, ScotRail had 'Sprinter' cars carried by road from Inverness to Invergordon, where they were replaced on the rails, and the accelerated train service was introduced as promised.

By summer the contract had been placed for a new bridge, 400ft long and of three spans, with concrete piers supporting a superstructure of steel with a concrete deck. This was completed at a cost of £2.5 million in time to be inaugurated on 9 May 1991, and through train services recommenced. The author's cynicism happily proved misplaced, and the North lines are with us yet.

The same flooding that washed away the Ness bridge also proved of benefit to rail, for it choked Inverness harbour with silt and debris, and so prevented its use by ships delivering petrol from Grangemouth refinery. Within days, BR's Railfreight Petroleum business was successfully carrying petrol into Inverness by rail.

A differing approach to alleviating interruptions to train services by flood damage was demonstrated by the Western Region in January 1990. Because of damage caused by the River Severn near Gloucester, the line thence to Lydney was closed on 28 January; this meant carrying passengers 28 miles by road. Within a few days, a temporary platform of scaffolding, complete with steps, ramp and lighting, was built at Over on the west bank of the Severn; trains terminated there, and the gap to be covered by road was reduced to 2 miles.

A heavy fall of snow succeeded by torrential rain and a sudden thaw caused intensive flooding around Perth in January 1993. The first sign of trouble to the railways that converge on that town was a bank slip on 14 January, which blocked the down track of the main line near Gleneagles. Then the swollen River Earn burst through its flood banks near Forgandenny, surged though an accommodation underbridge for a farm road and caused its collapse. The main line was now completely blocked. By the following morning, things were worse still: the central pier of the bridge that carried the line over the Water of May at Forteviot collapsed, and the steel spans were buckled.

Meanwhile, on the Highland line north of Perth, a 30yd length of embankment had been completely washed out, leaving the track hanging over the gap, and the River Tay was running so high at Perth that the bridge carrying the Perth-Dundee line over it was closed as a precaution.

The work of recovery began. After a radar survey of the bed of the Tay, the Perth-Dundee line was reopened on 22 January, and after a great deal of filling-in work, and inspection of bridges, the Highland line was reopened on 28 January. The work needed on the main line was much greater, and ScotRail introduced a temporary recast timetable. Through trains between Glasgow and Aberdeen were diverted via the Edinburgh & Glasgow line and the Forth and Tay Bridges to rejoin their usual route at Dundee. Inverness trains ran to and from Edinburgh. From Glasgow a train service ran as far as Gleneagles, whence there was a bus link to Perth, which connected with trains for Inverness, and also with a shuttle service to Dundee.

To restore the main line, it was found possible to fill in the accommodation bridge that had been swept away. The bridge over the Water of May was replaced by pipes of large diameter and an embankment. While this section of line was closed, the opportunity was taken to replace another bridge, at Dunning; work had earlier started on this, but treacherous ground had prevented its completion. The line was reopened on 19 April.

Mid-Wales had its problems too in the early 1990s. On 2 January 1991 floods damaged a bridge near Cemmes Road, and interrupted train services over the Cambrian for a day. On 11 June 1993 a flash flood swept down on the Talyllyn Railway at Brynglas, and main line and loop were buried beneath mud, debris, boulders, farm equipment and even gates. The embankment supporting the main line was eroded away. When trains recommenced the following day, they had to run through the loop as the main line was still unserviceable. In January 1994 the River Severn damaged the supports of Cilcewydd Bridge, by which the Cambrian crosses over it between Welshpool and Newtown. A temporary timetable with a bus link between these two points meant extended journey times and complaints. The bridge, however, had been built for double track, and was not so badly damaged as to prevent the space for the second track from being used as a footpath. Temporary platforms were built on either side of the bridge — named Cilcewydd East and Cilcewydd West — and from 17 January trains terminated at and commenced from these, while passengers walked across the bridge from one to the other. This arrangement lasted until the line could be reopened on 27 February.

The River Exe again overflowed on to the Great Western main line north of Exeter on the night of 30/31 October 1995. The line was closed for the following day; some trains were diverted via Yeovil and Honiton, but for most a bus link was provided.

The Aberdeen-Inverness line was blocked as a result of storms in September 1995 — the foundations of a viaduct were feared to have been affected, and there were many landslips. There was more trouble following another period of heavy rain at the end of June and the beginning of July 1997. Between Nairn and Keith this line was blocked in eight places, by washouts, floods and earthslips.

The Great Western main line north of Exeter was closed temporarily because of high river levels on 3/4 January 1998, and was flooded yet again following storms at the end of October.

On 9 April 1998 torrential rain fell across the South Midlands from Worcestershire to Cambridgeshire. Rivers burst their banks, and there were flash floods and landslips. All rail routes to Worcester were cut; so were the lines from Birmingham to Gloucester, where the line at Abbotswood Junction (south of Worcester) resembled a fast-flowing river, and from Birmingham to Oxford, with a washout near Fenny Compton. Kilsby Tunnel, on the West Coast main line, was flooded and closed for several hours. Conversely, at Evesham all roads into the town were blocked by floods and a rail shuttle provided the only access. Problems at Abbotswood Junction were repeated just over a year later, when 2in of rain fell on Worcestershire in 2 hours; ballast was washed away and water accumulated on the track to a depth of 1ft, bringing train services to a halt.

* * *

So to the events of the year 2000, which, as readers will scarcely need reminding, saw the most serious and widespread flood problems of recent years, and perhaps of any year in railway history. There was a harbinger of this on 27 April when torrential rain washed out the embankment supporting the Highland line over a length of some 400yd south of Culloden Viaduct. The Inverness-Aviemore section was then closed for about three weeks while repairs were made.

On 10 October the trackbed was washed out on the Stranraer line at Glenluce after torrential rain had caused a river to break its banks. The 12.39 Newcastle-Stranraer, a two-car Class 156 DMU, was derailed. The rear car tipped over and finished supported by trees; 20 passengers were slightly injured and eight of these needed hospital treatment.

After that, flood problems came thick and fast. On the remaining line in the Isle of Wight, the trackbed was washed away in eight places. The Kent & East Sussex Railway's extension to Bodiam, reopened only a few months earlier after years of effort, suffered a washout that left track suspended in the air. The greater problem in the South East, though, in mid-October, was widespread inundation.

Things got worse still. On 29 October a violent storm, followed by torrential rain, commenced in the South West and swept across most of England. The atrocious weather continued for several days. It brought washouts, inundations, landslips and gale damage. And it brought them to a railway system already in a state of near-paralysis, apparently self-induced, the effect of widespread engineering safety checks following the Hatfield disaster. In the innumerable subsequent delays and cancellations, it is virtually impossible to disentangle how much was due to which cause. It is said that some 70% of the rail network was out of action. Every part of Britain was affected, although the Scottish Highlands got off lightly.

So common did flood damage become at this period that problems which in normal times would have been news stories in themselves were reported only briefly; interruptions to train services were often attributed cursorily to 'flooding' without further detail. Such interruptions occurred at Ingatestone on the Great Eastern main line, between Upminster and Romford and between Wickford and Southminster, between King's Cross and Stevenage, at Armitage on the Trent Valley line, between Nottingham and Sheffield, on the Matlock branch, between Yeovil Junction and Exeter Central, on the Cambrian and Central Wales lines, and at several locations in Yorkshire, to mention but a few.

A notable washout did occur at Cowley Bridge Junction, where earlier troubles have already been recorded. On 30 October the River Exe sent much of its flow along the Great Western main line, and washed out 30ft of its embankment as well as the bridge carrying the former Southern branch to Barnstaple.

Heritage railways did not escape. Indeed, events on the Severn Valley Railway will serve as a microcosm of what was happening throughout most of Britain. By early in November the land was waterlogged, streams and culverts awash. South of Knowlesands Tunnel, a ditch running along the top of the west side of the cutting burst its banks; the water overflowed down the side of the cutting and washed it down on to the track. The permanent way staff made a temporary repair, and trains ran over the weekend of 4/5 November. Then on the night of 5 November 2in of rain fell on Bridgnorth. By morning there was a much larger washout of the cutting side, the temporary repairs were washed away, and a river flowed down the track through the tunnel. Where cutting changed to embankment, the river went over the side and washed away the ground; within a couple of days, track was suspended in the air for 100ft over a hole as much as 20ft deep, illustrated on the next page.

The first job, with the co-operation of neighbouring landowners, was to get contractors to cut a temporary drainage ditch to stem the flow of water. That done, reinstatement of the track could be considered, although it was clearly going to take weeks. A temporary train service terminating at Hampton Loade was arranged, and 0-6-0PT No 5764 was transferred by road from Bridgnorth to Kidderminster to help work it. Then the track overhanging the gap had to be removed, which meant assistance from contractors' plant. The very few sleepers that were damaged became a solid base for the new embankment. This was built, and the hole filled in, by contractors. Meanwhile, with the co-operation of Shropshire County Council and landowners, a new permanent land drainage system was being installed to prevent a recurrence. This involved laying over 500m of 600mm-diameter pipe.

A praiseworthy performance by the contractor building the embankment, followed by an equally praiseworthy one by the railway's own permanent way gang in laying the track on top of it, saw the line back in use as early as 23 November. Santa trains could traverse the entire line as planned — and their takings no doubt helped to pay the bills!

Other railways were affected too. On the Churnet Valley Railway, part of the trackbed was washed away after the River Churnet and the Caldon Canal burst their banks. The Llangollen Railway had to move rolling stock from a siding on an embankment that the River Dee was eroding away.

Still more storms swept across the South West on 8 December. At Cowley Bridge the main line, which had been reinstated in only six days, was washed out for the second time, and so was the Barnstaple branch. There were also washouts between Abergavenny and Hereford.

Yet washouts are no more than part of the story. Let us now turn to inundations.

The trackbed of the Severn Valley Railway near Knowlesands Tunnel was washed away by an overflowing stream during the appalling autumn of 2000. *(both)*
Ray Tranter, SVR

Chapter 8

Flooding: Inundation

To be precise, it is inundation of railways by fresh water that will be described in this chapter — salt water is reserved for the next. Records of early railways submerged by flooding from swollen rivers seem to be surprisingly few. I am inclined to suppose that the engineers who laid them out took into account the received wisdom of local inhabitants, and provided embankments across land at risk.

However, F. S. Williams records in *The Midland Railway* that in 1875 an exceptionally wet autumn caused the River Trent to rise 21ft. Burton-upon-Trent was flooded, Trent station became almost an island, and the lower part of Nottingham was like a sea. There was 2ft of water over the tracks, through which the trains passed. Near Newark the line was carried away and a temporary bridge built. The extensive flooding in Strathspey in 1892 has been mentioned in the last chapter.

There is also photographic evidence. Hereford Barton station was under water in 1886 — probably the River Wye had come

Below:
Hereford Barton station was inundated in 1886. *National Railway Museum*

up in flood. A well-known photograph shows a Great Western local proceeding along wholly inundated track at Creech, near Taunton, in 1894 — water is over the buffer-beam. Here, presumably, the nearby River Tone was the culprit. At Mitcham station, on the London, Brighton & South Coast Railway, the track was flooded up to the level of the platforms in 1900.

In Scotland, the Forth & Clyde Canal was built with headroom that was in effect unlimited, for sailing ships with masts to cross from sea to sea. It presented a considerable barrier to railways, which had either to cross over it, which meant a swing bridge with all its inconvenience, or to burrow beneath it. The North British Railway, building its Campsie branch (opened in 1848), thriftily made use of an existing structure, the Kirkintilloch aqueduct, which carried the canal over the Luggie Water. Its arch was large enough for the railway to be taken through it too, crossing over the Luggie while it did so to produce a three-decker structure. This was, perhaps, less of an economy than it first appeared, for the arch was only just large enough, and the Luggie was inclined to rise in spate. When it did, it rose above the level of the railway, and flooded the adjoining Kirkintilloch goods yard as well. Trains passing through the flood provided a spectacle for onlookers who gathered on the aqueduct above. This happened in the 1890s, probably earlier, and certainly later.

Railways in the low-lying parts of East Anglia were particularly liable to floods. The Southwold Railway, with its course close to the River Blyth, was often flooded; most of the railway's stock was based at Southwold, but during the winter the company made a point of stabling a locomotive and coaches at the other terminus, Halesworth, in case the line was breached by floods and a through train could not be run. In that event, according to Taylor and Tonks in *The Southwold Railway*, passengers were brought across the flooded marshes between the two trains by rowing boat. Somehow this accords with the popular perception of this undertaking!

The Southwold was blocked by floods on 26 and 27 August 1912, but on this occasion the region immediately to the north was much more seriously affected. There was exceptionally heavy rain at Norwich on 26 August; a rain gauge registered a fall of 7.34in between 4am and midnight. Just to the east of Norwich there was more than 8in, and throughout most of Norfolk and much of Suffolk there was more than 3in of rain.

Norwich, which then had no fewer than six possible railway routes to London, was cut off by rail from the outer world for the next 2½ days. The Great Eastern was affected by flooding in some 30 different locations. Photographs show the Yarmouth line at Whitlingham Junction disappearing beneath the surface of a lake that reaches as far as the eye can see. At Cantley the

Lowestoft-Norwich line does the same. Wagons stood up to their axleboxes in water at Norwich Trowse, and the Midland & Great Northern Joint Railway terminus at Norwich City suffered similarly.

Seven bridges on the Great Eastern were wrecked, and four more were damaged; they have been mentioned in the last chapter. The Great Eastern had a second experience of the same sort, but in its London district, in February 1919. Heavy snow followed by a quick thaw and continuous rain resulted in floods that inundated the railway in and around Stratford. Part of Stratford Works was under water, and so was Temple Mills Wagon Works. The railway was also flooded further out into Essex, at Chelmsford, Bishop's Stortford and elsewhere.

At the opposite end of Britain, there had been serious flooding at Elgin during the summer of 1915. Both the Highland and the Great North of Scotland Railway stations were under water, the latter sufficiently for trains to be diverted.

May is usually a dry month, but in 1932 it was exceptionally wet, particularly in South Yorkshire and the Midlands. Over 21-23 May there was a downpour for 30 hours, and in consequence the LNER was flooded at six places near Leeds, and in many other places from Nottinghamshire to Durham. The flooding was particularly bad at Arksey, north of Doncaster on the East Coast main line. Arksey itself remained above water, but on either side of the embankment apparently limitless sheets of water stretched away into the distance.

Left:
Floods from the Luggie Water also inundated the goods yard at Kirkintilloch, seen here from the point of view of the onlookers in the previous illustration.
East Dunbartonshire Council, William Patrick Library

Left:
The floods of 26 August 1912 inundated the Norwich City terminus of the Midland & Great Northern Joint Railway.
National Railway Museum

Left:
February 1919 saw the Great Eastern Railway under water at Temple Mills Wagon Works.
National Railway Museum

Above:
Elgin was flooded in 1915: the train is leaving over the Highland line but is hauled by a Great North of Scotland locomotive, presumably working through from Inverness to Aberdeen. *Great North of Scotland Railway Association*

Right:
Tracks at Nottingham Midland station were under water in May 1932. *Rail Archive Stephenson, T. G. Hepburn*

At Shaftholme the down line gave way early on 24 May; freight trains were diverted and all passenger trains used the up line — until that also collapsed, and for a while the East Coast main line was completely blocked. On the LMS, Nottingham Midland was also inundated in May 1932.

The pattern continued of intermittent but serious flooding, spaced widely in both time and place. November 1935 saw day after day of heavy and continuous rain in the South of England. Landslips were the main problem for the Southern Railway, but on 17 November Swanage station and goods yard were flooded up to platform level. Despite this, remarkably, the train service was apparently not affected.

In March 1947 the end of the freeze that had persisted over two months came in the form of a sudden rapid thaw and heavy rain. Meltwater ran off the frozen ground instead of soaking in, and according to A. J. Robertson in *The Bleak Midwinter*, the flooding that followed was the worst for 50 years. Thirty-one counties were affected; the Rivers Thames, Severn, Wye, Trent and Yorkshire Ouse were all in flood.

In railway terms, this meant that Nottingham Midland station was under water, again, with water on the tracks up to platform level. In the lower Thames valley, the Windsor branch of the Southern Railway was closed for several days. The LNER line from Liverpool Street to Stratford was flooded at Tottenham; trains were diverted via the loop from Lower Edmonton to Cheshunt, which at that period was little used. In the North, the River Derwent rose over the tracks at Malton. In the South, the River Rother burst its banks near Bodiam, but the Kent & East Sussex Railway's embankment was high enough — just — to rise above the resultant floodwater.

In Ireland the torrential rain of 8 December 1954, which washed out the Great Northern bridge over the River Tolka, also caused extensive flooding inland. The former Midland Great Western line between Dublin and Mullingar was worst affected; an up diesel train from Westport had its motors put out of action by flood water at Maynooth, and was rescued by an elderly 0-6-0. Subsequent trains were diverted from Athlone via Portarlington and the Great Southern & Western line to Dublin, but this too became flooded at Hazlehatch, and passengers had to complete their journeys by bus. Evening departures from Dublin for Sligo and Galway had to be cancelled when roads became flooded too.

Likewise the thunderstorms that did so much damage across southeast England on 5 September 1958 also caused inundations. At Beckenham Clock House station — a notorious spot that had earlier been inundated in October 1953 — floodwater on the track reached a depth of 2ft. On 8 October 1960, during the period of heavy rainfall in the West Country, flooding developed on the Minehead branch to a depth of 4ft near Dunster. Trains were terminated at Blue Anchor, whence buses traversed the flooded roads to Minehead; the signalman and the porter at Dunster were marooned in the signalbox overnight.

Flooding at Exeter later in the month has been mentioned in the last chapter; during the same period (26/27 October) rivers flowing down from Exmoor caused problems near Taunton, with lines flooded at Athelney and Creech. Heavy rain continued over the South of England, and by 3 November was causing problems to the lines running southwards from Tunbridge Wells to Eastbourne and Brighton. The former became flooded near Rotherfield and a bus link was instituted. On the latter, Uckfield station — not then the terminus that it is now — soon lay beneath deep floodwater, but no bus service could be provided as the local bus garage was also inundated. Flooding later also cut the line south of Barcombe Mills, although Uckfield dried out; it was 8 November before the railway was fully operational again.

Meanwhile on 3 November a small stream, which normally ran peacefully through Lewes, burst its banks and ran away down successive roads, through the cattle market and so into Lewes station. The tracks between the main-line platforms were soon flooded to platform level, and those to Brighton several inches over the rails. Electric power was switched off, and for the next few days a makeshift steam train service replaced electric trains between Eastbourne, Lewes and Brighton, where they connected with London trains. Motive power ranged from an 'M7' 0-4-4T to a 'West Country' Pacific; when water levels fell sufficiently, a Hastings six-car diesel-electric multiple-unit was added. The floods at Lewes were eventually beaten by the use of fire service heavy pumps on 11 November.

Further instances of flooded tracks occurred from time to time through the 1960s: at Mountain Ash on 9 March 1963, at Clock House (Beckenham) on 1 June 1964, and near Glastonbury on the Somerset & Dorset on 2 January 1966, a couple of months before closure.

The former Great North of Scotland station at Elgin was under water again in 1972. Walsall station, which had a history of inundation, was closed by floodwater as much as 5ft deep on 28 January 1978, reopening two days later. Early in 1980 the preserved section of the Kent & East Sussex was inundated, but subsequently carried over 1,000 sandbags needed to fill a breach in the bank of the Newmill Channel, which was inaccessible by road.

Exceptional flooding occurred in the Glasgow area on 12 December 1994. The underground Argyle line was inundated in the vicinity of Central Low Level station, where a train composed of two Class 314 electric multiple-units was immersed up to the top of the windows.

Right:
The internal rail system at the Associated Portland Cement Manufacturers' quarry at Swanscombe, Kent, was liable to be flooded. On 15 February 1969 — after the end of steam on British Rail — 0-4-0ST No 6 is plodding through the flood with a trainload of chalk.
David Idle

On the flooded section of line, power and signalling equipment had to be renewed; repairs took several months, during which period extra trains ran from Glasgow Central High Level to Motherwell.

A long cutting on the Midland main line at Draycott, between Derby and Loughborough, filled with rainwater to a depth of about half a metre several times in early 1995. This was considered to be a consequence of the filling-in of the closed Derby Canal, which had previously provided drainage.

Problems caused by the heavy rain at the end of June 1997 to the Aberdeen-Inverness line included inundation of Elgin station and goods yard. DMU No 158727 became marooned there in the flood, with water up to axle height. It was subsequently removed by road to Haymarket depot, Edinburgh, for repairs to be assessed.

The New Year of 1998 was marked by storms. Problems included flooding of the Severn Tunnel, which was closed on 4/5 January, and flooding of the Central Wales line at Llandeilo on 3 January. A steam special, hauled by Stanier 2-6-0 No 2968, had to terminate at Llandrindod Wells; it returned to Craven Arms and continued to Newport and its eventual destination of Gloucester, via Hereford rather than South Wales. Twenty-four hours of continuous rain combined with blocked drains to flood the Manchester-Bolton line at Agecroft, to a depth of 3in above the rails, on 7 March; trains were able to pass through at slow speed. Just over a month later, the heavy rain that fell across the South Midlands flooded Banbury station above rail level.

Storms on 23/24 October 1998 flooded part of the signalbox at Cardiff, causing the station to be temporarily closed. At the same period, DMUs were marooned in their depot at Newton Heath, Manchester, by flooding. In March 1999 the swollen River Derwent inundated Malton station well above the level of the rails.

So, again, to the floods of the year 2000. Their severity, extent and frequency were exceptional, but their locations often were not. When an East Coast main line express was halted by floodwater on 28 August following torrential rain — and then isolated by a landslide behind it — the location, Grantshouse, between Berwick and Dunbar, had a familiar ring. The previous trouble there was 44 years earlier, to the day.

When the deluge came to the South of England early in October, Uckfield station again disappeared under water. When the River Ouse rose and flooded Lewes, the sharply curved main-line platforms once again took on the appearance of a swimming pool with curved sides — as they had in 1960. This time there were no steam trains to come to the rescue, but when the Brighton main line became waterlogged south of Haywards Heath, a service of diesel trains appeared in lieu of the usual electric trains. Probably it was the first time that this section had ever been operated exclusively by diesels. Other lines where train services were cancelled included the Hastings line between Robertsbridge and Wadhurst, with water over the track at Etchingham, and between Ashford and Marden. Bletchingley Tunnel between Redhill and Tonbridge was flooded, and for some days a replacement bus service was provided.

On the Kent & East Sussex Railway's recently opened extension to Bodiam, where the washout has already been mentioned, about 1½ miles of track were inundated. The water still covered the track when the second outbreak of severe storms came at the end of the month, and indeed the track was still under water in mid-November. Another heritage railway affected at this time was Peak Rail, where the River Derwent rose sufficiently to inundate the track at Matlock.

On the national network, it is (as mentioned earlier) virtually impossible at this period of chaos to establish in all cases which hazard was responsible for which interruption to train services. On 1 November, however, Railtrack stated that 11 routes, in Surrey, Yorkshire, the West Country and South Wales, were closed by flooding — nor was reopening likely for many days. The following day the rapidly rising River Ouse interrupted East Coast main line train services at York; over the next few days intermittent attempts were made to run train services between York and Newcastle, only to see them withdrawn again. The York-Scarborough line was under water again at Malton on 6 November.

It was reported on 8 November that all six railway lines to Derby were flooded, and only one of the five routes in Nottingham was passable. Not surprisingly, Midland Mainline trains between Sheffield and St Pancras were not running. The East Coast main line was flooded at Doncaster where down trains terminated; up trains from Edinburgh were getting no further than Newcastle. In Scotland trains on the Bathgate branch were cancelled because there was flooding on the track. This list, even taken in conjunction with the previous chapter, is certainly incomplete, and probably not 100% accurate. Circumstances preclude it.

From 12 November, things started to return to some semblance of normality. But early in December, the Didcot-Oxford line was closed for several days by floods on the track.

Chapter 9

The Sea: Tidal Floods and Coastal Erosion

A railway that closely follows a coastline has half the traffic potential, one would think, of a railway further inland, for it can by and large gather traffic only from one side of the line, not both. Nevertheless, it is clear that in a great many instances that some compulsion or other moved engineers to lay out railways along the coast.

In some cases railways were combined with coastal protection or land reclamation works. When the Festiniog Railway was built in 1830s its lowest mile was laid out along William Maddocks's Traeth Mawr Embankment — 'The Cob' — built some 25 years earlier to reclaim a large area of former estuary behind it. This exposed location had its drawbacks, but the only occasion since the railway was built when The Cob was actually breached was, so far as I can trace, in October 1927. In a strong gale, heavy seas washed a hole in it and caused extensive flooding over the land behind. The damage was sufficiently severe to take until the following February to be made good. In the meantime trains terminated at Boston Lodge.

On the other side of the Irish Sea, the Dublin & Kingstown Railway was also built in the early 1830s. Inevitably the railway was close to the coast, but for almost a mile between Merrion and Blackrock it was laid out along an embankment built outside the low-water line, with the intention that the sea between it and the shore should be reclaimed. This was eventually done, but the railway's location left it exposed to heavy seas whipped up by onshore gales. These gave much trouble down the years, flooding the track and interrupting train services. At Blackrock station, for instance, a wall separated sea from platform, but in March 1937 a strong gale sent breakers over it and the track was inundated almost to platform level.

There are two principal ways in which the proximity of the sea has brought trouble to railways. Where the ground inland is high and a railway is located close to the shore, perhaps on a sea wall, gales and high tides bring waves that break on to the track, damaging it by washing out ballast and in some cases scouring away the wall or foreshore. Some lines in such positions have demanded regular coastal defence work down the years: locations include the Dublin-Wicklow line between Killiney and Wicklow, and the Cambrian Coast line, north of Barmouth, both of which have been protected by concrete blocks placed in quantity on the foreshore.

Elsewhere, railways have been laid out on land at or below sea level, perhaps some way inland but protected from the effects of the sea by flood banks. When gales and high tides breach these, extensive inundation results, covering railways and much else. There are other less general effects, such as the constant battles against corrosion fought on the Forth and Tay Bridges, while pier railways are so specialised a subject that I do not propose to cover them here. Their fates are in any event very much bound up with those of the piers they serve.

Of the first of the two types of location just mentioned, the famous example is that of the South Devon Railway as it follows its sea wall at Dawlish. The line was constructed in the mid-1840s; when the sea wall was being built, gales damaged it even before the mortar had set. In 1855 more than 50ft of the wall was washed away, and there was another washout in 1873. There have also been many problems in recent times, to which I shall return. Another railway damaged by the sea in its early years was the Dingwall & Skye, opened in 1870. Between Strathcarron and its then terminus at Strome Ferry it closely followed the shore of Loch Carron, a sea loch; the railway was severely damaged by gales and a high tide in December 1881.

At the opposite extreme of the map of Britain, a very high tide on 29 November 1897 overcame sea defences along much of the low-lying Essex coastline. On the London, Tilbury & Southend line some 2 miles of line were flooded between Pitsea and Benfleet, and ballast and sleepers were washed away.

The same tide affected the Great Eastern Railway's branch line from Wivenhoe to Brightlingsea, which followed closely the estuary of the River Colne; it was inundated to a depth of several feet. Ballast was washed away beneath the sleepers, and the brake van of the 2.30pm from Wivenhoe was derailed. The train came to a stand, and the passengers had to be rescued by boat. Late in 1903 another high tide swept away half a mile of ballast and track from this branch, and also affected the line from Wivenhoe towards Colchester Hythe, which had to be closed for some hours. On yet another occasion, the night of 6/7 January 1928, a very high tide washed out part of the railway embankment between Wivenhoe and Brightlingsea, and again damaged the track between Wivenhoe and Hythe.

The short-lived Campbeltown & Machrihanish Railway saw its train services interrupted by high tides on at least two occasions. In January 1915 a fierce storm accompanied a very high tide; waves broke over the railway at Campbeltown, covering it with debris and washing out the ballast. Train services had to be cut short until the line could be cleared and made safe. At the other end of the line, Machrihanish was once subjected to high tides, heavy rain and a westerly gale that combined to inundate the railway. When a driver attempted to take a passenger train through the flood, the water proved to be too deep and the locomotive fire was extinguished. This marooned the train with only the last coach on dry land. Another locomotive had to be summoned to draw the train out backwards.

Narrow-gauge locomotives are small, so the fire is nearer to the rails than it is on those of standard gauge. Another narrow-gauge line that experienced problems of the same type was the Tralee & Dingle. During a storm in 1927 the River Lee made a breach in its banks near Tralee, with the consequence that whenever a high spring tide coincided with a lot of water coming down the river, a flood occurred that inundated the track to a depth of as much as 3ft. Here again an over-bold driver had his locomotive fire put out. Subsequently the timetable warned passengers that, on the dates of spring tides, trains would not run to their usual schedule. The breach in the river bank was never repaired, at least not during the lifetime of

Right:
Inundation of the Belfast & County Down Railway was a long-standing problem where it crossed the Quoile Marshes near Downpatrick. *National Museums and Galleries of Northern Ireland, Ulster Folk & Transport Museum, L1309/5*

the railway, for it seems that allowing water to escape through it reduced the likelihood of flooding in low-lying parts of Tralee itself. So until the line closed, it offered the remarkable spectacle of narrow-gauge locomotives racing to beat the tide.

The Belfast & County Down Railway on its approach to Downpatrick crossed over the River Quoile near the tidal limit. Flooding of the Quoile Marshes hereabouts was a problem of long standing, and was probably caused by spring tides augmented by rainwater run-off. The trackbed is said to have been formed on rafts of timber bundles, the traditional method of making the foundation for both railways and roads through swamps. Despite floodgates, which seem to have been allowed to get out of repair, the floods on occasion rose high enough to cover the railway, with trains passing through several inches of water. This happened in the 1900s and in the 1930s, and probably at other times as well. A tidal barrier was eventually built in 1956 — after the railway had closed — but floods resulting from high river levels still occasionally affect the former trackbed, which is now used by the Downpatrick Railway Museum.

* * *

All those occurrences, however, fade into insignificance compared with the next series to be described: the East Coast Floods of 1953, on the Saturday/Sunday night of 31 January/ 1 February. What happened when the 7.27pm from Hunstanton met a tidal wave has already been described at the start of the Introduction. When those on board got back to Hunstanton in the small hours there was at least a welcome: the stationmaster (and, one may suppose, although it is not recorded, the stationmaster's wife) prepared a meal for the passengers. Afterwards they left for their homes in King's Lynn and Wisbech by taxi. The road evidently ran at a higher level than the railway.

But it must have been a terrifying ordeal for passengers and train crew alike, for they can have had no means of knowing what was happening or even, early on, how high the water would rise. Nor were they to know that this was but one incident, small in relation to the whole, in a widespread unfolding disaster.

All that winter Saturday a strong gale from the north west had been blowing up the North Sea. Two days earlier the moon had been full, and a spring tide was expected — a normal one. But the gale and the tide between them produced a colossal tidal surge. At Colchester the tide rose 4ft 3in above the predicted level, at Great Yarmouth more than 7ft above, and on the North Kent coast as much as 8ft. The tide combined with rough seas to overcome sea defences from the Humber to Kent, and through them the sea rushed inland.

Railways were affected to a greater or lesser extent at some 41 locations. Warning of trouble was minimal. G. F. Fiennes, who recalled these events in an article 'BR and the East Coast floods of 1953' for the 1982 *Railway World Annual*, states that the water rose so quickly and the onrush was so fierce that main lines, marshalling yards and motive power depots were inundated to a depth of 4 to 10ft in half an hour or less. Afloat in the rushing waters came signal posts, telegraph poles, sleepers, wooden huts, oil drums, carcases of drowned animals and all manner of debris. All this, when the water started to recede, was deposited upon railway lines. Where these remained *in situ* — for ballast and embankments were alike washed away — track was left unsafe or suspended, distorted, in the air. Electric signalling equipment failed, and telegraphs were badly affected. And where sea walls were breached, even when the tide went down, it was going to reappear twice a day until they could be repaired.

Fiennes himself was in Central Control when the word came that the 6.33pm Yarmouth South Town to Liverpool Street was standing in the floodwater not far out of Yarmouth. What was to be done? Faced with three choices — to propel back over a line that was already flooded, to stay put, or to attempt to go forward — his instruction was the latter. Two days later he was out inspecting the damage. From the track over which the train had passed, ballast had been washed away to leave a hole 3ft wide and 4ft deep. But whether the train passed over this, or whether the hole appeared subsequently, no one will ever know.

Early in the morning of 1 February, the 12.48am train from Colchester to Clacton was halted by the flood; water was pouring on to the track between Hythe and Wivenhoe.

Mercifully, this disaster was at its peak during the small hours of a Sunday morning, when few trains were on the move in the areas affected. No passengers lost their lives. But one railwayman did. The signalman at Trimley, on the Felixstowe branch, was cycling home from work at around 1am when, it seems, he met the oncoming flood. His bicycle was found in the road, his body in a nearby garden.

Several railwaymen had lucky escapes. The foreman at Harwich carriage sidings became trapped by the rapidly rising flood, although close to a crossing-keeper's hut. He was already waist deep when, by the intervention of Providence as Fiennes put it, there came, floating by, a ladder. This he was able to grab to use to ascend to the roof ridge of the hut, where he perched for the next 2 hours. When the flood swept in, an inspector at a Thames-side yard was rescued by his shunters through the roof of his office. The signalman at Yarmouth South Town was marooned in his box until rescued, after 21 hours, by boat. He was not alone in being rescued in this way.

The stationmaster from Harwich Town was at Dovercourt Bay when the water came up over the tracks soon after midnight. He needed to get back to Harwich — not just to get home but, as a conscientious railwayman,

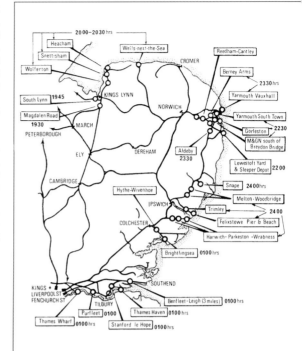

East Anglia at 6am on 1 February 1953 — 145 miles of railway flooded or cut off.

to find out the conditions and to start making arrangements for would-be travellers in the morning. He and his wife struggled on foot along the flooded line to Harwich in the dark, tripping over debris and stumbling into holes where the ballast was washed away. They got as far as a signalbox at Harwich, where they spent the rest of the night marooned. The stationmaster at Tilbury set out on a light engine to examine the line towards Pitsea. The track gave way over a damaged culvert and the engine was derailed beneath him.

Perhaps the most bizarre occurrence in the whole disaster came early on. At New Holland Pier station, the Hull ferry broke loose from her moorings. Her funnel then came into contact with a signal gantry and wrecked it. The pier was damaged too. On 1 February trains terminated at New Holland Town until early afternoon, when the service on to the pier was resumed with hand signals.

On Sunday the overall extent of the damage became clear. Here are some of the main problems — not an exhaustive list. Immingham Dock station was flooded. Between Mablethorpe and Sutton-on-Sea several miles of track were under water. The tidal River Great Ouse had inundated not only the Hunstanton branch but also the main line south of King's Lynn. South Lynn station and marshalling yard were flooded too. Wells station and yard had been inundated to a depth of 4ft. A flood from the breached bank of Oulton Broad had inundated Lowestoft station, and one from Breydon Water had done the same for Yarmouth South Town, both the station and the motive power depot. Yarmouth Vauxhall was also under water. Inland from these, many lines were breached by floodwater from the tidal rivers in a manner reminiscent of the 1912 flood, although this time from a different cause.

Further south, the East Suffolk line near Woodbridge, the Felixstowe branch and the Snape branch were all affected. The Harwich branch was unusable beyond Wrabness, so the stations at Parkeston Quay and Harwich Town were out of action. The ramp for the Harwich-

139

Zeebrugge train ferry was seriously damaged. The Colchester-Clacton line was cut between Hythe and Wivenhoe, and the Brightlingsea branch, ever at risk, had been washed out over a length of 3 miles.

On the London, Tilbury & Southend line, 3 miles of track between Benfleet and Leigh-on-Sea were submerged up to 10ft deep beneath a vast flood. The line was flooded also between Stanford-le-Hope and Tilbury (where the Riverside station was inundated), on the Thames Haven branch, and between Grays and Purfleet, including a large rail-served industrial area. At the Shell sidings, the buoyancy of empty tank wagons was demonstrated when the rising water floated more than 20 of them off the rails. When it fell, it grounded them again — almost anywhere but on the rails.

South of the Thames estuary, the main damage was to the main line from London to Ramsgate, between Herne Bay and Birchington-on-Sea. Although the line runs half a mile inland on a low embankment, when the sea wall was breached 5,000 acres of low-lying land were flooded; the railway embankment was washed out and track distorted in many places over a length of nearly 2 miles. The line was also damaged by flooding near Whitstable, as also were the Sheerness and Grain branches, and the North Kent line to Dartford.

Appalling though this catalogue of horrors may appear, it was little compared with what was suffered at the same time by the railways of the Netherlands.

At home, railwaymen immediately set about the task of setting things right. For passenger traffic, this at first meant extemporising bus links past flooded and damaged sections. It was doubly fortunate that this disaster came on a Saturday/ Sunday night, for on the morning after there were no hordes of commuters expecting transport to London. Railwaymen had Sunday in which to prepare for them. The breach in the Southend line caused particular problems. Isolated at Shoeburyness terminus were 35 locomotives and 326 coaches, regularly stabled there overnight and at weekends, ready for the morning rush into London. Without them, it was extremely difficult to maintain train services on the London side of the floods. This applied particularly to the locomotives, which were equipped with the Hudd automatic train control apparatus with which the Southend line had been provided, uniquely, in 1948. No other lines in Britain yet had ATC — or, as it later became known, automatic warning system — apart from the former GWR lines, which used their own system. So these locomotives could not simply be replaced by others drawn from elsewhere. Something more than a bus link to Benfleet was needed.

Southend, fortunately, had (and has) an alternative route to London, from the separate terminus at Southend Victoria. This led as far as Shenfield with steam trains and thence, electrified, over the main line to London. And at the London end the electrification ran not only to its usual terminus at Liverpool Street, but also from Bow Junction to the LT&S terminus at Fenchurch Street. Why that link had been electrified I do not know — perhaps for just such an emergency as this. The link certainly was not used regularly by electric trains; before it could be, several 'ghost trains' were urgently run to scrape the steam-locomotive-induced soot from the overhead wires. And so the substitute commuter train service was arranged: extra steam trains between Southend and Shenfield, and non-stop electric trains between Shenfield and Fenchurch Street. Subsequently the chairman of the Southend Travellers' Association — not, I suspect, an organisation given to over-fulsome praise of British Railways — complimented the railway on the efficiency with which it was done.

Even while the arrangements were being made on the Sunday, a separate problem was arising at Benfleet. This station served Canvey Island — and of all localities affected during these floods, Canvey Island suffered the worst. It was totally inundated. The residents had to evacuate their homes, and in doing so they made for Benfleet station. In the opposite direction came a stream of relatives anxious to help. From being a little wayside station, Benfleet had been thrust into prominence as a temporary terminus through which, that day, 10,000 passengers passed.

All this accentuated the need to recover the locomotives and rolling stock trapped at Shoeburyness. The full rigour of the flood between Leigh and Benfleet was now reduced, and the track on its embankment was emerging from the waters. But only when the tide was low; when each high tide approached, the sea flooded in through the breached sea wall and submerged it again. Repairs to the up line were nevertheless extemporised, and over this track, which in normal circumstances would have been considered unsound, locomotives and coaches were brought out at slow speed between one tide and the next. Light engines came in columns of three; other locomotives headed trains of empty stock. In this way on Tuesday 3 February nine engines and three 11-coach trains successfully reached Benfleet before the tide came up again.

The Southern Region had been faced with diverting London-Ramsgate trains from Faversham via Canterbury East, the loop at Kearsney near Dover, and Deal, a very circuitous route. However, at Canterbury it crossed over the Ashford-Ramsgate line, which offered a much shorter route from Canterbury to Ramsgate. To link the two, a spur had been put in at the request of the Military during World War 1, and subsequently lifted. It had been similarly reinstated, and lifted, during and after World War 2. Now it was put in for a third time, as a fully signalled double line, and opened on 23 February. The length of route taken by the diverted trains, which continued for the next few months, was much reduced.

Emergency arrangements had to be made not only for passenger traffic but also for goods and parcels to and from the stricken areas — such as 4,200 boxes of fish for London, which were stuck at Parkeston Quay. Traffic was augmented by the supplies and materials needed for recovery. This meant, largely, arranging for carriage by train to or from the nearest suitable railhead; inward traffic, which could not be handled at all, was held back for the time being in marshalling yards, and train ferry wagons were diverted via Dover-Dunkirk.

The work of recovery got under way. Some lines could be reopened in hours, some in days, others took months. A vast quantity of fill, hardcore and ballast was needed; much of the fill for East Anglia originated in the colliery tips and ironworks slag heaps of the Midlands. It was brought by train initially to Whittlesea or March, and thence worked forward to different

BRITISH RAILWAYS

PROGRAMME OF ALTERED PASSENGER
TRAIN SERVICES IN CONNECTION WITH THE

FLOODING OF THE LINE

IN CONSEQUENCE OF FLOOD
DAMAGE THE LINE BETWEEN
FAVERSHAM AND BIRCHINGTON-ON-SEA
WILL BE CLOSED UNTIL FURTHER
NOTICE

COMMENCING MONDAY, 23rd FEBRUARY, 1953
AND EVERY DAY UNTIL FURTHER NOTICE

TRAINS WILL BE DIVERTED AND A SERVICE OF
BUSES HAS BEEN ARRANGED AS SHEWN HEREIN

AVAILABILITY OF RAIL TICKETS

Only rail tickets will be available on the special bus services
connecting with trains by which such tickets are normally available.

Passengers holding rail tickets routed via Herne Bay may travel
by the alternative rail service via Selling, without additional charge.

O/18367 AIS 18253   McCorquodale, London, S.E.—3388.

Above:
The great escape! Three ATC-equipped locomotives, from the many that had been isolated at Shoeburyness but were desperately needed at the London end of the LT&S line, pick their way gingerly along flood-damaged track between Leigh and Benfleet on 3 February 1953. When the tide returns, the track will disappear again beneath the waves. *Hulton Archive*

Left:
British Railways Southern Region announces diversions following the floods of February 1953. *R. N. Forsythe collection, courtesy British Railways Board*

destinations according to need. During that February Whitemoor Yard — through which passed much of the freight traffic for East Anglia — was moving 2,000 wagons a week more than the previous February.

The Kent River Board decided to construct as a first stage a new sea wall, which would eventually become the second line of defence, along the seaward side of the main line between Herne Bay and Birchington. Large quantities of chalk for this were delivered by rail from quarries near Knockholt and Ramsgate. For loading at the latter point, a new siding about half a mile long was built. At the delivery end, the down line was temporarily reinstated with additional crossovers, and floodlights. In the first six days of the operation, trains brought in more than 15,000 tons of chalk, and the rate of delivery was later stepped up to 7,000 tons a day.

By means of this sort, the lines affected were steadily reinstated. Hunstanton was open again on 10 February, and Yarmouth South Town on 18 February. Wrabness to Parkeston Quay reopened on 5 February, but it took longer, until 23 February, to reach Harwich Town. On the LT&S, train services were reinstated by stages until a full service was operating again from 19 February; 6 miles of route had been completely re-ballasted. On the Southern, trains started running again to Grain and Sheerness on 2 March, and on the same day over the main line from Faversham as far as Herne Bay. It was several months more before the line was reinstated throughout. Over the little Brightlingsea branch, British Railways hesitated over the cost of repairs, and considered closure. But there were strong protests that the town, and particularly its famous trade in oysters, would suffer severely. These were successful, and in November 1953 it was announced that the branch would be reopened. It ran successfully for many years afterwards.

For their bravery on the night of 31 January/1 February, four railwaymen — the guard of the Hunstanton train, an inspector at Yarmouth, a signalman at Leigh and the stationmaster at Parkeston — were awarded the British Empire Medal.

* * *

In the North West, the main line of the former Furness Railway follows the coastline for some 60 miles, and much of its infrastructure is closely associated with sea defence work. As such it has from time to time been damaged, for instance at Kent's Bank, where in October 1954 the unusually wet weather was associated with gales and accompanied by high tides. Holes 20ft wide and 10ft deep were torn out of the stone pitching that protected the line along this length. Another trouble-prone location is between Nethertown and St Bees, where the single line follows a series of reverse curves on a shelf above the sea. Following storm damage in 1996 the line was closed for a time for repairs, with materials brought in by rail.

The extensive flooding in the West Country in October 1960 was equally associated with storms and gales. In consequence heavy seas washed out the ballast at several points on the main line where it follows the coast between Teignmouth and Dawlish. Trains were allowed past at 5mph.

There have been many problems on this stretch. On 7 March 1962 heavy seas washed away ballast and left track undulating over subsidences in the trackbed. Repairs were made, but twice during the next 48 hours conditions worsened and one or both tracks were closed again for a time. In a storm on 11 February 1974, waves 60ft high broke over Dawlish station, demolishing the down platform and leaving the wreckage scattered over the track. On 1 September 1988 waves were breaking over passing trains, and on 17 December 1989 the sea wall was again damaged in strong winds and high seas, with ballast washed away.

Meanwhile another problem had arisen after semaphore signalling in the area was replaced in 1986 by multi-aspect colour-light signalling controlled from Exeter, with full track circuiting. Salt water short-circuited the track circuits and displayed false 'line occupied' indications at the signal centre. Between Dawlish Warren and Teignmouth, therefore, track circuits were replaced by electronic axle counters in 1991. These offered much greater resistance to adverse conditions, and not only distinguished whether a train had entered and left a section, but also the direction of travel; on this length, where conditions so often dictated single-line working, the up line, furthest from the sea, was signalled for bi-directional working.

In January 1996 the sea wall was damaged extensively during a period of high winds and spring tides. A large cavity was found under the down line; it was reported that summer maintenance had been reduced, leaving cracks unfilled and vulnerable to ingress of water. The line was closed three times in two weeks. A package of repairs was subsequently announced by Railtrack, although the poor condition of the sea wall was still giving cause for serious concern the following winter. As recently as 7 December 2000 the storm once again sent waves breaking over passing trains.

The Cambrian line to Aberystwyth closely follows the shore of the Dovey estuary, between Machynlleth and Borth. This is a section long subject to problems of flooding, but on 2 January 1976 a high tide combined with a gale gusting up to 100mph to produce a flood that did serious damage. Near Ynyslas, track over two half-mile lengths was undermined to a depth of 8ft, and flood walls and lineside fences were carried away, the debris being carried 200yd inland. Near Dovey Junction a quarter of a mile of embankment was washed away to a depth of 10ft. At Dovey Junction itself branches of trees and other debris were left blocking the track, and there was more damage between Dovey Junction and Machynlleth.

On this last section, and at the junction, repairs were completed by 6 January, but on the more seriously damaged sections west of Dovey Junction there was a long delay. Six weeks went by while British Rail waited for approval from the Department of the Environment to spend the sum needed for repairs, without affecting the grant-aid for the operating deficit. Repair works then took 5,000 tons of stone and 3,000 tons of ballast; they cost £150,000 and were completed on 14 April, just in time for the Easter holiday traffic.

On the Belfast-Larne line of Northern Ireland Railways, recent coastal erosion has caused singling of the double track between Carrickfergus and Whitehead, only the further inland of the two lines now being used.

Minehead station, on what is now the West Somerset Railway, was originally (I understand) higher than its surroundings, but, as a result of filling-in, its surroundings are now higher than the station. On the evening of 28 October 1996 a high tide combined with high winds overcame the sea defences, and seawater engulfed the station and the locomotive shed. Electrics were put out of action, including the half-barrier level crossing, and rolling stock was standing in water over the axles. Improved sea defences had been planned, and this flood, the latest of several to affect Minehead town, provided an impetus for the work to go ahead.

The work proved doubly beneficial for the West Somerset Railway, for the stone required was brought in by rail. The initial contract was for 90,000 tons of stone, quarried in the Mendips, to be brought to Minehead, quite the most notable example of through freight traffic between the national network and a heritage railway.

The stone trains commenced in March 1997. Locomotives and wagons were provided by English, Welsh & Scottish Railway, which operated the trains successively over the tracks of Railtrack and the West Somerset. EWS provided the driver and shunter, while the WSR provided a conductor driver over its line and manned its signalboxes. At Minehead a new siding was laid by the WSR, where stone was unloaded by contractors. Since this siding was long enough for only half a typical stone train, the WSR did the necessary shunting.

EWS usually powered trains with Class 37 diesels, although on at least one occasion two Class 33s were used in multiple. The need from time to time move light engines, without occupying a separate path over the single line, resulted in the remarkable sights of passenger trains and at least one stone train double-headed by an EWS diesel and a WSR steam locomotive. And on 10 July 1997 EWS No 37713, hauling a 25-wagon, 1,115-ton stone train, failed to make it up the bank from Bishops Lydeard to Crowcombe, so 2-6-2T No 4160 was detached from the 16.40 Minehead-Bishops Lydeard at Williton and sent to the rescue. It assisted the Class 37 successfully to the summit, before returning to continue with its own train.

The stone trains ran until June 1998, keeping a vast quantity of heavy lorries off the roads and so helping to convince the populace of west Somerset that those running the WSR were more than just a bunch of puffer-nutters — if indeed they needed to be convinced.

144

Chapter 10

Avalanches and Landslips

Avalanches of snow are a familiar risk to railways in mountainous countries overseas, and are far from unknown in the Highlands of Scotland. But they have caused little if any damage to its railway system — presumably by luck or good judgement routes were usually laid out away from locations where avalanches are a recurrent risk.

Avalanches of rocks, earth and stones, and landslips, are another matter. They are not uncommon when ground is sodden after heavy rainfall; they have blocked lines and caused serious accidents. In just such circumstances in the early morning of 24 December 1841 there occurred a severe landslip in Sonning Cutting on the Great Western Railway, which had been opened the previous year. A large mass of earth fell from the side of this deep cutting and buried the down line to a depth approaching 3ft. Into it ploughed 2-4-0 locomotive *Hecla* hauling the 4.30am goods train from Paddington. Immediately behind the tender were marshalled two coaches conveying 3rd Class passengers. These vehicles would scarcely seem like coaches to our eyes — no more than open wagons with bench seats, they had sides only 2ft high. Remarkably primitive though this seems to us now, to their clientele at the time they were an improvement upon their other main options for travel — to walk, however far the distance, or to clamber aboard one of the many carriers' wagons that moved goods up and down the turnpike roads. Nonetheless, the effects of the slip were disastrous. On running into it the locomotive and tender turned over on to their sides, and the coaches were crushed

Right:
The 1872 slip at Dove Holes, as depicted in F. S. Williams's *The Midland Railway.* Author's collection

Above:
Top brass of the South Eastern Railway inspect repair works following a bad landslide at Folkestone Warren, on the occasion of the reopening of the line on 9 March 1877. The gentleman in the Cossack-style hat is said to be Sir Edward Watkin. *National Railway Museum*

against them by the weight of the rest of the train. Eight passengers were killed and 17 severely injured. At the inquest Brunel himself was asked why the coaches were marshalled thus; he explained that if they were put at the back of a slow-moving goods train, they were at still greater risk — of being run into from behind by a faster train. This accident marked the start of the long and gradual process of improving the standards of the lowest classes of passenger accommodation.

Eleven years later and much further down the line to the West, there was a serious rockfall between Teignmouth and Dawlish in December 1852. The cliff above the railway gave way and descended on to the track where it runs along the sea wall. Initially passengers and goods were conveyed by road between the two places; after a day or two, damage had been made good sufficiently for trains to run up to either side of the blockage, there to exchange passengers who walked past it, while labourers worked night and day to restore the railway fully.

The northern part of the Midland Railway's line to Manchester was early on beset by problems. The autumn of 1866 was exceptionally wet, and towards the end of the year, when the line had been opened for freight but not yet for passenger trains, signs of downward movement were noticed in a hillside along which the line ran near Buxworth. First a road bridge was found to be damaged, then a viaduct, built on a curve, was found to have become straight with large cracks opening up in the masonry. Eventually, over a period of days, some 16 acres of hillside, composed of clay and shale, slipped down towards the river at its foot, taking with them and demolishing not only the railway but road, stone walls, and a farmhouse with its outbuildings. Trees were twisted off their roots.

It took a gang of 400 navvies ten weeks to remedy matters. The foot of the landslip was drained by excavation of a great many underground headings, and a timber viaduct was built to carry the railway. Some years later this was replaced by an embankment of which ashes were the principal ingredient, as being less likely than clay to slip. Earth, stone and clay were also used in smaller amounts. Uphill from the embankment, across the hillside, a drainage trench 7ft deep was dug to intercept surface water, and a 4ft-diameter cast-iron pipe carried the water away through the embankment. The result was a success.

On 19 June 1872 there was a tremendous thunderstorm a few miles to the south. In consequence a landslip demolished the north portal of Dove Holes Tunnel and filled in the entrance. Traffic was halted for several weeks until repairs could be completed.

The line from Helmsdale to Wick experienced a similar problem, of lesser extent but with immediate consequences that were more serious, on 6 August 1874 within a few days of the opening of the railway. The sides of a shallow cutting near Altnabreac, on the section that would later become notorious for snow problems, were weakened by a long-lasting downpour. Rock weighing in total about 1½ tons fell upon the track, and an up train collided with it. The locomotive and the first two coaches were derailed, but fortunately no one was seriously injured.

At the opposite end of Britain, the South Eastern Railway's coast-hugging line between Folkestone and Dover traversed a stretch of undercliff known as Folkestone Warren for 2 miles between Martello and Abbotscliff Tunnels. Records of landslips here go back long before the railway, to 1765, and during the 19th century eight slips were recorded. The railway was seriously affected by one in 1877, which took three months to repair. There was more serious trouble here in the 20th century, which will be mentioned below.

* * *

The Callander & Oban line, which was opened in stages between 1870 and 1880, had several locations where the line was subject to falls of loose rock or boulders from the mountainside above. There were several rockfalls on to it in Glen Ogle in the early 1870s, and the line was patrolled regularly. Another length at risk was that where the line ran alongside Loch Lubnaig nearer to Callander. A railway cottage that survives (although the railway here does not) was clearly positioned so as to give a view down the line from its door.

The length most at risk, however, was between Loch Awe and Taynuilt, where the line passed through the Pass of Brander below the steep slopes of Ben Cruachan. From the start a speed limit was imposed, 25mph by day or 12mph after dark. Then, on 17 August 1881, a falling boulder struck a train and derailed several carriages. The precautionary measure, set up at the suggestion of C&O Company Secretary John Anderson, took the form of a wire fence, originally 9ft high and later increased to 10ft, running along the hillside some distance above the railway. In this fence, however, the wires were in effect signal wires, holding off the semaphore arms on nearby signal posts. In the event that a falling boulder broke through the fence, the arms would go to danger. A trial length proved satisfactory, and the fence or screen was extended over more than 3 miles, with 16 signals. It became nicknamed 'Anderson's Piano'. A short length was also installed on Loch Lubnaigside.

In the Pass of Brander, the signals had semaphore arms controlling trains in both directions, on all posts except those at the ends. This double-arm arrangement was not unconventional at the period when they were first put up, but with the passage of time they have become almost if not wholly unique. The installation, now with upper-quadrant semaphores, remains in use and has apparently given good service down the years, although occasionally boulders have bounced over the screen. Indeed, on 8 August 1946 one of them derailed the engine and coaches of the 6.5am from Oban to Glasgow, fortunately without deflecting them over the edge of the hillside shelf that supports the railway. This train was more fortunate than the next to be described.

* * *

On the Cambrian Coast, on 13 January 1883, an afternoon of heavy rain gave way to a dark and stormy evening. Through this the 5.30pm from Dovey Junction (then called Glandovey Junction) was making its way towards Barmouth; it comprised 2-4-0 No 29 *Pegasus*, three carriages and a guard's van. At Friog rocks between Llwyngwril and Fairbourne, the line runs along a shelf cut into the steep hillside above the sea; higher above the railway ran the turnpike road. Towards the northern end of the shelf, the railway was about 50ft above the sea, the road about 70ft above the railway, and the hillside was as steep as 45°, composed of shaly rock overlaid by peaty loam. This hillside shelf section of the railway was considered to be liable to falls of earth and stone — although none had occurred for two years — and was patrolled by a watchman who met every train at its commencement. The 5.30 in due course came to the watchman, who had just walked the length and so was able confidently to give the driver a green caution light to proceed, which the train did while observing the speed restriction of 4mph.

Nevertheless, some 30 tons of loam and stones came down on to the track, either just before the train arrived or at the moment when it did so. The engine, tender and the first two coaches were derailed, and the engine and tender were tipped over the cliff. For an engine named after a mythological winged horse, there is cruel irony in her final downward flight to the beach; during it she became detached from her tender and appeared to have turned a complete somersault. Driver and fireman were both killed.

The front coupling hook of the first coach had fortunately broken; fortunately too, no passengers were travelling in this coach, for it still finished up hanging over the edge of the shelf, suspended by the coupling from the next coach, which was also thrown on to its side. The final coach and van remained upright. Among the passengers was Captain R. D. Pryce, a director, who had already had a narrow escape in one of his company's trains, the one that was halted short of the flood-damaged bridge at Pontdolgoch described in Chapter 7. The immediate cause of the avalanche was found to be the collapse of the retaining wall supporting the turnpike road, over a length of about 30ft; material continued to fall immediately after the accident. Gasquoine, in *The Story of the Cambrian* (1922), commented that during the rest of the company's history, no similar accident happened at Friog or anywhere else on its system. Rash words indeed!

Fifty years later, on 4 March 1933, the 6.10am passenger and mail train set out from Machynlleth for Pwllheli. The morning was fine and clear, and the heavy snow of a few days earlier had thawed. The train comprised 0-6-0 No 874, three bogie coaches and a bogie milk van. It ran on to the hillside shelf section, then, when it was half a mile short of the site of the earlier accident, the retaining wall of the road above once again gave way and brought an avalanche down on to the track. This was severe enough to lift engine and tender, and sweep them over a parapet wall and away over the edge of the cliff down on to the beach. Once again the tender became uncoupled from the leading coach; the train was undamaged, and the guard, assistant guard and lone passenger were unhurt, but the driver and fireman lost their lives.

There were some slight differences from the earlier event. The railway was at this point some 90ft above the sea, the road 100ft above the railway. The railway was by now part of the Great Western, and the speed limit had been raised by stages to 15mph. The watchman had been withdrawn three years before in favour of motor trolley inspections and temporary watchmen when required. The road had become the A493, had been tarred and was carrying motor traffic. On 3 March an exceptionally large lorry, weighing almost 23 tons, had passed *en route* from London to Barmouth, diverted, because of snow, from the direct road inland. After it had passed, a crack was observed along the road, parallel to the parapet wall and 2-3ft from it, at the point where the fall subsequently occurred. Yet the precise cause of the avalanche, at the particular moment that it fell, was never fully established — perhaps, even, it was the vibration of the train itself.

Lt-Col Mount, who investigated the accident on behalf of the Ministry of Transport, suggested that the line might be protected by mechanical appliances in addition to or instead of a watchman. What the GWR did was to construct a concrete avalanche shelter over the length concerned, which was for many years the only one of its kind in Britain.

* * *

At Folkestone Warren on 19 December 1915 a movement of the ground supporting the railway was, fortunately, observed by three soldiers who formed a military guard — this was at the height of World War 1. It was night-time, but moonlit, and they were able to warn the driver of a train from Ashford, which stopped shortly after leaving Martello Tunnel. Scarcely had the passengers descended — they were guided back to Folkestone on foot — when the ground under the track subsided. This left the locomotive, a 'D' class 4-4-0, and four of the six coaches suspended ominously over the gap.

The slip continued, bringing down trees and large pieces of cliff. Some landed on the railway, some continued down towards the sea. Thousands of tons of material came down; the line, where not buried, was left twisted and kinked and was moved bodily towards the sea — at one point, as much as 160ft.

The railway was not repaired immediately. Dover was at that time closed as a Channel Port, and the workforce needed could not be spared. A motor-bus link was provided between Folkestone and Dover, and a few trains took a very long diversionary route to Dover via Canterbury. But in any case, slippage of the land continued, and it was three years before it appeared to have ceased. Soon after the war ended, however, the work of restoration commenced, and the line was reopened on 11 August 1919.

This was not the end of the story. In 1934 it was reported that the Southern Railway was, as a precautionary measure, seeking powers for a diversionary line that would bypass the affected length by means of a 3½-mile tunnel beneath the cliffs. Then in 1936/7 there was a further bad slip, which moved much of the western part of the Warren, below the railway, down towards the sea by as much as 90ft. The Southern then evidently decided to get to the root of the problem, sinking deep test boreholes in 1938 and applying soil mechanics tests. The Southern Region of British Railways resumed the work in 1948-50.

The Warren lies over a bed of gault clay, and it was eventually shown that erosion by the sea at its foot, and pressure from a high water table behind, were resulting in a sheer failure in the gault clay over the lower greensand. Massive concrete sea walls were therefore built over several years, both to prevent erosion and to retain fill at the toe of the slope. To supplement existing short drainage headings, which ran back into the Warren, a new drainage tunnel, of 6ft 6in diameter, was bored far enough to penetrate the cliffs behind; this was successful in lowering the water table in its vicinity by 20ft.

Such problems are not unique. For much of the way between Whitehaven and Workington in Cumbria, the railway runs along a stone-walled shelf, just above the sea and below the cliffs. At Micklam Point the cliff takes the form of a steep concave slope rising to 200ft; the ground is badly faulted and there are old mine workings too. In the 1950s it was found that waterlogged earth was moving steadily downwards, carrying the railway with it, out over the beach. Lifting and slewing the tracks to correct the level and curve were regular tasks for the permanent way gang, but in 1955 it was reported that the movement had become so marked that as much as 5in a day was recorded, and 95lb/yd flat-bottom rail was buckled overnight. Remedial drainage work was carried out, and the movement reduced.

* * *

Such problems are long-term ones, but at the other extreme, of all the natural phenomena that result in railway disasters, few appear with such terrifying suddenness, and so little warning, as avalanches and landslips. This was all too amply demonstrated on 19 January 1918 near Little Salkeld on the Settle & Carlisle line. Driver Whitworth had charge of compound 4-4-0 No 1010 hauling a down express of 11 bogie vehicles. The train was running freely downgrade at about 55mph. It was a little before 4pm, still daylight. Rounding a gentle curve he looked half a mile ahead to the cutting where, until its removal three years before, Long Meg distant signal had stood; he and other drivers retained the habit of thus observing the line ahead. All was clear. Driver Whitworth turned to attend to something within the cab, and less than half a minute later he looked out again. Where the line had been clear there was now, immediately ahead, a large pile of earth over the rails. He instantly applied the brakes, but as he did so the engine struck the obstacle. It reared up in a cloud of flying mud and spray, ran on for 200yd on the ballast and came to a stop leaning over to the left. The first vehicle, a van, finished on its side broadside on to the track; the next, a bogie 3rd Class coach, mounted on top of it; the remainder, although the track was damaged, finished more or less vertical. Nevertheless, casualties were severe: six passengers killed, another dying later from the effects, 37 passengers injured or shocked, and nine Midland Railway employees slightly injured.

Within the hour before the accident, the foreman platelayer for the length had twice passed the site of the accident and observed nothing amiss. Col J. W. Pringle, Inspecting Officer, eventually pieced together the cause. The line lay in a cutting through ground rising to the east, and with a gentle undulation north and south. The landslip happened where the cutting intersected the depression, which was the lowest point in this undulation. Normally this was dry — the ground was sufficiently porous for rainwater to drain away through it. But earlier in the month there had been hard frost, followed successively by 3in of snow on 16 January, a sudden rapid rise in temperature on the night of 18 January and rain on 19 January. Pringle deduced that, while the snow melted and the rain fell, the ground remained partly frozen, interrupting the natural drainage and causing the water to pond up in the waterlogged depression until, at the crucial moment, it burst through on to the track. The debris was so wet that even several hours after the fall it could be shovelled only with difficulty; such a semi-fluid mass of mud could well have erupted on to and covered over the track in the short time available.

* * *

Landslips have continued to be an unwelcome accompaniment to unusually wet conditions, whether caused by heavy rainfall or sudden thaw — or both combined. Between the wars the Southern Railway experienced problems with landslips that accompanied the wet autumns and winters of those years. A storm at Christmas 1927 produced a landslide that blocked for a week both tracks in the cutting north of the old tunnel at Merstham. November 1935 saw day after day of heavy, continuous rain. On Sunday 17 November this resulted in

150

a serious landslide in a deep cutting between Winchfield and Hook. A train was derailed, and the down local line was obliterated under the debris over 100yd or more. At Botley on the Eastleigh-Portsmouth line slippage resulted in serious subsidence under the down line. Shareholders were warned that the cost of making good these and other landslips was £55,000.

The thaw that followed the severe cold spell of early 1940 was accompanied by several slips in cuttings. One which had fatal consequences occurred in the cutting north of Watford Tunnel on the LMS, just as a Northampton-Euston train was passing on the up slow line. It derailed the locomotive and four coaches, and one passenger was killed.

The storms that swept across southeast England on 5 September 1958 caused at least 23 landslips on the Southern Region alone. Both tracks were blocked between Swanley and St Mary Cray, and the main line to Brighton was blocked by a chalk fall near Quarry Tunnel. On 1 October 1960, at an early stage in the storms that hit the West Country that autumn, the 1.10am Waterloo-Plymouth newspaper train ran into a landslide on Honiton bank. Commendably quick action by the engine crew brought the train to a stand without derailment, but both lines were blocked. It was probably the cumulative effects of that wet autumn that brought the side of the cutting down on to the track at the eastern mouth of Wiveliscombe Tunnel, near St Germans, early on 30 January 1961. The 5.10am from St Austell ran into the fallen rock, and its diesel locomotive and first four coaches were derailed.

Shortly after midnight on 14 August 1966, during torrential rain, the 22.10 sleeping car train from Glasgow to Euston via Dumfries ran into a landslide near Sanquhar. The driver had cautiously kept speed low, and although Type 4 No D311 and the first ten vehicles were derailed, no one complained of injury. One of the passengers was so grateful for the actions of the train crew in atrocious conditions that she sent a cheque for £300 to be shared between four of them. Disaster was again averted by an alert railwayman on 17 September 1968. The driver of a London-Dover train, passing through a steep cutting near Selling, saw rocks, mud and trees collapse on to both tracks ahead, but was able to stop before colliding with them.

* * *

The Callander & Oban line had been blocked by a landslide in Glen Ogle in 1963, and was blocked again on the night of 26/27 September 1965. This time the blockage was not cleared. Closure of the line from Dunblane through Callander to Crianlarich had already been agreed by the Minister of Transport; it was to take effect from 1 November, accompanied by diversion of passenger trains between Glasgow and Oban via the West Highland line as far as Crianlarich. It was stated that to clear the debris from the avalanche and do the necessary remedial work would cost £30,000 and take about a fortnight. Rather than that, Glasgow-Oban trains were diverted earlier than had been expected, and between Callander and Crianlarich a bus service replaced trains until the closure date. Nonetheless, this premature closure was a fruitful source of controversy.

The Crianlarich-Oban section remained open, and as liable as ever to avalanche problems in the Pass of Brander. Torrential rain fell across north Argyll on 28 July 1979, and avalanches blocked both railway and main road at Falls of Cruachan. 'Anderson's Piano' played its part, and halted a train short of the avalanche. On 2 January 1981 heavy rain and melting snow produced further avalanches near the same place and again blocked railway and road. History repeated itself further, in a small way, for the 01.00 night mail from Glasgow to Oban was to be withdrawn, making its last run on 3 January. It was prevented from doing so on that date by the blockage, and it turned out that the night mail of 2 January was the last.

Another line closed prematurely as a result of a landslip (although not so prematurely as the C&O) was the one-time main line of the Midland Railway between Bristol and Mangotsfield. It was scheduled to close from Monday 29 December 1969, but on the previous Saturday morning both tracks through a cutting at Fishponds were blocked by a landslide. The line was closed forthwith.

Above:
On a golden evening in June 1951 the school train from Callander to Killin climbs Glen Ogle. Near this spot, 14 years later, an avalanche would bring about premature closure of the line. *W. J. V. Anderson*

* * *

A railway that might well have gone the same way as the eastern part of the Callander & Oban was the Skye line to Kyle of Lochalsh. This was blocked by rock falls between Strathcarron and Strome Ferry at least twice during 1969/70. In this case they were caused by adjacent road-building operations, which may perhaps be considered as adding insult to injury!

A new route was being built for the A890 to avoid the ferry crossing of Loch Carron; it was to run between the railway and a very steep hillside, and so required much removal of rock. These operations caused a landslide that blocked the track for nearly six weeks in May/June 1969, and a further rockfall blocked it again from November 1969 until March 1970.

The railway was very much under threat of closure at this period, but nonetheless a substantial avalanche shelter was built at the worst-affected spot, to shelter both rail and road. Notice of closure of the railway was given by British Railways late in 1971, but after a sustained campaign of opposition, the line was eventually reprieved. The avalanche shelter was certainly needed, for photographs taken when it was still new show substantial amounts of fallen debris on its roof and, when I visited it in the year 2000, fair-sized trees were growing there. The main road, for all its construction in the late 1960s, is but single track with passing places — which are quite far apart so far as the length through the avalanche shelter is

Above:
The early-1970s avalanche shelter, seen here in 2000, protects both the Kyle line and the adjoining A890 near Strome. *Author*

concerned. With road and rail disappearing side by side into portals of apparently identical dimensions, it looks very much as though the designer thought that before long his work would be sheltering not road and rail, but a dual carriageway road. Happily, 30 years on, the railway is still with us.

A disaster to the East Coast main line near Burnmouth, where it runs along the hillside above the sea, was averted in May 1983. A neighbouring farmer discovered that the track had been undermined by a landslide that had carried 4,000 tons of debris down on to the beach. An accumulation of groundwater was the cause. The cure was to build a new length of line, about 1,000m long, 25m further inland at a cost of £1.6 million.

* * *

On 31 January 1995 an avalanche on to the Settle & Carlisle line caused a derailment followed by a collision with a most distressing result. Although the guard of the derailed train was evidently a kindly man, most solicitous of his passengers' welfare, he was killed, and he might well not have been (as is made clear by the accident report) had he carried out the basic duty of protecting his train. Yet the report also makes clear that there were shortcomings elsewhere — particularly in the operation, in event of emergency, of radio links that by this date had become available between trains and control offices.

The day had been one of typically horrendous Settle & Carlisle weather, torrential rain resulting in localised floods, which, at 17.00, closed the section between Blea Moor and Settle Junction. The 16.26 Regional Railways train from Carlisle to Leeds, composed of a Class 156 two-car DMU, reached Kirkby Stephen. There it was held while the decision was taken that it should run as far as Ribblehead with passengers for intermediate stations, then return to Carlisle. If any attempt was made to arrange a replacement bus onwards from Ribblehead, in which event the train would have returned northwards empty, no mention is made of it in the accident report.

The train was carrying passengers and travelling northwards at about 60mph after dark in heavy rain near Ais Gill when, at about 18.46, it struck a landslide of earth and stones. This had fallen from the west side of a cutting, and derailed the front car, throwing its nose across on to the up line. The driver, although injured, made an emergency radio call to Railtrack Control, giving details of the accident and asking Control for both lines to be protected. This Control agreed to do. The guard may have been aware of this. Either he, or the driver, switched the train's headlamps from white to red — the driver could not afterwards remember. The guard helped passengers from the front coach, where the lights had gone out, back to the rear one where they had not. Then for some reason or other he went back into the front car. What he did not do, despite the Railtrack Rule Book's clear requirement, was to protect his train by placing detonators on the line ahead of it.

Meanwhile, for Control to protect the train was no simple matter. The call had been answered, according to the arrangements in force, at Crewe Control, at 18.48. The controller concerned had no detailed knowledge of the relevant signalboxes, nor was he trained in the use of radio — he knew nothing of arrangements to make group calls to warn all trains in the area of an emergency. He had instead to alert York Railtrack Control, which actually controlled the Settle & Carlisle line, by telephone. York Control then advised the signalmen concerned; this was all done quite quickly, but not quickly enough, for by then events had moved on.

The 17.45 from Carlisle to Leeds, composed likewise of a Class 156 DMU, entered the Kirkby Stephen to Blea Moor (Ribblehead) section at 18.49 after a routine station stop. By default, no warning of the floods, nor of the need to return to Carlisle, was passed to the crew. Not that it would have made any difference if it had. The train was travelling at full power when the driver faintly saw two red lights less than a quarter of a mile ahead. He made an emergency application of the brakes and was escaping from his cab when he was thrown to the floor by the collision. This was 6 or 7 minutes after the initial derailment. If, in that space of time, detonators had been placed on the line, or if a radio warning had been given to the 17.45, it appears that the collision could have been prevented.

Neither driver was killed, although the driver of the first train had to be cut free from his cab. Some passengers were injured. The guard of the first train was found on the ground beside his train, close to an open doorway; he was seriously injured and, sadly, later died. The emergency services performed with credit, appearing on the scene at this remote location as soon as 19.20.

The report of HM Railway Inspectorate (by then part of the Health & Safety Executive) was published only towards the end of 1997. This delay of almost three years goes unremarked in the report itself, apart perhaps from a mention that the inquest on the guard was resumed only in November 1996.

The delays in publication of this and other recent accident reports are in marked contrast to the promptness with which the Inspectorate acted in former times. When the down Midland express hit a landslip on the Settle & Carlisle line on 19 January 1918, Col Pringle was able to make his inquiry — despite wartime conditions — in time to date his report 9 February. After the Elliot Junction accident on 28 December 1906, he was taking evidence at Dundee on 1 January 1907 — despite its being an important holiday — and dated his report 26 February. As long ago as 1869, when the Great North of Scotland Railway's snowplough was involved in the fatal accident on 28 December, Col Hutchinson was able to travel to the North, make his investigation, and return to Whitehall in time to date his report 31 January 1870.

It is clear from the Ais Gill report that during the interim between accident and report the Inspectorate was able to discuss remedial measures with the railway authorities, as had not been the case with Glanrhyd Bridge. Even so, there seems to have been little sense of urgency — it was not until 13 May, apparently, that Railtrack issued a reminder notice to train crews about the need for physical protection of the line even when radio had been used.

Furthermore, this was an accident that generated a lot of public concern and comment, yet for almost three years the public was left to uninformed speculation about its cause.

* * *

Right:
Repair works continue by
night at the Polmont
embankment slip at the
end of October 2000.
Gabion baskets are being
filled to form a new
bank for the burn.
Sandy Simpson

The wet conditions resulting from the widespread and heavy rainfall of autumn 2000 produced landslips in many places. On or about 30 October, on the Edinburgh-Glasgow Queen Street line 60yd east of Polmont station, serious slippage of the embankment was associated with a scour by a burn passing beneath the line. The up line had to be closed during repairs, with single-line working on the down line, reducing ScotRail's recently introduced quarter-hourly service to one-hour intervals.

On 8 November there was massive slippage of the embankment at Heck near Doncaster on the East Coast main line. Adjoining land had been inundated by floods, and some 20,000 tons of soil fell away from the embankment over a length of half a mile, which necessitated closure of the railway. It was reported that 200,000 tons of fill were needed, and large amounts of limestone were positioned along the foot of the embankment, on both sides of the line. Nevertheless, the railway was reopened as early as 21 November, although work continued well into December.

Other slips that caused cancellation or reduction of train services at this period were reported between Preston and Lancaster, at Ben Rhydding near Ilkley, between Liverpool Lime Street and Huyton, between Wivelsfield and Hassocks, and near Manningtree.

The Llangollen Railway was twice blocked by landslips from the base of an adjoining hill fort known as Glyndwr's Mount, the first occasion being during November, with a repeat on 11 December. This second phase of the stormy weather in early December also produced a landslide that blocked the Exeter-Plymouth line, another that blocked the Central Wales line near Llandovery, and yet another that derailed an empty train at the approach to Honiton Tunnel.

'Santa specials' on the Bluebell Railway were affected by slippage of an embankment on 12 December, which meant that journeys had to be curtailed, and on the East Somerset Railway the first train of 2001 encountered a rockfall on to the track, fortunately without damage.

Problems also spread to Ireland. Northern Ireland Railways' Belfast-Bangor commuter line was blocked by a landslide on 8 December. At the same period, following weeks of heavy rain, a landslide between Dalkey and Killiney blocked the Dublin Area Rapid Transit line to Bray for almost a week. On 23 December it was the turn of NIR's Belfast-Larne line to be blocked by a landslide. These two latter events rebounded on operation of Santa trains by the Railway Preservation Society of Ireland — the editor of its magazine *Five Foot Three* affected to suppose that they might be connected with an enquiry he had received just before, from someone writing a book about disruption of railways by landslides, etc. Sorry — I had not expected them to be laid on specially — honest!

155

Chapter 11

Gales and
Other Disasters

Gales frequently accompany other forms of harsh weather, and their effect, when combined with snowfall, in producing snowdrifts has already been described. So have the effects of onshore gales combined with spring tides in producing floods. But there are some circumstances in which it is the effect of the gale itself that is the most severe.

Lineside telegraph lines were much at risk from severe gales, particularly in cold weather when the wires were coated with ice or snow; in these conditions, not only were wires blown down, but poles also snapped off. Towards the end of 1872 there was widespread disorganisation of railway telegraphs from this cause, and in March 1881 the blizzards that swept across the Settle & Carlisle line damaged the telegraph lines in the same way. Further south on the Midland main line a hurricane wrecked the block telegraphs in 1916. On the Festiniog Railway, at a date probably between the wars, a blizzard brought several telegraph poles down; a down gravity slate train and an up passenger train both collided with fallen poles. Other problems of fallen telegraph poles, such as those associated with the snows of 1941 at Newcastle, and 1960 near Aberdeen, have already been mentioned.

Recent years have seen a marked decline in the extent of traditional pole routes for telephones and telegraphs, but this has perhaps been matched by corresponding expansion in overhead electrification. This has brought its own problems, for in high winds pantographs disconnect from the catenary and on occasion damage it, while the catenary itself is also susceptible to gale damage. Delays from such problems are no rarity, but some problems are worse than others. On Boxing Day 1998, for example, there was an increasing gale all day over western Scotland, and the wires came down at Bishopton upon the last train from Gourock to Glasgow. Since, I understand, it was adjacent to a high-security area, it could not be rescued until morning. The storm at the end of October 2000 brought down overhead cables in many places, and in the small hours of 27 February 2001, during a blizzard, the pantograph of the locomotive hauling a down freight train on the West Coast main line near Beattock became caught up in the overhead wires. The sleeper from Euston to Edinburgh and Glasgow was one of several trains stuck in the queue behind it, and was eventually drawn back to Carlisle that afternoon.

Gales blow down buildings and parts of buildings — an early example was the locomotive shed of the London, Brighton & South Coast Railway at New Cross, which lay in ruins after a gale on 30 October 1863. They also demolish structures, and parts of structures. One of the earliest examples of this was the most dramatic and notorious of all railway disasters, the fall of the Tay Bridge on the night of 28 December 1879, when nearly 80 people died. It is said to have been the only railway accident from which there were no survivors. As an example of the striking down of over-confident technology, it ranks in the public mind, as L. T. C. Rolt suggested in *Red for Danger*, alongside the loss of the *Titanic*.

As such, it presents an equal problem to the author of a book like this, for so much has already been written about it that it is scarcely practicable to put anything not already well-known into the space available. For that reason I have given equal coverage to events less celebrated. So far as the Tay Bridge is concerned, the reports of the subsequent Court of Inquiry alone ran to well over 1,000 pages, and there have been innumerable articles, and

several entire books, written about the
subject since and down to the present day.
Many of these cast doubt upon the inquiry's
conclusions; some will be found in the
Bibliography. I have not had the opportunity
to study the inquiry reports in all their detail
— and as I come to write this I rather wish
I had, for I find that subsequent publications, supposedly reliable, differ in such basics as the
year in which the bridge was opened, and the direction, east or west, of the gale on the night
in question!

Construction of the bridge was authorised by Act of Parliament in 1870, and it would enable
the North British Railway to fill one of the two gaps in its route from Edinburgh to Aberdeen
— the Firth of Tay and the Firth of Forth, which were then crossed by ferries. It was designed
by Thomas Bouch, who had a long record of skilful and economical design of railways and
particularly of their bridges and viaducts. Many of these were standing until recent years,
although often subject to weight restrictions. He also had, although this was not so well known
at the time, a long record of skimping supervision of construction and lack of attention to its
details.

Both the contractors and the design of the bridge were changed during construction.
What eventually emerged was a structure of strikingly flimsy appearance, almost 2 miles
of lattice girder spans supported for the most part by groups of cast-iron columns on
masonry foundations. For most of the way the single track ran on top of the spans; but for
the central 13 spans, the 'high girders', the railway ran through them so as to achieve the
clearance necessary for shipping in the channel below. The bridge was completed in 1878,
and was passed by the Board of Trade's Inspecting Officer, Major-General Hutchinson,
who put a 25mph speed limit on it and expressed regret that he had not had the opportunity
to observe the effects of a high wind when a train was crossing. The bridge was opened for
traffic, and traversed by Queen Victoria in the Royal Train the following year. Bouch was
knighted.

On a wild night, soon after 7pm on the last Sunday of 1879, the down mail from Burntisland — where passengers from the Forth ferry had joined it — approached the south end of the bridge. The train comprised a 4-4-0, still at that period a large engine, five passenger coaches and a van, all of which were four-wheelers except for one that had six wheels. The signalman at the south end of the bridge passed the train staff for the single line to the fireman, and then found, so strong was the gale, that he could return to his box only by crawling on all fours. From the box he and another railwayman watched the train's tail lights grow smaller. A fierce gust of wind shook the signalbox, and at the same time they saw a brilliant flash of light on the bridge, then darkness. The block instruments went dead. The two railwaymen attempted to walk out on to the bridge but the gale was too strong. Then, from the shore, when the moon shone through a gap in the clouds, they could see that all 13 of the high girders had gone. With them had gone their supporting columns. Divers later located the spans on the sea-bed, the train still within them, only the last two coaches badly damaged.

The Court of Inquiry comprised William Barlow, President of the Institution of Civil Engineers, Col Yolland, Chief Inspecting Officer of Railways, and Henry Rothery, Wreck Commissioner. The immediate cause of the collapse was established as fracture of lugs on the cast-iron columns to which iron ties were secured to provide lateral bracing. The columns, it seems, had then buckled at their joints. Bouch considered that the rear coaches had been derailed by the gale and had collided with the high girders, and this had initiated the collapse. But the Court of Inquiry decided that the columns at the north end had collapsed first. During the Inquiry it became clear that trains had been exceeding the speed limit. Much more seriously, the design of the bridge was inadequate, construction methods were defective, and maintenance (for which Bouch received a retainer) deficient. The bridge was unsound. All three members of the court concurred in this; Rothery, in a minority report, went further and put the blame squarely on Bouch.

Bouch was a broken man, and died a few months later. The Board of Trade, and General Hutchinson, came under a lot of criticism for having passed the bridge as fit for service. The Board's response was robust. While safeguarding the public, they must nonetheless take it that designers and engineers were responsible and competent. The only alternative was for the whole process of design and construction to be supervised by Government officials. In this case, Hutchinson had expressed reservations upon which those in positions of responsibility had not acted.

The principle expressed in that response seems as relevant now as then. But in technicalities, both the design of the bridge and the inquiries of the court were constrained by the accumulated knowledge of the 1870s. With knowledge gained more recently, and particularly in the light of certain subsequent gale-related accidents that are described later, it

158

Tay Bridge Disaster, 1879.

DUNDEE

does seem increasingly clear that although Bouch had a great deal for which to answer, his theory as to the cause of the accident should have been treated with greater regard than evidently it was.

As an indication of the ferocity of the storm that night, it is recorded that in the village where this is being written, which lies about 50 miles due west of the Tay Bridge, some of the inhabitants took refuge in the manse, being convinced that the end of the world was at hand. And, another 30 miles or so to the west, at Ardkinglass Estate where the owner, anticipating a later generation of miniature-railway builders, had constructed a 2ft-gauge line, the station building was blown down.

Other railway buildings suffered similarly from time to time. In 1881 a gale blew off part of the roof of the engine shed at Southwold, and in 1894 the signalbox at New Galloway was blown down on to the track. A hurricane in November 1899 blew down the corrugated iron fitting shop in the Festiniog Railway's Boston Lodge works; in 1927 the storm that breached The Cob blew down all the station buildings, likewise of corrugated iron, at Beddgelert on the Welsh Highland Railway. London was struck by a small tornado on 8 December 1954, which tore down part of the roof of Gunnersbury station, injuring six waiting passengers and blocking both lines with debris. On the Cromford & High Peak Railway during the hard winter of 1962/3, gales blew down the engine shed at Sheep Pasture Top, and carried away the roof of the shed at Middleton.

* * *

Gales also blow trees down across tracks. In the days when the lineside had to be kept clear of trees for fear of the fire risk from steam locomotives, fallen trees were evidently less of a problem than today. But the problem did occur. The postal sorter in the TPO running between Inverness and Wick had a narrow escape near The Mound in 1895. What was described as a 'tornado' struck the district, felling innumerable trees, many of them upon the railway, including one that crashed on to the train while it was in motion. It struck the rear of the sorting carriage, smashing it to pieces, at a moment when the sorter fortunately was working at the front. The train completed its journey nonetheless, with much of the sorting carriage covered with sheeting.

In September 1946 a locomotive had its chimney knocked off when it collided with a tree blown down across the track in a gale on the Midhurst branch of the Southern Railway. The cab was damaged too, but the enginemen again escaped injury. A gale in 1953 brought much of a plantation of conifers down on the Great North of Scotland line near Elgin.

Around 01.30 on Friday 16 October 1987 the signalman on duty at Salisbury looked out of his box and observed to his surprise that around the station the hanging baskets of flowers —

Left:
The consequence of a
gale in 1953 on the Great
North of Scotland line
between Keith and Elgin.
*Great North of Scotland
Railway Association/
Edwin Innes, Keith*

which normally hung vertically as flower baskets do — were streaming out horizontally. The wind, which had been rising earlier, was now very strong indeed; it developed into the great hurricane that swept across southeast England on that morning.

Horizontal hanging baskets proved to be the least of the problems. Around 5,000 trees were blown down to block lines of the Southern Region, around 2,000 more were blown down on the Eastern, and 600 more on the surface lines of London Transport. There were innumerable cases of railway buildings being damaged, and of parts of buildings from outside the boundary fence landing on the tracks. Very few trains were directly affected in the course of their journeys; mercifully, as with the 1953 floods, the disaster was at its worst at a time when few people were travelling. In any case, by 04.00 the supply of electricity to the Southern Region had failed and it was at a standstill; not long afterwards there was a total blackout in London and the Home Counties. But a few trains did hit fallen trees. At Merstham a train hit a tree, and then another fell on top of it. The 22.52 down mail ran into a tree at Pokesdown near Bournemouth, and on the Eastern Region two trains did so at Hatfield Peverel and Ingatestone respectively. Other trains found their way barred by fallen trees, then more trees fell behind them, barring the way back. Like this the 01.45 Waterloo-West of England and the up Mail from Weymouth were both trapped at Weybridge, and a down newspaper train was trapped at Greenhithe.

But, even if there had been power, few public trains could have moved that morning. Between Tonbridge and Hastings there were 300 trees down across the tracks. On Sole Street Bank, near Rochester, the tracks were invisible beneath a blanket of fallen oaks. The Oxted line was badly affected, and both approaches to Greenhithe Tunnel were covered by fallen trees. Other places badly hit included Barnehurst, Bexleyheath and Balcombe. On the Eastern Region there were fallen trees on the overhead wiring at Upminster, Harlow, Walthamstow, Bromley by Bow, Purfleet, Forest Gate … and so on.

Of railway buildings, Dover Western Docks had lost most of the glass from the roof, and at Bournemouth the wind tore the glass from the roof and blew it around the station. Many stations were damaged to a lesser extent — the total cost of repairs to Southern Region stations was estimated at £500,000. On the Eastern Region, Limehouse station roof was blown off, damaging the overhead wiring. Benfleet station canopy was blown away, as was the roof of Clacton station.

Making unauthorised appearances on railway property were greenhouses, garden sheds, corrugated iron, plastic sheeting, scaffolding, the roof of a factory at Grays and, at Leigh-on-Sea, beach huts, boats and a cockle shed.

From 04.00 onwards, while the gale was at its fiercest, railway managers were starting to plan recovery and railwaymen of all grades were struggling into stations and depots, often from homes themselves damaged, and spontaneously starting to clear up. They armed

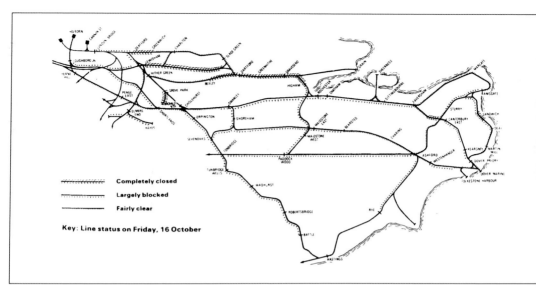

Key: Line status on Friday, 16 October

- ~~~~~~~~~~~ Completely closed
- ············· Largely blocked
- —————— Fairly clear

themselves with saws from emergency kits and with chainsaws, and used whatever motive power was available for transport. Southern Region chartered a helicopter to survey lines and find the worst trouble spots. Clearing fallen trees meant not only cutting them up but operating special trains to remove the timber. Sadly, one railwaymen was killed when a 20-ton tree root fell on him. Troops from the Royal Engineers and the Parachute Regiment came to help out on the Brighton line; on the Eastern Region, contractors Balfour Beatty sent wiring teams, who should have been electrifying the East Coast main line near Doncaster, down to Essex to help restore the overhead wires.

The wind did not drop until lunchtime, and about that time traction electricity was restored to the Southern Region. On the Eastern Region it came on during the afternoon. By astonishing effort from all concerned, lines were gradually reopened through the weekend, and on the Southern, on Monday, 94% of scheduled trains ran at the morning peak. And British Rail is nowadays considered to have been inefficient!

* * *

The storms of 29-31 October 2000 brought down about 1,100 trees and tree branches across the tracks of the national rail network, and some more on London Transport lines. Although far more trees came down in 1987, those blown down in 2000 were far more widespread. Among the many localities affected by fallen trees were the Piccadilly Line near Hounslow, the main line near Acton, the Bedford-Bletchley branch, and the main line between Coventry and Birmingham International. Near Birmingham a train was halted by a fallen tree, and another tree then came down on top of it. At Eastbourne the gale blew down the station clock tower, damaging the roof. Near Peterborough the roof of a warehouse was blown on to the line, at Skegness a portable building, and near Hull a garden shed. All this came at the height of the dislocation following the accident at Hatfield.

During the blizzard that swept across the Highlands on 6 February 2001, as mentioned in Chapter 3, a substantial oak tree was blown down foul of the Highland main line at Killiecrankie. ScotRail's 06.48 Inverness to Edinburgh, formed of 'Turbostar' set No 170423, struck it while travelling at some 60mph. The windscreen was shattered, one pair of wheels was derailed, and the driver made an emergency stop that brought the train to a stand within about a quarter of a mile and upright. He suffered cuts to his face and a woman passenger injured her leg. The other 39 passengers were uninjured.

Passengers were later rescued by train. Another train of the same type was brought up from Perth, coming to a stand nose-to-nose with the derailed train. Its passengers were then able to descend by ladder from doorway to trackbed, helped by British Transport and local Police, and walked along to the replacement train to resume their journey.

Their footprints could still be seen in the trampled snow two days later when I travelled from Perth to Inverness — the train in which I was travelling was clearly and very reasonably subject to a severe speed restriction past the site. The tree, to judge from the massive sawn-up fragments still lying around, must indeed have been a very large one growing apparently outside the boundary fence. From the limited amount of damage to the train, it seems likely that only the topmost branches were foul of the loading gauge. It appeared that after hitting the tree the train passed beneath the A9 main road, which is carried over the railway on a concrete viaduct, before coming to a stand.

In the aftermath of this accident, things were cleared up with commendable promptitude, given the delayed responses to other recent accidents. The line was reopened later the same day, and when I travelled trains were not merely running but running pretty well to time.

* * *

When gales have such marked effects upon the supposedly immobile lineside, it is little wonder that they have had equal or greater effect on trains that in principle are mobile. Wagon sheets from time to time have been blown off wagons, notoriously on the exposed Settle & Carlisle line. Much more dramatically, a gale on 8 January 1965 blew seven new motor cars off the train that was transporting them, while it was crossing Ribblehead Viaduct. Two of the cars landed in the valley below; to clear the debris of the others from the track, a snowplough was brought in.

Garsdale, just up the line, is subject to gales of up to 100mph. Here, in the early morning of 21 December 1900, a locomotive was being turned on the turntable. The gale was so strong that the locomotive was caught by the wind and started to revolve out of control. The signalman called out a ganger and five other men to assist; material, probably cinders or sand, was shovelled on to the circular rail upon which the wheels of turntable ran in the turntable pit, and this eventually had the desired effect. Subsequently a stockade of old sleepers was built around the turntable to provide shelter from the gale.

MIDLAND RAILWAY. _____ _____ 1900

P. F. 45.

From *Hawes Junction* To *Settle*

Mr Bilcock Inspector

Dear Sir

As the Pilot Engine No 1310 was turning on the Turntable this morning the Wind being so strong the Engine got beyond control the following are the Names who was called out to Assist called out by Signalman time called out 5.30 am till 6.30 am J Sutton

Doubt has sometimes been cast upon the authenticity of this event, with the supposition that it was no more than a tall story or leg-pull, so I am indebted to Dr W. R. Mitchell for providing a copy of the Midland Railway memo that confirms it; the first page appears as an illustration. The ganger was clearly applying to his inspector to make sure his men got their money for being called out.

A strong gale could set railway wagons in motion. On 22 November 1881 two wagons were blown out of a siding at Afon Wen, Cambrian Railways, into the path of a passenger train. At Chelford, on the London & North Western line from Manchester to Crewe, a wagon blown by the gale was the cause of a serious fatal accident on 22 December 1894. The wagon had been fly-shunted into a siding, but was blown back out of it and collided with more wagons, which were being shunted similarly into another siding. It was derailed, and came to rest fouling the up main line; almost immediately it was run into by a heavy double-headed express travelling at speed. In the resulting pile-up 14 people were killed. This was the day that New Galloway signalbox was blown down.

In November 1899 a strong gale blew a train of Festiniog Railway coaches out of Portmadoc Harbour station and on to the main line. As they passed round the 90° curve they came broadside-on to the wind. The bodies of the bogie coaches were carried on spherical mountings; the wind now blew the bodies off their bogies and over on to their sides. There were other instances of gales blowing Festiniog coaches off the track, though seldom so dramatically, to a total of at least five occasions between 1886 and 1914.

* * *

A terrific gale was blowing from the South West when the Furness Railway mail train for Barrow left Carnforth at 4.34am on 27 February 1903. It comprised a four-coupled tender locomotive and ten items of rolling stock: from the front, they were a Furness mail van, two LNWR vans, two LNWR coaches and another LNWR van, all of which were on six wheels, followed by an eight-wheeled LNWR bogie brake van, an FR six-wheeled coach, an FR four-wheeled brake van and a Midland Railway four-wheeled brake van. On board the train were 34 passengers, two guards and a Post Office clerk.

Just after the train had crossed the viaduct over the River Kent near Arnside, it ran into some telegraph wires that had been blown down. These knocked off the engine's headlamp, and about 20 minutes were needed to cut the train free, after which it continued. About 5.30am, as it was approaching the 500yd viaduct over the Leven estuary, between Cark and Plumpton Junction, it struck some more blown-down wires. Sparks flew, and the driver shut off steam. Then the sparks ceased and, thinking he was clear, the driver opened up again. But as the train ran on to the viaduct, vacuum was lost in the braking system, and halfway across the viaduct the brakes brought the train to a stand.

The fireman got down. The gale, broadside-on, was now so strong that it was almost impossible to stand without holding on to something, but he struggled to the front of the locomotive. There he found a piece of telegraph wire pressing against the vacuum brake hose, and which had partly raised the hose off the plug. He replaced the hose, then, as he returned to the footplate, he observed the gale overturn the first two vans on to the up line. In the dark, he could see no further down the train.

The second guard had been travelling in the bogie brake van. When the train stopped he got out and walked up the train to join the head guard in the composite, but as he was stepping into it, the near side of the van arose and the van fell over on to its side on the up line. Both men were covered by luggage, but the second guard got clear first and rescued the head guard, who was pinned down. The second guard managed to get out and then, buffeted by the gale, he could see that the entire train, apart from engine and tender, had been blown over on to its side.

The two guards together hastened to turn off the gas supplies in the gas-lit LNWR vehicles, and so prevented a conflagration. The fireman got word of the accident to the signalman at Plumpton Junction, and all trains were stopped before another could arrive. All the passengers were extricated, or extricated themselves, and were able to walk along the viaduct to some railway cottages. No one was killed, although all on board the train were injured to a greater or lesser degree. It might have been very much worse. If the train had been on the up line it would have gone over into the estuary.

By daylight it could be seen that the front van was being held partly upright by the coupling with the tender; it was thought that the rear van had toppled first and taken the rest of the train with it. The Furness company's harbourmaster at Barrow, 10 miles upwind, registered by anemometer a mean wind speed between 4.30 and 8am of 100mph; he considered that gusts had reached 120mph. As an example of just what the wind can do to a train, the Leven Viaduct accident was a very remarkable demonstration indeed.

* * *

Yet it was by no means the only one. The little trains of the 3ft-gauge railways that served the west coast of Ireland were exposed to the full fury of Atlantic gales. On 12 December 1883 a train of the West Donegal Railway, opened the previous year, was brought to a stand by a headwind sweeping down from Barnesmore Gap. Six weeks later a train, all but the locomotive, was blown off the track on a sharp curve by a westerly gale. The three vehicles that comprised it fell to the inside of the curve; Maj-Gen Hutchinson, perhaps by now considered to have a deep knowledge of the effects of gales, was sent to inspect and considered that excessive supererelevation was a contributory factor. The same day the same thing happened to a train of the Londonderry & Lough Swilly Railway as it approached Letterkenny. On the Donegal, as traffic increased, it sometimes became necessary to divide trains for the ascent to Barnesmore Gap against a gale.

On the West Clare Railway, during the winter of 1888/9, two trains were derailed by a gale on the same day near Quilty station. After that an anemometer was installed at Quilty, and some vehicles were weighted down with concrete slabs. When the wind reached 60mph only these were allowed to run on the section affected; when it reached 80mph, all traffic was stopped.

The Tralee & Dingle Railway experienced similar problems. On 24 November 1898 the three passenger coaches of a train were blown over. It is possible that the condition of the track was poor, and that a strong gust coincided with a roll induced by the track. Another T&D train was blown off the rails on 24 December 1912.

The climax of this series of events came with the Owencarrow Viaduct disaster on 30 January 1925. This viaduct carried the Burtonport extension of the Londonderry & Lough

Swilly Railway over the valley of the Owencarrow River in the bleak and windswept northern part of County Donegal; it was 380yd long with a maximum height of rather more than 30ft. A strong gale was blowing that day when a Letterkenny-Burtonport train ran on to the viaduct. Three coaches, all six-wheelers, were blown over against the parapet; within a few yards they broke through it and fell. They did not fall far, because at that point a short length of rocky embankment intervened between the two parts of the viaduct, and they therefore came to rest upon it; but one of the coaches finished upside down and, since its roof had been broken off, its passengers fell into the valley below. Of the 14 passengers on the train, four lost their lives and five were injured.

Subsequently coaches running on the extension were weighted down by cast-iron slabs in each compartment. An anemometer was provided at Dunfanaghy Road station; when the wind reached 60mph, open wagons were excluded from trains, and when it reached 80mph all traffic was halted. In January 1927 the anemometer recorded a gust of 112mph.

In England, the light iron viaduct at Staithes, on the North Eastern Railway's Loftus-Whitby line, was equipped with a wind gauge. This rang a bell in a signalbox so that traffic would be suspended while the gale remained too strong.

Mountain railways are inevitably exposed to strong winds. When the electric Snaefell Mountain Railway was built in 1895, ascending to the summit of the Isle of Man's highest mountain, it was equipped with the Fell central rail. This had and has two purposes. The clasp brakes with which cars are fitted not only serve for braking purposes but also provide lateral stability in high winds.

On Snowdon the railway runs along a very exposed ridge as it climbs from Clogwyn towards the summit. Wind speed is monitored via the University of Bangor's automatic weather stations at Clogwyn and Summit, and by hand-held anemometers operated by the railway's own staff. The policy is not to run trains above Clogwyn when the wind speed there is greater than 35mph; when it exceeds 41mph trains do not go above Rocky Valley, which is about ⅛ mile below Clogwyn. These limits are not related to the stability of rolling-stock but to the effect on passengers should they have to leave the train on the mountain in the event of breakdown. It has been calculated that the carriages should be stable in side winds of 68mph.

* * *

Reduced visibility in fog has always been one of the greatest difficulties encountered in railway operation, and has contributed to serious accidents from early days to more recent times. The London & Greenwich Railway experienced a triple collision in fog at the approach to London Bridge as early as 1840. In the recent past there was the disastrous accident in fog at Lewisham in 1957 — a collision leading to a bridge collapse.

Yet fog has ever seemed not so much exceptional as predictable, its consequences foreseeable. Furthermore, since the earliest days railway engineers have taken ingenious and successful action to alleviate its effects. The detonator or detonating fog signal was invented by E. A. Cowper in 1841, at a period when much signalling was still being done by hand and flag. It was tried out on the London & Greenwich and adopted soon after on the London & Birmingham Railway. Automatic train control was introduced by the Great Western in 1906 and installed widely throughout its system. Colour-light signals, their lights better able to penetrate fog than those of semaphores, were widely installed in the 1960s and subsequently. And it must be admitted that withdrawal of the smoke-producing steam locomotive, however much one may regret it, has helped to render thick fogs less common than they were. All in all, fog seems to have been too commonplace an occurrence, and too regularly overcome, to be treated as a disaster.

Excessive heat on the other hand seems in the British climate to be much less likely to lead to accidents, yet the accident at Felling on the North Eastern Railway in 1907 resulted from this cause. To be precise, the cause was not so much an excessively high temperature, as a sudden extreme rise in temperature. The date was 26 March, and a sharp overnight frost gave way to a clear morning with exceptionally hot sun. This beat down upon the rails of the NER as they ran, aligned east-west, along a cutting deep enough to provide shelter from the slight breeze, but with its south side at such an easy slope that it offered no shade.

The fishplates were done up tight as was the custom in the winter. The line fell on a gentle gradient and in these circumstances there was a tendency for the rails to creep towards its foot. There, it was found subsequently, the expansion which should have been taken up a little at each joint could be concentrated wholly at a single one. At around 1.35pm the track could no longer take it, and suddenly buckled into the form of an S, about 2ft long and 5in towards the side of the cutting.

The distorted track was observed from an overbridge by a man who, as it happened, was deaf and dumb. However, through an intermediary he managed to attract the attention of the driver of a passing steam-roller. This man, seeing what was wrong, immediately ran to Heworth signalbox, which was close to the bridge but on the far side of it from the damaged track, which could thus not be seen by the signalman.

The signalman, busy in his box, had dispatched a light engine down the line at about 1.32 with no problem. By 1.42 he had already pulled his signals off again for the next train, the Liverpool-Newcastle express running via Leeds and Sunderland, which had been accepted by the box in advance at Felling. His immediate reaction when confronted by an over-excited stranger, shouting that the rails were twisted, was not to take him seriously.

'Who are you, and what has twisted the rails?' he responded.

Within a few seconds he had understood the gravity of the situation, but by then it was too late. The express was passing his box at about 40mph under clear signals. A few hundred yards further on the locomotive, a 4-4-0, left the rails and fell over against the side of the cutting; the first two coaches overran it and fell on to their sides foul of the up line, and all the remaining vehicles were derailed or partially so. Eight passengers were seriously injured, of whom two subsequently died.

Serious problems of track buckling in heat arose again in 1969. During the 1960s many miles of continuously welded track with flat-bottom rail were laid, replacing jointed track with bullhead rail. Initially, potential problems of expansion were alleviated either by laying continuously welded track only in warm conditions, or by warming it artificially. That this was inadequate was demonstrated in the unusually hot summer of 1969. During June and July there were three derailments caused by buckled continuously welded track. One of these, at Lichfield, involved a freight train, but the other two, at Somerton and Sandy, involved express passenger trains. Subsequently standards of de-stressing continuously welded rail were improved, and additional ballast shoulders were provided.

On 15 June 1986 track-buckling derailed a Glasgow-Euston express at speed as it passed through a junction while approaching Motherwell. The track had been laid in extremely cold weather, while the afternoon of the accident was exceptionally hot.

A very strange incident relating to excessive heat was reported in *The Railway Gazette* for 15 September 1911. On an intensely hot day the previous week, a Great Central local train had come to a stand some miles out of Marylebone with vacuum brake failure. Close investigation disclosed that one of the brake hoses was charred, with a hole burned through it. The obvious possible causes appeared to be a spark from the locomotive, the dropping of a lighted match, or glowing ash from a cigarette or pipe. But these were discounted for two reasons. First, if any of them were correct, it was most surprising that it was not a frequent occurrence. Second, it seemed unlikely that a spark, or ash, would not only lodge on the curved surface of the India-rubber brake hose, but stay there long enough to ignite what was not a quick-burning substance. So it was suggested that part of Marylebone station roof had acted as a burning-glass, and that the breeze set up by the moving train had caused the hose to smoulder until it burned through. Perhaps. At any rate, the brakes, as the paper pointed out, had failed safe.

Lightning has occasionally affected railways, usually in the telegraph department. 'In thunderstorms,' wrote F S. Williams alarmingly in *Our Iron Roads*, 'the electric fluid has been known to flash along the telegraph wires, and to fling the telegraphic instrument across the office at the heads of clerks yards away.' In the violent thunderstorm of 5 September 1958, lightning struck the stationmaster's house at Reigate, and a signalbox at Sanderstead. The block telegraph was knocked out on the line from East Grinstead to Tunbridge Wells, and recourse had to be made to time-interval working.

* * *

For a railway structure to be struck by lightning is rare, but for one to be attacked by marine boring worms must be almost if not entirely unique. Yet in 1980 it was discovered that they had reduced many of the timber piles of Barmouth Bridge to a state reminiscent of Gruy``re cheese. The culprit was the shipworm *teredo norvegica*, a mollusc that bores holes up to 1in diameter in timber.

Barmouth Bridge, half a mile long, carries the Cambrian Coast line over the estuary of the River Mawddach. It was built originally in 1867 and reconstructed in 1903-6; for most of its length it has a timber superstructure that is carried on 113 groups of timber piles. I can think of no larger timber bridge remaining in use on British railways.

The first indication of trouble was found during routine maintenance in April. A temporary weight restriction was placed on the bridge, which had the effect of restricting its use to DMUs and so causing suspension of freight trains on the line to the north of it; with closure of the Caernarfon-Afon Wen line some years earlier, this no longer had any alternative standard-gauge access.

That October all trains over the bridge were withdrawn so that the extent of the infestation could be established; this could only be done by sampling, by removing pieces of timber from the piles. A passenger train service was maintained both south and north of the bridge — some DMUs were left on the isolated section — and a network of temporary bus services was set up. But the line had been proposed for closure and reprieved in the 1970s, and there were widespread and justified fears that repairs would be considered too expensive. There was a strong local campaign for repair and retention.

The investigation was followed by sufficient repair work to enable the bridge to be reopened temporarily the following May, for use by DMUs, while funding was sought for the total cost of repairs, estimated at £1.7 million; to this, BR initially pledged £0.5 million. No special funding was forthcoming from the Government, however, which required BR to fund the work from its regular Public Service Obligation grant.

So the work was done gradually: replacing some 30 of the bridge's 498 timber piles completely, encasing most of the piles in glass-reinforced cement, and placing stone pitching around the groups of piles to prevent formation of the scour pools which, for shipworms, are a favoured habitat. It took until 1986 to complete, and the bridge was then ceremonially reopened to locomotive-hauled trains with a special train from London. The following year it was being used by steam specials.

* * *

From a highly specialised problem in a single location, let us move finally to a problem that in recent years has become regrettably widespread: leaves on the line. In days gone by the fire risk from steam locomotives made it necessary for linesides to be kept clear of overgrowth, but, after the end of steam, restricted funds meant that the extent of clearance was much reduced. As we have seen, at one location, Seer Green, the consequence of this was disaster when snow brought trees down over the track. Generally, the consequence has been less severe but more widespread, particularly where broad-leaved trees such as sycamores, chestnuts and ashes have grown up to deposit their leaves upon the railheads in autumn. There, particularly in light rain, they are squashed by the wheels of passing trains at a pressure of more than 30 tons per square inch to form a hard, slippery coating on both railhead and wheels.

The problem has been accentuated by simultaneous development of electric and diesel multiple-units with disc brakes. These have steadily superseded trains fitted with brake shoes, which had the beneficial side-effect of scraping any accumulation of leaves off wheel treads.

Leaves on the line: Southern Region makes its
apologies, c1980. *R. N. Forsythe collection, courtesy
British Railways Board*

The result has been an increasing tendency for trains to lose adhesion. This is a nuisance while they are attempting to accelerate, for it leads to delays and damaged rails. It is far more serious while braking. Wheels lock and slide, which causes flats on the treads and prevents trains from stopping where intended, with all the dangers that that implies.

The problems first seem to have become conspicuous on the electrified Liverpool-Southport line in the late 1970s, when the fleet of traditional EMUs was replaced by new Class 507 trains with disc brakes. But it soon became very much more widespread on the extensive — and well-wooded — Southern Region. In the autumn of 1981 its most modern EMUs, the Class 508s, were unable to cope. Their compressed-air-operated disc braking system incorporated electronic apparatus intended to detect wheel slide and reduce brake application appropriately. In the worst cases, however, it was found that brake application was reduced to nothing. The whole fleet had to be temporarily withdrawn. Then in November 1985 crushed fallen leaves on the rails were found to be a significant factor in a collision at Copyhold Junction, near Haywards Heath, making it impossible for the driver of one of the trains to bring it to a stand before the impact. With introduction of further disc-braked trains the problem became common throughout much of Britain.

Several possible remedies were considered, but according to C. Pritchard in 'The Sandite Story' (*Railway World*, November 1994), that which eventually became most frequently used was, remarkably, a spin-off from the abortive development of the Advanced Passenger Train in the 1970s. To maintain its adhesion at speed, a system of jetting sand-bearing gel on to the rails was developed in British Rail's research laboratories at Derby. The material was given the name Sandite. Trials were then carried out with it on the steep banks of South Devon, applying it from a train to the rails with the intention of reducing slippage, which damaged wheels and rails alike. It proved effective, and the treatment was found to last for the passage of several trains; but it was not quite economical enough to be adopted, for damaged rails were not eliminated and still needed costly replacement.

Sandite was first used in earnest on the route between Ilkley and Leeds, where trains were slipping excessively. Holbeck depot and the Area Laboratory at Doncaster between them produced a rugged workaday mobile unit to apply Sandite and, after a few teething troubles, the problem was solved. Sandite was used again on the Liverpool-Southport line, where some of the superseded EMUs were converted to lay it. Precautions were found to be needed to prevent its insulating properties affecting track circuit operation; metallic particles were later added to it.

During the early 1980s further trials were carried out on the Shepperton branch in attempts to understand the overall problem in detail, and to develop solutions to it. So that trials could continue outside the leaf-fall season, a Class 508 was modified to apply a slippery fluid to the rails while applying its brakes, the resulting loss of adhesion being monitored by scientists on board. The tests were done at a location well short of Shepperton terminus, and by night; the rails were cleaned before normal train services recommenced. But on 21 April 1982 this was not done properly. All unaware, the driver of the first train, the 06.34 from Waterloo formed of set 508031, approached Shepperton terminus at normal speed and applied his brakes as usual. The train sailed through the station, passed the Ian Allan offices, and collided with the buffer stops. The first car rose up on these and finished projecting high above the pavement of the street beyond, teetering on the brink. Fortunately, no one was injured.

From these trials, some trains were provided with a 'panic button' to return full control of the brakes to the driver in the event of a slide, and some were fitted with 'scrubber blocks' to scrape accumulated leaf debris off the wheels. Various methods of removing leaf mulch from rails were tried too, such as high-pressure water cannons. Vans equipped with these and accompanied by water tank wagons have operated as rail-cleaning trains, topped and tailed by locomotives. But Sandite has evidently been found to be the most effective cure for the problem and has come into widespread use.

It has usually been applied from superannuated and converted EMUs and DMUs, although a few Class 37 diesel-electric locomotives have also been equipped for this purpose. Sandite-laying vehicles are fitted with storage tanks or hoppers, electric pumps and jets to deliver the material to the rails, where the wheels spread it over the railheads. Typically, a couple of runs are made every 24 hours through known problem locations.

Some of these vehicles have been adapted for other purposes outside the leaf season — they have also been used to spread de-icing fluid, or for route-training of drivers. The principle has logically been taken further by Railtrack with development of Multi Purpose Vehicles — MPVs — which not only clear leaf mulch with high-pressure water jets and lay Sandite, but can also be used to spray weedkiller, to apply de-icing fluid to third rails, or to clear snow.

* * *

Evidently the solutions to natural hazards are, like the problems, interlinked. Such problems, particularly floods and snow, have over the past year been much more severe than usual — even while I have been writing these lines in April 2001 a snowstorm has been blowing past the window. And they inflicted themselves upon a British railway system already in a state of collapse, consequent on the defective manner in which it was privatised. On a railway — a guided transport system where the track steers the trains — to make one company responsible for steering the trains and another responsible for starting and stopping them seems about as sensible as splitting up a chain of restaurants by making one company responsible for front-of-house and another for kitchens and cooking. Such systems are at best extremely cumbersome, at worst highly dangerous. This has, sadly, been demonstrated by the railway system. It is axiomatic that for safety, efficiency and economy, track and trains on any particular line of railway must be under the same management. And matters have been made worse still, in the aftermath of accidents, by an increasing tendency for the powers that be to seek to apportion blame, at the expense of getting things running again, establishing the cause, and preventing recurrence.

Yet if there is one thing that emerges from consideration of railways and natural disasters, it is that from the beginning to the present day the nature of railways is such that they inspire great loyalty in those who run them. I have no doubt that this bond between railwaymen — whoever their employers may be — will ensure that together they will continue successfully to overcome natural hazards in the future as in the past.

Bibliography

Acworth, W. M. *The Railways of England* (John Murray, 1889)
   The Railways of Scotland (John Murray, 1890)
Anderson, P. and Smith, W. A. C. 'Scotland in the Snow' in *British Railways Illustrated*,
   March 1995
'Andred' 'Winter's Worst' in *The Railway Magazine*, April 1991
Bailey, E. 'Filters, motors, door grooves, ducts ...and money' in *The Daily Telegraph*,
   13 February 1991
Baker, A. C. 'Tales of the West Highland Line' in *The Railway Magazine*, April 1993
Biddle, G. and Simmons, J. (eds) *The Oxford Companion to British Railway History*
   (Oxford University Press, Oxford, 1997)
Bishop, W. H. 'Over the Narrowest Narrow Gauge' in *Scribner's Monthly*, August 1879,
   reproduced in *Heritage Group Journal* (Festiniog Railway Heritage Group,
   Nos 26-9, 1991/2)
Boyd, J. I. C. *Narrow Gauge Railways in Mid-Wales* (Oakwood Press, Lingfield, 1965)
   Narrow Gauge Railways in North Caernarvonshire, Vol I: *The West* (Oakwood Press,
   Salisbury, 1981)
   The Festiniog Railway (Oakwood Press, Blandford, 1975)
   The Isle of Man Railway (Oakwood Press, Lingfield, 1962)
'British Railways and the January Floods' in *The Railway Magazine*, May 1953
Butcher, R. *On-Track Plant 2000* (NPT Publishing, Waterlooville, 2000)
'Caberfeidh' (MacKenzie, C.) 'Reminiscences of the TPO Services in the Highlands,
   1873-1923', originally printed in *Notes* of the Association of Head Postmasters, 1925/6,
   reproduced in *Railway Philately*, March, June and September 1996
Carlson, R. E. *The Liverpool & Manchester Railway Project 1821-1831* (David & Charles,
   Newton Abbot, 1969)
Cartwright, R. and Russell, R. T. *The Welshpool & Llanfair Light Railway* (David & Charles,
   Newton Abbot, 1972)
Chapman, C. 'On the borderline' in *Railway World*, February 1981
Christiansen, R. *Forgotten Railways: North and Mid Wales* (David St John Thomas/
   David & Charles, Newton Abbot, 1984)
Clowes, P. ' "Line Blocked" in the Peak' in *The Railway Magazine*, January 1993
'Coast Erosion Works in Folkestone Warren' in *The Railway Magazine*, September 1954
Cordner, K., Harris, M., Kardas, H. and Perren, B. 'Storm Force' in *Modern Railways*,
   January 1988
Cozens, L. *The Mawddwy Railway* (Author, 1954)
Darby, M. *Early Railway Prints* (HMSO, 1974)
Davidson, M., Currie, I. and Ogley, R. *The Hampshire and Isle of Wight Weather Book*
   (Froglets Publications, Westerham, 1993)
Dow, G. 'Deluge over the Border' in *Railway World*, September, October and November 1968
Doyle, O. and Hirsch, S. *Railways in Ireland 1834-1984* (Signal Press, Dublin, 1983)
Dunbar, Billy *Newtownstewart Remembered* (Strule Press, Omagh, 1987)
Earnshaw, A. 'Sir Thomas Bouch CE: Hero or Villain' in *BackTrack*, September/October 1991

170

Ellis, C. Hamilton *British Railway History* (George Allen & Unwin Ltd, Vol I 1954,
   Vol II 1959)
   London Midland & Scottish Railway (Ian Allan Ltd, 1970)
   The Midland Railway (Ian Allan Ltd, 1955)
   Twenty Locomotive Men (Ian Allan Ltd, 1958)
Fayle, H. *Narrow Gauge Railways of Ireland* (Greenlake Publications Ltd, 1946)
Ferguson, N. 'Snow in the Highlands' in *British Railway Journal*, Christmas 1993 and
   Winter 1994
Fiennes, G. F. 'BR and the East Coast floods of 1953' in *Railway World Annual 1982*
   (Ian Allan, 1981)
Flood in October and November 2000 (Telegraph Books, 2000)
Fryer, C. E. J. *The Girvan & Portpatrick Junction Railway* (Oakwood Press, Oxford, 1994)
   The Portpatrick and Wigtownshire Railways (Oakwood Press, Oxford, 1991)
Gasquoine, C. P. *The Story of the Cambrian* (Christopher Davies (Publishers) Ltd,
   Llandybie, 1973 (reissue of 1922 edition))
Glen, A. E. and Glen, I. A., with Dunbar, A. G. *Great North of Scotland Railway Album*
   (Ian Allan Ltd, 1960)
Gould, D. *The South-Eastern & Chatham Railway in the 1914-18 War* (Oakwood Press,
   Salisbury, 1981)
Grieve, H. E. P. *The Great Tide: the story of the 1953 flood disaster in Essex*
   (Essex County Council, Chelmsford, 1959)
Harbottle, M. 'Maintaining Services after Heavy Snowfalls' in *The Railway Magazine*,
   January 1960
Hoole, K. *Railway History in Pictures: North-East England* (David & Charles,
   Newton Abbot, 1969)
Hoole, K. and Malton, J. *North Eastern Railway: Diagrams of Snow Ploughs*
   (Nidd Valley Narrow Gauge Railways, Knaresborough, 1969)
Hope, T. 'At War with the Weather' in *The Railway Magazine*, November 1999
Howat, P. *The Lochaber Narrow Gauge Railway* (Narrow Gauge Railway Society,
   Huddersfield, 1980)
Idle, D. *North Yorkshire Moors Railway Stock Book*, 6th ed (North Yorkshire Moors Railway,
   Pickering, 2000)
'Inclement End to West Country Branch' in *The Railway Magazine*, March 1963
Ingenious Engineers (ScotRail, Glasgow, 1993)
Jackson, R. P. 'Snow' in *Great North Review*, Spring 1990
Kelling, K. 'Whatever the Weather' in *Railway World*, October 1998
Kennedy, M. *The LMS in Ireland* (Midland Publishing, Leicester, 2000)
Kidner, R. W. *The Cambrian Railways* (Oakwood Press, South Godstone, 1954)
Lambert, A. J. *Highland Railway Album* (Ian Allan Ltd, 1974)
Law, J. N. C. 'Sir Thomas Bouch — a scapegoat?' in *The Railway Magazine*, March 1965
Leleux, S. *The Leighton Buzzard Light Railway* (Oakwood Press, Lingfield, 1969)
Longbottom, K. 'By Goods Train to Gweedore' in *The Railway Magazine*,
   November and December 1949
McConnell, D. 'The Carrbridge Disaster of 1914' in *BackTrack*, July 2000
   'The Carrbridge Disaster of 1923' in *BackTrack*, October 2000
McCutcheon, A. *Railway History in Pictures: Ireland* (David & Charles, Newton Abbot, 1970)
McGowan, P. and Murray, R. 'A Week to get Back on Track' in *Evening Standard*,
   11 February 1991
McGregor, J. *100 Years of the West Highland Railway* (ScotRail, Glasgow, 1994)
Macmillan, N. S. C. *The Campbeltown & Machrihanish Light Railway* (Plateway Press,
   Brighton, 1993)
Macnab, I. *A History and Description of the Isle of Man Railway*
   (Greenlake Publications Ltd, 1945)
Marsden, C. J. 'New Devon Sea Wall Signalling' in *The Railway Magazine*, June 1991
   'Shifting it with "Sandite" ' in *The Railway Magazine*, September 1992
   'What causes wheelslip problems?' in *The Railway Magazine*, January 1995

Marsden, C. J. and Slater, J. N. 'Disaster!', supplement to *The Railway Magazine*, April 1994

Marshall, J. *A Biographical Dictionary of Railway Engineers* (David & Charles, Newton Abbot, 1978)

    The Cromford & High Peak Railway (Martin Bairstow, Halifax, 1996)

Mitchell, W. R. *Garsdale* (Castleberg, Settle, 1999)

Nairne, D. *Memorable Floods in the Highlands* (Inverness, 1895)

Newlands, A. 'The Highland Railway: The Cloud-Burst at Carr-Bridge, 1914' in *The Railway News*, 20 March 1915

Nock, O. S. *Scottish Railways* (Thomas Nelson & Sons Ltd, Edinburgh, 1950)

Parkes, G. R. *Railway Snowfighting Equipment and Methods* (Author, Hyde, Cheshire, 1961)

Patterson, E. M. *The County Donegal Railways* (David & Charles, Dawlish, 1962)

Pritchard, C. 'The Sandite Story' in *Railway World*, November 1994

Rimmer, A. E. *The Cromford & High Peak Railway* (Oakwood Press, Lingfield, 1971)

Robertson, A. J. *The Bleak Midwinter: 1947* (Manchester University Press, Manchester, 1987)

Rolt, L. T. C. *Red for Danger* (Pan Books Ltd, 1971)

Rose, D. 'Cloud Burst over Carr-Bridge: The 1923 Disaster' in *Journal of the Highland Railway Society*, Issues 45 and 46

Semmens, P. W. B. 'Snow on the Line' in *The Railway Magazine*, April 1963

    'Wintry Journey on the "Thames-Clyde Express" ' in *The Railway Magazine*, March 1963

Slater, J. N. 'Historic Railway Disasters', supplement to *The Railway Magazine*, April 1993

Slindon, F. 'The Settle & Carlisle line and the snows of 1947' in *Railway World*, February 1981

Smith, M. 'How Blizzards Stopped the GWR 100 Years Ago' in *The Railway Magazine*, April 1991

'Snow' in *Great North Review*, February 1995

Southern Railway, Annual Report, 1936

'Storm Damage in the Home Counties' in *The Railway Magazine*, November 1958

'Storm Damage in the West' in *The Railway Magazine*, May 1962

'Storm Damage Repairs in Furness and West Cumberland' in *The Railway Magazine*, July 1955

'Storm Damage Repairs in Wales' in *The Railway Magazine*, July 1976

Tatlow, P. *Highland Railway Miscellany* (Oxford Publishing Co, Poole, 1985)

Taylor, A. R. and Tonks, E. S. *The Southwold Railway* (Ian Allan Ltd, 1979)

Teasdale, J. G. 'Snow-bound: Being a Report on the Accident ... near Annitsford on Thursday, 15 March 1888' in *National Railway Museum Review*, Spring 2001

The Climate of Scotland: Some Facts and Figures (HMSO, 1989)

'The Fight against snow and ice' in *The Railway Magazine*, March 1963

The Glasgow & South Western Railway 1850-1923 (Stephenson Locomotive Society, 1950)

Thomas, D. St J. 'Widespread Damage to Railway System' in *Devon Flood Story — 1960* (David & Charles (Publishers) Ltd, Dawlish, 1960)

Thomas, J. *The Callander and Oban Railway* (David & Charles, Newton Abbot, 1966)

    The Skye Railway (David & Charles, Newton Abbot, 1977)

    The West Highland Railway, 4th ed (House of Lochar, Isle of Colonsay, 1998)

Thomas, J., revised Paterson, A. J. S. *A Regional History of the Railways of Great Britain, Vol 6, Scotland: The Lowlands and the Borders* (David St John Thomas/David & Charles, Newton Abbot, 1984)

Thomas, J. and Turnock, D. *A Regional History of the Railways of Great Britain, Vol 15, North of Scotland* (David & Charles, Newton Abbot, 1989)

Thomas, R. H. G. *London's First Railway* (B. T. Batsford Ltd, 1986)

Thrower, D. 'Could some of our railways go under?' in *The Railway Magazine*, August 2000

Toal, E. 'The "Lost" Train' in *Rail News*, March 1978

Tomlinson, W. W. *The North Eastern Railway: Its Rise and Development* (Andrew Reid & Co Ltd, Newcastle-upon-Tyne, 1914)

Vallance, H. A. 'How Railways Fight the Snow', paper read to the Railway Club, 31 May 1935

    The Highland Railway (Pan Books Ltd, 1972)

Vaughan, A. *Grime & Glory: Tales of the Great Western 1892-1947* (John Murray, 1985)

Vignoles, K. H. *Charles Blacker Vignoles: romantic engineer* (Cambridge University Press, Cambridge, 1982)

'When the way is less than permanent' in *The Railway Magazine*, May 2000

'When winter's challenge came' in *London Transport Magazine*, February 1963

Whishaw, F. *The Railways of Great Britain and Ireland (1842)*, reissued in facsimile (David & Charles, Newton Abbot, 1969)

Whitehouse, P. B., in collaboration with Powell, A. J. *The Story of the Tralee & Dingle Light Railway* (Locomotive Publishing Co Ltd, 1958)

Williams, F. S. *The Midland Railway: Its Rise and Progress*, 5th ed (Author, Nottingham, 1886)

Our Iron Roads: Their History, Construction and Administration, 4th ed (Bemrose & Sons, Derby, 1883)

Wrottesley, A. J. *The Great Northern Railway* (B. T. Batsford, 1979)

Periodicals

(Articles of particular interest are detailed above)

BackTrack

British Railway Journal

British Railways Illustrated

Evening Standard

Festiniog Railway Magazine

Five Foot Three

Friends of the West Highland Lines Newsletter

Great Eastern Journal

Great Eastern Railway Magazine

Great North Review

Heritage Group Journal (Festiniog Railway Heritage Group)

Heritage Railway

Highland Railway Journal

Illustrated London News

LMS Magazine

London & North Eastern Railway Magazine

London Transport Magazine

Modern Railways

Moors Line

National Railway Museum Review

Rail News

Railway Gazette

Railway Observer

Railway Philately

Railway World

Severn Valley Railway News

Southern Railway Magazine

Talyllyn News

The Courier and Advertiser

The Daily Telegraph

The Engineer

The Press and Journal

The Railway Gazette

The Railway Magazine

The Railway News

The Scotsman

The Times

Railway Inspectorate, Accident Reports

The full titles of these reports are, as befits official documents in Victorian times, often extremely long-winded, while the body to which reports have been made — Board of Trade, Ministry of Transport, and so on — has varied down the years. The Inspecting Officers' methods of working — meticulous investigation, hearing evidence, giving their opinion as to causes, proposing means to prevent recurrence — has remained refreshingly constant. Reports into the following accidents have been consulted:

Abbots Ripton, 1876	Glanrhyd Bridge, 1987	Seer Green, 1981
Ais Gill, 1995	Huntly, 1869	Sun Bank Halt, 1945
Elliot Junction, 1906	Leven Viaduct, 1903	Vriog (ie Friog) Cutting, 1883
Felling, 1907	Little Salkeld, 1918	Vriog Cutting, 1933

Index